An Adventure Where Kids Discover Who God Is!

Gospel Light's
Kids Time
For Ages 3-12

TREASURE seekers

Includes CD-ROM with Island Music & More!

This 13-Session Course is Perfect for:
- Small and Large Churches
- Summer Children's Programming
- Preschool and Elementary Children, Ages 3 to 12

REPRODUCIBLE

How to Make Clean Copies from This Book

You may make copies of portions of this book with a clean conscience if

However, it is ILLEGAL for you to make copies if

★ you (or someone in your organization) are the original purchaser;

★ you are using the copies you make for a noncommercial purpose (such as teaching or promoting your ministry) within your church or organization;

★ you follow the instructions provided in this book.

★ you are using the material to promote, advertise or sell a product or service other than for ministry fund-raising;

★ you are using the material in or on a product for sale; or

★ you or your organization are not the original purchaser of this book.

By following these guidelines you help us keep our products affordable.
Thank you,
Gospel Light

Permission to make photocopies of or to reproduce by any other mechanical or electronic means in whole or in part any designated* page, illustration or activity in this book is granted only to the original purchaser and is intended for noncommercial use within a church or other Christian organization. None of the material in this book, not even those pages with permission to photocopy, may be reproduced for any commercial promotion, advertising or sale of a product or service or to share with any other persons, churches or organizations. Sharing of the material in this book with other churches or organizations not owned or controlled by the original purchaser is also prohibited. All rights reserved.

* Do not make any copies from this book unless you adhere strictly to the guidelines found on this page. Only pages with the following notation can be legally reproduced:

© 2006 Gospel Light. Permission to photocopy granted. *Treasure Seekers*

NOTE

Because church liability laws are inherently complex and may not be completely free of doubtful interpretations, you are advised to verify that the legal rules you are following actually apply to your situation. In no event will Gospel Light be liable for direct, indirect, special, incidental or consequential damages arising out of the use, inability to use or inappropriate use of the text materials, forms or documentation, even if Gospel Light is advised of or aware of the possibility of such damages. In no case will Gospel Light's liability exceed the amount of the purchase price paid.

Gospel Light in no way guarantees or warrants any particular legal or other result from the use of *Treasure Seekers*.

While Gospel Light attempts to provide accurate and authoritative information regarding the subject matter covered, *Treasure Seekers* is sold with the understanding that Gospel Light is not engaged in rendering legal or other professional services, and is sold subject to the foregoing limited warranty. If legal or other expert assistance is required, the services of a competent professional should be sought.

Forms are shown for illustrative purposes only. They should not be relied on for any legal purpose or effect until they have been reviewed by a competent attorney in your state who is experienced in laws relating to churches.

Senior Managing Editor, Sheryl Haystead · **Editor,** Rachel Kim · **Contributing Editors,** Debbie Barber, Suzanne Bass, Mary Davis, Dana Hwang, Marion Park, Lynnette Pennings, Christina Zeeb · **Art Directors,** Lenndy McCullough, Samantha A. Hsu · **Designer,** Zelle Olson

Founder, Dr. Henrietta Mears · **Publisher,** William T. Greig · **Senior Consulting Publisher,** Dr. Elmer L. Towns · **Senior Consulting Editor,** Wesley Haystead, M.S.Ed. · **Senior Editor, Biblical and Theological Issues,** Bayard Taylor, M.Div.

Scripture quotations are taken from the *Holy Bible, New International Version*®. Copyright © 1973, 1978, 1984 by International Bible Society. Used by permission of Zondervan Publishing House. All rights reserved.

© 2006 Gospel Light, Ventura, CA 93006. All rights reserved. Printed in the U.S.A.

How to Use This Guide

If you are a teacher or a small-group leader, follow these simple steps to lead your class in a discovery of God's characteristics.

1. Read "*Treasure Seekers* Overview" on pages 9-10 and the "Scope and Sequence" on page 11 to get an understanding of the purpose and goals of this curriculum.

2. Look at "Advice and Answers for Schedule Planning" on pages 14-18, choose the schedule that best fits your situation and decide which centers you will include.

3. Read the teaching tips articles (pp. 34-42) for each center you will lead, taking note of the ways you can make each center an effective learning experience for the kids in your group.

If you are the children's director or coordinator of *Treasure Seekers*, follow the above steps and add a few more!

1. Pay special attention to "Getting and Keeping the Very Best Staff" on pages 19-21. Remember to start recruiting early—several months before *Treasure Seekers* begins.

2. Read "Outreach Ideas," "Partnering with Parents," "Decorating Ideas" and "Theme Ideas" on pages 26-33 for exciting ideas to motivate interest in *Treasure Seekers*, special ways to involve parents, eye-catching decorating ideas and more!

3. Photocopy the materials you need for each session and distribute to small-group leaders or teachers.

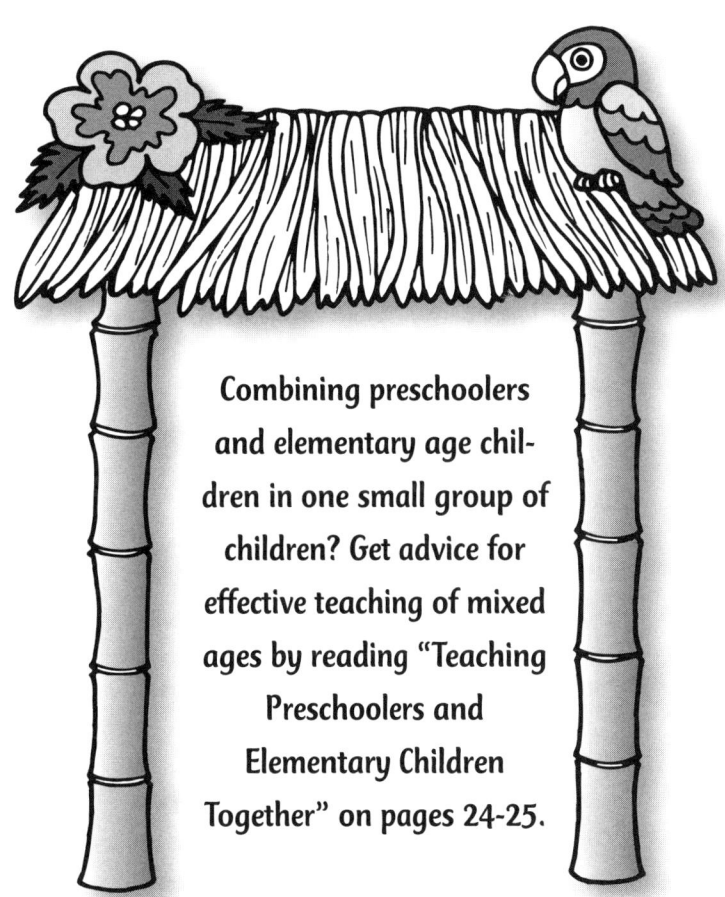

Combining preschoolers and elementary age children in one small group of children? Get advice for effective teaching of mixed ages by reading "Teaching Preschoolers and Elementary Children Together" on pages 24-25.

Contents

How to Use This Guide 3

Coordinator Information 7

This section contains concise and practical information that can help you plan and lead the *Treasure Seekers* program.

Treasure Seekers Overview 9

Treasure Seekers Scope and Sequence 11

Leading a Child to Christ 12

Advice and Answers for Schedule Planning 14

Getting and Keeping the Very Best Staff 19

Publicity Guidelines and Schedule 22

Teaching Preschoolers and Elementary Children Together 24

Outreach Ideas 26

Partnering with Parents 27

Decorating Ideas 29

Theme Ideas 33

Bible Story Center Tips 34

Art Center Tips 36

Game Center Tips 37

Coloring/Puzzle Center Tips 39

Worship Center Tips 40

Treasure Seekers Lessons 43

In this section are 13 lessons to lead your students in a treasure-hunting adventure, discovering the attributes of God.

Lesson 1 God Creates 45

Lesson 2 God Knows Me 59

Lesson 3 God Is Wise and Good 73

Lesson 4 God Keeps His Promises 87

Lesson 5 God Is Holy and Perfect 101

Lesson 6 God Loves and Forgives Me 115

Lesson 7 God Provides 129

Lesson 8 God Is with Me and Protects Me 143

Lesson 9 God Answers Prayer 157

Lesson 10 God Is Powerful 171

Lesson 11 God Is Merciful 185

Lesson 12 God Strengthens 199

Lesson 13 God Is the One True God 213

Resources 227

This section includes helpful resources that you can customize for use in your church.

Certificates 229

Family Treasure Talk 231

Parent Letters 232

Patterns 234

Planning Page 238

Publicity Flyers 239

Puzzle Answers 242

Song Charts 246

CD-ROM

On the CD-ROM you will find all the music for *Treasure Seekers*, a pdf of the entire book and individual lessons ready to e-mail.

Coordinator Information

This section contains concise and practical information that can help you plan and lead the *Treasure Seekers* program. Included in this section is an overview of the course, the scope and sequence, guidelines for recruiting, publicity suggestions, as well as tips for each of the activity centers in this program.

Treasure Seekers Overview

Welcome to *Treasure Seekers*, a 13-lesson adventure for children ages 3-12. The thrill of treasure hunting is combined with the excitement of discovering God as the greatest treasure of all.

The Purpose and Goals

The purpose of *Treasure Seekers* is to give children a solid understanding of who God is, and the amazing ways in which His character and actions can make a difference in our lives. In today's world, so much of everyday life seems separated from the plans and promises of God. This course is designed to help both preschool and elementary age children connect their daily lives with their growing awareness of God.

Each session provides the opportunity to guide children in exploring a foundational characteristic of God. Children need to know such truths as: God Creates, God Knows Me, God Is Wise and Good, God Loves and Forgives Me. In all, children are introduced to 13 of God's attributes, helping them begin to understand who God is and what God is like (see p. 11 for a complete scope and sequence).

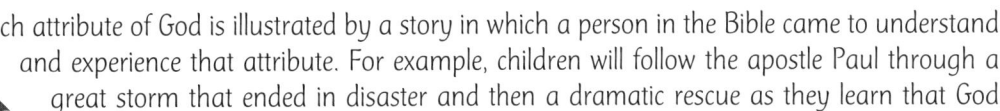

Each attribute of God is illustrated by a story in which a person in the Bible came to understand and experience that attribute. For example, children will follow the apostle Paul through a great storm that ended in disaster and then a dramatic rescue as they learn that God Strengthens. They will walk with Daniel into a den of lions as they learn that God Is With Me and Protects Me. They will hear of Jesus' birth, death and resurrection as the great story of God's love and forgiveness.

As each characteristic of God is presented, children will be led to consider the way in which they can respond to God. Thus, children will learn not only that God Is Merciful, but also that "We can forgive others because God shows mercy and forgives us." As children learn that God Is Powerful, they will also learn that "We can praise God for His help, because of His great power." Children will discover not only that God is a great and powerful being, but also that God is always present and active in the daily patterns of our lives.

In approaching this course, it is helpful to consider the different ways in which children view God: as a kindly old man dressed in a robe and sporting an impressively long beard? as a stern and strict enforcer of all the petty rules imaginable? as a remote and mysterious manipulator of events and people? as a year-round Santa Claus?

While a child's view of God may range from the fanciful to the fearful, after 13 *Treasure Seekers* sessions, your children will be well on their way to developing a loving and trusting relationship with the God who made us all and whose desire is for each person to come to know and love Him.

Special Features

- Each Bible story offers creative storytelling techniques to involve children in an active way. In addition, a unique Treasure Chest Option gives the teacher of elementary-age children a fun code or puzzle to help children focus on the attribute of God being presented in the lesson.
- Because children learn in diverse ways, *Treasure Seekers* is filled with variety to appeal to kids' many learning styles. In each session, the students may participate in active games and creative art activities that will help them express what they learn, solve fun word codes, sing songs, etc.

© 2006 Gospel Light. Permission to photocopy granted. *Treasure Seekers*

- The Worship Center provides ideas for worship and prayer as well as large-group participation in lively, kid-appealing games and songs.

- In each lesson, Bonus Island theme ideas are suggested to help create even more island excitement for your students and leaders—and keep attendance and enthusiasm high. You'll find a variety of decorating ideas, snacks, games, family participation ideas and more!

- Get a quick overview of each lesson's activities by referring to the Planning Page. This page can also function as a supply list for quickly collecting the materials your leaders and teachers need.

- *Island Music* CD offers fresh and fun music that will keep your kids singing about God and the adventure of discovering who He is all week long. Make a copy for every child to take home!

Best of all, you'll appreciate the flexibility of this course! Every church and every group of children is different. Whether you are a large church with separate groups for each age level or a small church that combines preschoolers and elementary age children together in one group, you can use this curriculum to meet your needs. The activity and schedule choices provide you with the opportunity to customize the lesson to make a perfect fit for your church. You'll find the resources you need to increase students' involvement as well as build the relationships with your students that will make the difference between simply leading kids in fun activities and guiding them in a life-changing discovery of who God is.

Treasure Seekers Scope and Sequence

	Attribute	Life Focus	Bible Story	Bible Memory Verse	Early Childhood Adaptation
1	**God Creates**	We can praise God for all the things He has made for us to enjoy.	Genesis 1—2:25	"I will praise you, O LORD, with all my heart; I will tell of all your wonders." Psalm 9:1	"O LORD, . . . I will tell of all your wonders."
2	**God Knows Me**	We can thank God for knowing us and loving us.	1 Samuel 16:1-13	"I praise you because I am fearfully and wonderfully made." Psalm 139:14	"I praise you because I am . . . wonderfully made."
3	**God Is Wise and Good**	We can trust in God's wisdom and goodness, even in difficult times.	Genesis 37; 39—45	"The LORD is good, a refuge in times of trouble. He cares for those who trust in him." Nahum 1:7	"The LORD is good."
4	**God Keeps His Promises**	We can thank God for keeping His promises.	Genesis 12:1-7; 15:1-7; 18:1-19; 21:1-7.	"The LORD is faithful to all his promises and loving toward all he has made." Psalm 145:13	"The LORD is faithful to all his promises."
5	**God Is Holy and Perfect**	We can obey God's commands because He is holy and perfect.	Exodus 19:1—24:18	"There is no one holy like the LORD; there is no one besides you; there is no Rock like our God." 1 Samuel 2:2	"There is no one holy like the LORD."
6	**God Loves and Forgives Me**	We can be a part of God's family because of God's love and forgiveness through Jesus.	Selections from the Gospels	"For God so loved the world that he gave his one and only Son, that whoever believes in him shall not perish but have eternal life." John 3:16	"God so loved the world that he gave his one and only Son."
7	**God Provides**	We can trust that God cares for us and will give us everything we need.	1 Kings 17:7-16.	"My God will meet all your needs according to his glorious riches in Christ Jesus." Philippians 4:19	"My God will meet all your needs."
8	**God Is with Me and Protects Me**	We can depend on God to protect us in times of worry or trouble.	Daniel 6:1-28	"Do not fear, for I am with you; do not be dismayed, for I am your God. I will strengthen you and help you." Isaiah 41:10	"I am with you; . . . I will . . . help you."
9	**God Answers Prayers**	We can pray to God because He promises to hear and answer our prayers.	Acts 12:1-19	"Call upon me and come and pray to me, and I will listen to you." Jeremiah 29:12	"Call upon me . . . and I will listen to you."
10	**God Is Powerful**	We can praise God for His help, because of His great power.	Matthew 8:23-27; Mark 4:35-41; Luke 8:22-25	"No one is like you, O LORD; you are great, and your name is mighty in power." Jeremiah 10:6	"LORD; you are great."
11	**God Is Merciful**	We can forgive others because God shows mercy and forgives us.	Luke 15:11-32	"You are forgiving and good, O Lord, abounding in love to all who call to you." Psalm 86:5	"You are forgiving and good, O Lord."
12	**God Strengthens**	We can obey God and not give up, because He is our strength.	Acts 27:1-44	"The LORD is my strength and my shield; my heart trusts in him, and I am helped." Psalm 28:7	"The LORD is my strength . . . and I am helped."
13	**God Is the One True God**	We can worship God because He is the one true God who loves us.	1 Kings 18:16-39	"The LORD is the true God; he is the living God, the eternal King." Jeremiah 10:10	"The LORD is the true God."

Leading a Child to Christ

Many adult Christians look back to their childhood years as the time when they accepted Christ as Savior. As children mature, they will grow in their understanding of the difference between right and wrong. They will also develop a sense of their own need for forgiveness and feel a growing desire to have a personal relationship with God.

However, the younger the child is the more limited he or she will be in understanding abstract terms. Children of all ages are likely to be inconsistent in following through on their intentions and commitments. Therefore, they need thoughtful, patient guidance in coming to know Christ personally and continuing to grow in Him.

Pray

Ask God to prepare the students in your group to receive the good news about Jesus and prepare you to communicate effectively with them.

Present the Good News

Use words and phrases that students understand. Avoid symbolism that will confuse these literal-minded thinkers. Remember that each child's learning will be at different places on the spectrum of understanding. Discuss these points slowly enough to allow time for thinking and comprehending.

a. God wants you to become His child. Do you know why God wants you in His family? (See 1 John 3:1.)

b. You and I and all the people in the world have done wrong things. The Bible word for doing wrong is "sin." What do you think should happen to us when we sin? (See Romans 6:23.)

c. God loves you so much, He sent His Son to die on the cross for your sins. Because Jesus never sinned, He is the only One who can take the punishment for your sins. (See 1 Corinthians 15:3; 1 John 4:14.) On the third day after Jesus died, God brought Him back to life.

d. Are you sorry for your sins? Tell God that you are. Do you believe Jesus died to take the punishment for your sins? If you tell God you are sorry for your sins and tell Him you do believe and accept Jesus' death to take away your sins, God forgives all your sin. (See 1 John 1:9.)

e. The Bible says that when you believe that Jesus is God's Son and that He is alive today, you receive God's gift of eternal life. This gift makes you a child of God. This means God is with you now and forever. (See John 3:16.)

Give students many opportunities to think about what it means to be a Christian; expose them to a variety of lessons and descriptions of the meaning of salvation to aid their understanding.

Talk Personally with the Student

Talking about salvation one-on-one creates the opportunity to ask and answer questions. Ask questions that move the student beyond simple yes or no answers or recitation of memorized information. Ask open-ended, what-do-you-think questions such as:

- "Why do you think it's important to . . . ?"
- "What are some things you really like about Jesus?"
- "Why do you think that Jesus had to die because of wrong things you and I have done?"
- "What difference do you think it makes for a person to be forgiven?"

When students use abstract terms or phrases they have learned previously, such as "accepting Christ into my heart," ask them to tell you what the term or phrase means in different words. Answers to these open-ended questions will help you discern how much the student does or does not understand.

Offer Opportunities Without Pressure

Children normally desire to please adults. This characteristic makes them vulnerable to being unintentionally manipulated by well-meaning adults. A good way to guard against coercing a student's response is to simply pause periodically and ask, "Would you like to hear more about this now or at another time?" Loving acceptance of the student, even when he or she is not fully interested in pursuing the matter, is crucial in building and maintaining positive attitudes toward becoming part of God's family.

Give Time to Think and Pray

There is great value in encouraging a student to think and pray about what you have said before making a response. Also allow moments for quiet thinking about questions you have asked.

Respect the Student's Response

Whether or not a student declares faith in Jesus Christ, there is a need for adults to accept the student's action. There is also a need to realize that a student's initial responses to Jesus are just the beginning of a lifelong process of growing in the faith.

Guide the Student in Further Growth

There are several important parts in the nurturing process.

a. Talk regularly about your relationship with God. As you talk about your relationship, the student will begin to feel that it's OK to talk about such things. Then you can comfortably ask the student to share his or her thoughts and feelings, and you can encourage the student to ask questions of you.

b. Prepare the student to deal with doubts. Emphasize that certainty about salvation is not dependent on our feelings or doing enough good deeds. Show the student places in God's Word that clearly declare that salvation comes by grace through faith. (See John 1:12; Ephesians 2:8-9; Hebrews 11:6; 1 John 5:11.)

c. Teach the student to confess all sins. This means agreeing with God that we really have sinned. Assure the student that confession always results in forgiveness. (See 1 John 1:9.)

The Preschool Child and Salvation

- The young child is easily attracted to Jesus. Jesus is a warm, sympathetic person who obviously likes children, and children readily like Him. These early perceptions prepare the foundation for the child to receive Christ as Savior and to desire to follow His example in godly living. While some preschoolers may indeed pray to become a member of God's family, accepting Jesus as their Savior, expect wide variation in children's readiness for this important step. Allow the Holy Spirit room to work within His own timetable.

  - Talk simply. Phrases such as "born again" or "Jesus in my heart" are symbolic and far beyond a young child's understanding. Focus on how God makes people a part of His family.

    - Present the love of Jesus by both your actions and your words in order to lay a foundation for a child to receive Christ as Savior. Look for opportunities in every lesson to talk with a young child who wants to know more about Jesus.

© 2006 Gospel Light. Permission to photocopy granted. *Treasure Seekers*

Advice and Answers for Schedule Planning

Begin your planning for *Treasure Seekers* by choosing when you will schedule the program. This 13-lesson curriculum can be used effectively for second hour programs, midweek programs, Sunday School, or summertime Sunday morning or weekday programs.

No matter when or where *Treasure Seekers* takes place, there are two main format options—Self-Contained Groups and the Learning Center Plan. Read the following descriptions and select the learning format that fits your needs.

Self-Contained Groups

If you are confined to a single room or have a small number of children, Self-Contained Groups may be your best option. In this format, groups of six to eight students are formed. Each group has a teacher who leads his or her group in the activities. (If the size of the group is larger, additional teachers or helpers are needed.)

The greatest benefit of Self-Contained Groups is that teachers are able to form meaningful relationships with the students since they remain together during the entire session.

Self-Contained Groups are often a good option for small churches.

Learning Center Plan

The Learning Center Plan offers an exciting recruiting and schedule variation for *Treasure Seekers*. In this plan, each teacher prepares and leads only one activity. Guides (adults, teenagers or even responsible seventh and eighth graders) lead groups of students to rotate between the centers. In other words, each teacher leads only one part of the lesson. This specialization simplifies teacher preparation and often improves teaching effectiveness, as well as making it easier to recruit teachers. The Learning Center Plan also keeps inexperienced teachers from feeling overwhelmed. Teachers who don't enjoy leading games or who are apprehensive about telling Bible stories can leave those tasks to others more skilled in those areas.

The Learning Center Plan is often a good option for medium or large churches.

What do students do and who leads them?

- Students are placed in small permanent groups (six to eight children is the best size). As much as possible, form groups with children of similar ages.

- Each group has at least one guide who leads the group to various centers. (Color code name tags for easy group identification.)

- Each group, along with its guide(s), visits each center during each session. All groups participate at once in the Worship Center.

> If you want to combine preschool and elementary children in the same group, read "Teaching Preschoolers and Elementary Children Together" on pages 24-25.

If you have large numbers of children, two groups may participate in one center at the same time.

What do teachers do?

- Each teacher takes responsibility for one center, remaining at the center and instructing each group as it visits the center. (Note: If both preschool and elementary-aged children will visit the same center, teachers modify activities as shown in each lesson.)

- During the Worship Center, teachers (and guides) sit with students and participate with them in the activities.

What are the centers?

- One room or outside area is designated for each of the *Treasure Seekers* learning centers. Post a large sign to identify each center.

- Decorate centers (see Decorating Ideas on pp. 29-32) and give centers fun, interesting names: Treasure Point (for the Bible Story Center), Parrot Landing (for the Art Center), Coconut Hut (for the Game Center), Underwater Adventure (for the Coloring/Puzzle Center) or The Beach (for the Worship Center). Choose from the centers suggested in the following diagram:

(Optional: The Bonus Island Ideas offered in each session can be used as an additional learning center.)

How do I plan the time schedule?

• The centers in *Treasure Seekers* can be taught in any order, but each center should last the same amount of time. For example, in a one-hour program, groups would remain in each center for 15 minutes and groups would be able to participate in three centers. (Add 5 minutes to the first center each group attends to provide for a brief welcome time.)

• Allow 5 minutes for groups to move from center to center, following a preestablished route.

If you have more time for each session, additional centers may be added or the time in each center may be lengthened (generally it is best to limit the time in each center to a maximum of 25 minutes in order to keep student interest high). Use the chart below as an example of how to schedule groups. (Note: As the number of children in your program grows, add teachers or helpers to each center to maintain a ratio of one leader for every six to eight children. You may also add duplicate centers.)

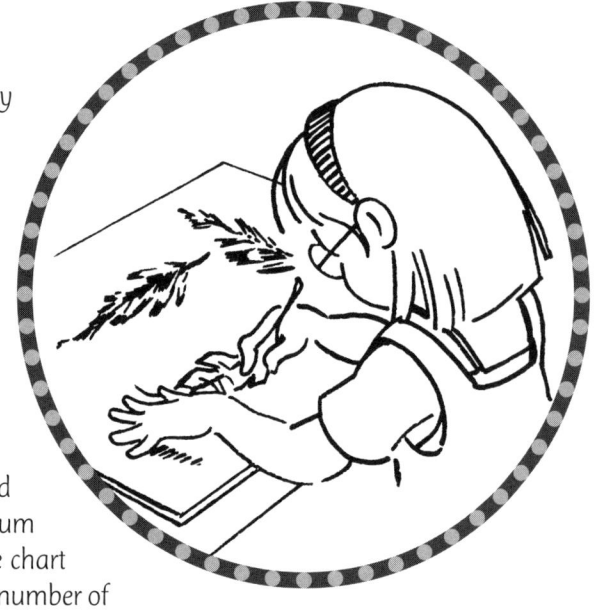

Sample One-Hour Schedule

	11:00-11:20	11:25-11:40	11:45-12:00
Group 1	Welcome and Bible Story Center	Game Center	Worship Center
Group 2	Welcome and Game Center	Bible Story Center	Worship Center

How do I make the Learning Center Plan run smoothly?

• Predetermine the route each group will travel, including room and building entrances and exits. Ask guides to walk their routes in advance to become familiar with all locations.

• Establish a signal for notifying groups when it's time to move to the next center.

• Provide labeled tables or other areas where students may leave their projects and belongings during the session.

• Provide color-coded name tags to identify each group.

Schedule Options

You can adapt the sample schedule on page 16 to the needs and interests of your church. (See schedule options on p. 18.) Other centers can be added or substituted in order to meet the needs of younger or older students. In addition to the centers suggested in this course, many churches include centers for such things as snacks, recreational outdoor games (soccer, baseball, volleyball), children's choir and elective classes (cooking, woodworking, etc.).

When planning the schedule, remember to include a variety of activities in an order that will meet the needs of children. For example, if students have been sitting in the adult worship service before coming to *Treasure Seekers*, plan an active center at the beginning of the session. If students attend *Treasure Seekers* after being in Sunday School, provide a snack at the beginning of the session.

For help in planning each session's schedule, give each leader and teacher a copy of the planning page on page 238.

OPTION 1
(60-75 minutes)

Worship Center
15 minutes

Bible Story Center
15-20 minutes

Game Center
15-20 minutes

Art Center
15-20 minutes

OPTION 2
(75-90 minutes)

Adult Worship
15 minutes

Game Center
15-20 minutes

Bible Story Center
15-20 minutes

Art Center
15-20 minutes

Worship Center
15 minutes

OPTION 3
(75-90 minutes)

Game Center
15-20 minutes

Bible Story Center
15-20 minutes

Art Center
15-20 minutes

Worship Center
15 minutes

Snack Time
15 minutes

OPTION 4
(75-95 minutes)

Worship Center
15 minutes

Bible Story Center
15-20 minutes

Game Center
15-20 minutes

Coloring/Puzzle Center
15-20 minutes

Art Center
15-20 minutes

© 2006 Gospel Light. Permission to photocopy granted. *Treasure Seekers*

Getting and Keeping the Very Best Staff

One of the most important elements in staffing a successful program is planning how you will recruit and organize your staff. However you do it, keep in mind that the best learning and the most fun take place when there is a teacher or helper for every six to eight children.

The optimum plan for staffing is to have the same teachers in place for the entire course. Both teachers and children benefit from regular interaction. Having long-term teachers creates a wonderful opportunity for spiritual growth in students as they build relationships with adults who are faithful in demonstrating God's love.

> If you are using *Treasure Seekers* with preschoolers, they will benefit greatly from consistent teachers. Young children need the security of familiar faces. This security creates a familiar and positive atmosphere, resulting in fewer separation and/or discipline problems and more positive learning!

While it may be easier to recruit teachers to teach one session at a time, such short-term staffing creates other problems. Many churches have found that rotating teachers frequently not only makes learning and growth difficult for children, but it also creates a heavy workload in administration (distributing curriculum, orienting a constant stream of new teachers, etc.).

Here are some options if long-term commitment is difficult in your situation.

- Ask teachers to teach for a shorter time period—four weeks at a time instead of 13 weeks.

- Find two teams of teachers and helpers who will each teach for two weeks at a time. Then plan to rotate the two teams so that they alternate teaching two weeks at a time. Over the course of the program, teachers and children become familiar with each other and can benefit from regular interaction.

- If you must rotate some teachers on a weekly basis, make sure that you have a number of consistent people who can greet and interact with children and parents on a weekly basis.

Recruiting Tips

Recruiting teachers and helpers is one of the key tasks to making *Treasure Seekers* an effective and fun learning experience for the children of your church and community. Keep the following tips in mind as you seek the volunteers and then match their talents to the tasks to be done:

- Pray for guidance in finding the people God wants to serve in this ministry.

- Start early—at least three months before the *Treasure Seekers* program begins!

- Keep all the leaders of all your children's ministries aware of and praying about staffing needs.

- Develop a written job description for each staff position.

- Make a list of potential teachers and helpers. Consider a wide variety of sources for volunteers: church membership list, new members' classes, suggestions from adult teachers or leaders,

lists of previous and current teachers, and survey forms. Get recommendations from present teachers. Don't overlook singles, senior citizens, youth and collegians. Some churches ask parents to teach during the summer months, giving school-year teachers a break. Be sure to follow your church's established procedures for screening volunteers.

- Look for team members with interests and abilities in specific areas. For example, the teaching team for 24 children might consist of three adults: one who prepares and leads the Bible Story Center each week, one who prepares and guides the Game Center and a third adult who prepares and leads the Worship Center. While each team member has the primary responsibility to lead only one center, all team members are involved throughout the session as helpers.

- Recruit a separate team of teachers and leaders for each center. Each team might consist of two or more adults who enjoy teaching together, or consider asking a family with teenagers to work together to form a teaching team.

- Prayerfully prioritize your prospect list. Determine which job description best fits each person's strengths and gifts.

- Personally contact the prospects. Sending a personal letter or a flyer (see p. 21) to each prospect or calling the prospect are good first steps. Follow up to answer any questions or to see if the prospect has made a decision. Show the prospect the **Treasure Seekers** manual and *Island Music* CD. Ask the prospective volunteer what he or she would most enjoy doing as a leader or teacher in *Treasure Seekers*.

- Provide new volunteers with all the needed materials, forms, helpful hints and training that will help them to succeed. For all teachers and helpers, you may want to schedule one or more training meetings at which you distribute curriculum, review the schedule and procedures, sing the songs together, etc.

- During the volunteer's time of service, make sure the volunteer knows who will be available to answer questions or lend a helping hand. Look for specific actions and services contributed by the volunteer and offer your thanks!

- Plan a thank-you brunch or dinner for teachers and their families. Even if they don't attend, they'll be grateful for your appreciation!

Recruiting Announcements

The teachers and helpers who will be your *Treasure Seekers* teachers and helpers will appreciate clear, concise information about the program—and a little added inspiration couldn't hurt! Here are some attention-grabbing recruiting announcements.

Hunt for Treasure!

Come join the exciting adventure at *Treasure Seekers!*

If you'd like to discover buried treasure every single Sunday, we're now taking applications for Island Guides who can show God's love to kids, use their imaginations and have fun discovering the treasure of who God is!

Treasure Seekers starts on_____

and continues through_____

at_____

Discover Your Island of Treasure!

_____ _____
(date)   (date)

_____
(times)

Come join a team of treasure seekers on a 13-week island getaway!

Treasure Seekers has exciting songs, fun games, worship activities and great Bible stories that will give kids new ways to discover who God is. But that's not all! You'll keep kids coming back for more through awesome art projects, tasty snacks, wacky games and more!

Act now to ensure your spot as an Island Guide in this 13-week adventure!

© 2006 Gospel Light. Permission to photocopy granted. *Treasure Seekers*

Publicity Guidelines and Schedule

Well-planned publicity is critical to the success of any event, so take time to carefully schedule each part of your publicity plan. Publicity ideas are endless (bulletin board displays, banners, coloring poster contests, parent letters, etc.), but be sure to include these basics: church bulletin and newsletter announcements, posters and flyers. Here is a suggested schedule:

Publicity Schedule

12 WEEKS BEFORE:
- Determine the exact dates on which each publicity piece will be released.
- Assign publicity tasks.

8 WEEKS BEFORE:
- Print a teaser announcement in your church bulletin and/or newsletter.

6 WEEKS BEFORE:
- Display posters in well-traveled areas at your church facility and in your community.

4 WEEKS BEFORE:
- Print information about *Treasure Seekers* in your church newsletter and mail flyers to children.
- Print announcements in your church bulletin on a weekly basis.

1 to 3 WEEKS BEFORE:
- Continue bulletin announcements.
- Make verbal announcements during church worship services.

Publicity Ideas

Posters and Flyers

Use the posters and flyers on pages 239-241 to get the attention of children and families and invite them to participate in *Treasure Seekers*. You may also use the art on pages 234-237 to make your own posters and flyers, telling information about *Treasure Seekers*. Display the posters in a variety of locations around your church.

Church Website

Add information about *Treasure Seekers* to your church's website. Consider adding an online registration feature and a course outline and schedule that will help parents become familiar with the course. Create interest in *Treasure Seekers* by adding a photo of several kids and teachers dressed in island clothing and carrying a treasure chest.

Information Booth

Decorate a booth or table in the church lobby from which to recruit teachers and helpers and preregister children. Decorate the booth or table with an island motif (see "Decorating Ideas" on pp. 29-32). Prepare promotional flyers, registration forms and volunteer sign-up sheets for use at the booth.

Kickoff Event

Prepare for and publicize the upcoming *Treasure Seekers* course with a kickoff event. Schedule the kickoff event two to three weeks before *Treasure Seekers* begins. Invite children and their parents to discover what the fun is all about. Publicize the event by distributing flyers to families in your church and community. Set up three or four fun island games or activities and offer a snack or two. Choose ideas from the Bonus Island activities suggested in each lesson. Place a registration booth near the center of all the action so it is convenient for parents to register their children. Display flyers and posters at the booth.

- Each activity needs at least one adult or older teenager to be in charge. Encourage all adult and teen helpers to dress in island clothing.

- Consider asking individual families in your church to sponsor activities. Each family would be responsible for purchasing supplies, setting up the activity and leading the activity during the event. In addition to having people who lead activities, have several helpers greet parents and encourage children to try an activity that is lacking participation.

- Each activity needs a designated area. In most situations, the activities can be set up outside, preferably on a lawn. One simple way to mark each area is with stakes in each corner. Then tie a rope from stake to stake, marking the boundaries of the area. If using a parking lot, draw boundaries for each area with chalk. Each activity area needs a large sign identifying the activity. Restrooms need to be open and clearly marked.

© 2006 Gospel Light. Permission to photocopy granted. *Treasure Seekers*

Teaching Preschoolers and Elementary Children Together

Whenever possible, it's recommended that you group preschool- and elementary-age children separately for *Treasure Seekers*. Teaching is most effective when children are grouped with others at similar developmental levels. While there is some benefit in mixing children of various ages together, it is difficult to prevent the oldest children from feeling that the activities are "baby" stuff because the younger kids are also involved. Even among children of similar ages, you are likely to find a variety of skills and abilities.

However, if there aren't enough children to form separate groups for preschool- and elementary-age children, you may need to combine children of both age levels together. The tips and ideas in *Treasure Seekers* will help you combine children from a wide variety of ages and still provide effective teaching.

Game and Art Center Tips

• Use the games and art activity ideas suggested for the age level of the majority of children in your class. If needed, modify the games and art activities as suggested in each lesson for either older (elementary) or younger (preschool) children. The modifications use the same or similar materials so that you don't have to collect and prepare an entirely new set of materials.

• Use the Bible memory verse that corresponds to the age of the majority of children in the group. However, in individual conversations with children, use the age-appropriate Bible memory verse, suggestions and discussion questions found in the lesson.

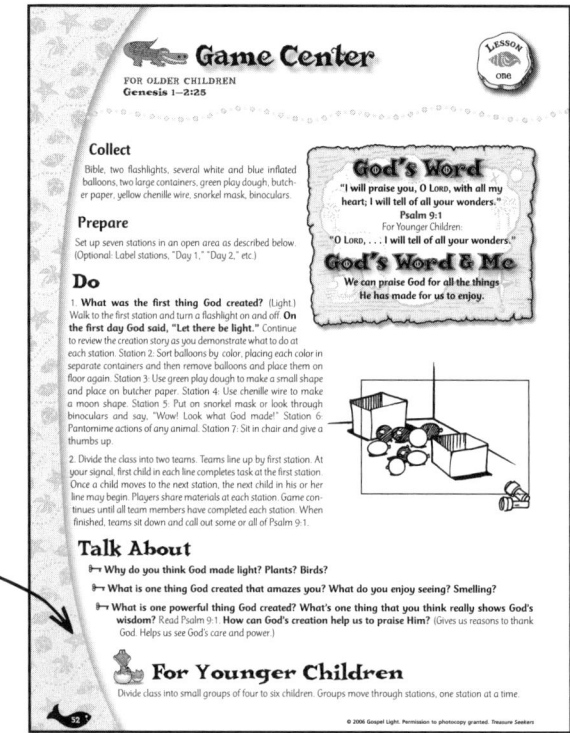

• Have the older children help lead the games or have younger children cheer on their teams as the older children play.

Bible Story Center Tips

• Even if children of varying ages are combined for art and game activities, consider keeping the Bible Story Center as a center through which small groups of children of similar ages rotate. Then the leader of the center can tailor the story to each particular group, ensuring that all children are taught the Bible story on their own level.

• If you have primarily elementary-age children, use the Bible Story Center Option for Older Children. However, provide for preschoolers the lesson's coloring page as a way to involve them and extend their interest in the story.

- If you have mostly preschoolers, use the Bible Story Center Option for Younger Children. Invite elementary-age children to participate by acting out the story or drawing Bible story murals.

Worship Center Tips

- While preschoolers are not likely to feel comfortable volunteering for the fun team games and other activities, they will still enjoy cheering for their teams.

- Make sure that the teachers and helpers of the preschoolers sit among the children to provide security and attention.

- Set aside space for preschoolers to sit at the front of the Worship Center area so that they are able to see.

- Make a copy of the *Island Music* CD for each child to take home. Familiarity with the songs will help preschoolers feel comfortable in the large-group setting. Although preschoolers may not be able to remember all the words of a song, they will easily catch on to and sing the song's chorus and can still participate by doing the song's motions and/or by clapping or by playing rhythm instruments such as maracas. If a song doesn't include motions or clapping, add them.

Outreach Ideas

Because *Treasure Seekers* is packed with loads of exciting hands-on learning activities, you won't want any student to miss it! And since this program is also a great place for unchurched kids to learn about God in a relaxed, inviting atmosphere, you'll want to publicize it—even beyond your church! Here are ideas to help you not only plan to invite children to participate in *Treasure Seekers* but also to follow up on visitors.

Invitation Ideas

- Keep accurate enrollment records for your ongoing children's programs. Several weeks prior to the beginning of *Treasure Seekers*, send flyers (see pp. 239-241) or make phone calls to children who have either stopped attending your church or who have visited recently.

- Offer a small island-related prize to any child who brings a friend to attend *Treasure Seekers*. (Note: Adapt one of the flyers on pp. 239-241 for use as an invitation children can give to friends.) Each week be prepared to welcome visitors by having a greeter(s) who can help visitors find the appropriate classrooms, make name tags available, and record contact information on registration forms. Consider recognizing visitors each session during the Worship Center. (Note: Prepare enough name tags so that visitors have same tags as other children.)

- Plan with the adult ministry coordinator to offer a parenting or other special-interest class at the same time children will be participating in *Treasure Seekers*.

- Make a large outdoor banner or paint a large sign and hang it in a visible place outside your church.

- Mount flyers in businesses frequented by children and their families (grocery stores, laundromats, etc.) and on community bulletin boards.

Follow-Up

- Invite parents to attend a special celebration as part of the final *Treasure Seekers* session (see invitations on p. 233). Children sing songs for their parents, families may tour classrooms and everyone enjoys an island snack or potluck meal. Encourage teachers and leaders to make a special effort to introduce themselves to parents and look for natural opportunities to build friendships, answer questions about the church, etc.

- During the 13 weeks of *Treasure Seekers*, encourage teachers and leaders to contact their students, including absentees, visitors or irregular attendees. Provide already-stamped postcards, prepared mailing labels, and address and phone lists.

- Take one or more photos of children during *Treasure Seekers* and ask leaders and teachers to personally deliver photos to children's homes at the end of the program. (Obtain parent permission for use of photos.)

- Make a *Treasure Seekers* Memory CD with lots of photos showing the variety of activities in which children participated. Send each CD to children who attended and include an invitation to other upcoming church programs.

- Pray for the teachers, leaders and helpers and remind them to pray for the children in their groups, asking God to bring to their minds appropriate ways to keep in touch with the children and to nurture them in Christ.

Partnering with Parents

In Deuteronomy 6:7, God commanded parents to teach their children about Him "when you sit at home and when you walk along the road, when you lie down and when you get up." The most important learning in life takes place not in churches, schools or scout troops but in families. The hours and days parents and children spend together are the prime opportunities for building long-lasting spiritual foundations!

Choose one or more of the following ideas for ways you can help parents in their awesome responsibility of spiritually teaching their children.

- Send home the Parent Letter (p. 232) to each parent at the beginning of the program and include a copy of the *Treasure Seekers* Scope and Sequence so that parents are aware of the content and goals of this course.

- Offer a free or low-cost kid-friendly Bible to parents when they register their children for *Treasure Seekers*. Especially if your program will attract visitors or unchurched children, it's wise not to assume that every family will have a kid-friendly Bible.

- Consider giving each parent a copy of the first page of each session. As parents read the devotional, they will develop an understanding not only of how they can model and demonstrate the focus of the session but also how they can talk with their children about the session's Bible truth.

- If you don't use the Coloring Page or Puzzle Page in each session, send them home with children each week. Include an introductory letter with the first lesson's Coloring or Puzzle Page, explaining that these pages can provide an opportunity for parent and child to talk about the way in which Bible people came to know more about who God is.

- Give parents of elementary-age children a copy of the Family Treasure Talk page (p. 231) and the *Treasure Seekers* Scope and Sequence page (p. 11). Encourage parents to use these with their children each week to read and study either the session's Bible story references or the Bible Memory Verse.

- Make a copy of the *Island Music* CD for families to listen to at home or in the car.

- Ask parents to support *Treasure Seekers* by providing a special snack or by preparing the materials for an art activity or game. Invite the parent to join in on the fun! (See invitations on p. 233.) Observing the way in which teachers and leaders talk with children about the session's Bible content will model for parents effective ways of spiritual education. (Note: You may want to invite each parent to schedule a session when he or she will observe a full class session with his or her child.)

• For the length of *Treasure Seekers*, invite parents to attend a parent support/prayer group that meets together twice a month or weekly to pray for their children, their teachers and each other. Enlist several parents to serve as hosts for this group. Hosts call parents to invite them to participate, arrange meeting space (homes, if possible), provide snacks, etc.

• Establish a group Bible memory verse contest in which all parents and children work together to memorize a certain number of the memory verses from *Treasure Seekers*. If the goal is met, promise an island party celebration. Using the patterns on pages 234-237, make a fun poster on which to record the number of verses memorized (large paper palm tree to which each parent and each child who can say a verse adds a palm branch, or a treasure chest in which coins are added for each verse memorized). (Avoid identifying individual memory efforts.) Display the poster in a central area and have several people serve as Bible memory listeners. During arrival or dismissal, parents and children repeat verses.

• Plan Family Days several times throughout the course as suggested on the Bonus Island Ideas pages in various lessons.

© 2006 Gospel Light. Permission to photocopy granted. *Treasure Seekers*

Decorating Ideas

No matter where you choose to hold your program, decorating the rooms where the action will take place can add fun and excitement to the proceedings! Children and teachers both will enjoy spending time in an island atmosphere. A few simple decorations can transform an ordinary classroom into part of *Treasure Seekers*. Use a variety of real items and/or painted backdrops. Use the art patterns on pages 234-237 to help you create the perfect atmosphere for both fun and learning. Recruit people who love to plan and prepare for a party as your decorating team.

Before the program begins, invite your congregation to loan or donate island-related items. Include any or all of the following: artificial palm trees or plants, beach towels, beach chairs, real wooden trunks or chests, fake jewels, discarded costume jewelry, play coins, sand buckets and shovels, stuffed animals, fish and/or parrots.

If you cannot leave decorations on the walls from week to week, consider simply attaching island items to rolling bulletin boards to be brought in during the sessions. You may also make murals on large sheets of butcher paper. Roll up murals after each session.

Create a Place

Name and label one or more rooms, especially if you are using a center method with this course. Places such as Treasure Point, Parrot Landing, The Beach, Coconut Hut, Coral Bay, etc., can create enthusiasm for this course. Decorate each room appropriately. Here are three ideas (see sketches on pages 30-32):

• Treasure Point

Create a room full of treasure! Use black electrical tape to make a large X on the floor. Add signs saying "X marks the spot!" and "Ahoy! Ye found the buried treasure!" Paint signs on cardboard to look old and weathered, or use old pieces of wooden fencing. Suspend signs from the ceiling, or attach to entrance door.

As a focal point, set out a large treasure chest filled with jewels, coins and golden treasures. Use a real wooden trunk or chest, or construct a chest using a cardboard box (see instructions on p. 234).

Arrange burlap fabric on the floor, placing boxes or crumpled newspaper underneath to make an uneven surface. Set the chest on a level spot on the burlap. (Optional: Scatter some sand on top of the burlap.) Fill the chest with crumpled paper. Then place treasure items on top.

For treasure, use plastic bead strings, acrylic jewels, discarded costume jewelry, play coins, and extra-large gold and silver sequins. Add ornate gold- and silver-colored items such as candlesticks, goblets and plates, or use metallic spray paint to paint items. Arrange objects to spill over the sides of chest and onto the burlap. Place several Bibles among the treasures. Prop an old rusted shovel against the wall.

Create a huge island treasure map and place on one wall. Tape together two large sheets of white butcher paper. Paint the paper with brewed tea to give it an aged appearance. Draw a simple treasure map (see clip art on p. 235). Then carefully singe (and quickly extinguish!) the edges of the map. Attach map to wall.

• Parrot Landing

Play games or create art projects surrounded by a grove of palm and flamboyant trees that are inhabited by colorful parrots. Enlarge onto butcher paper the Palm Tree and Flamboyant Tree patterns found on page 236, paint and attach to the walls. (Optional: Simply cut trees out of green and brown butcher paper.) Add tropical flower cutouts.

Place artificial or real plants around room. Tack artificial flowering vines around windows and doorways.

Make vines (using twisted paper), paper leaves and tissue paper flowers. Cut leaves from green construction paper and glue to the vine. Use tissue paper and chenille wire to form large paper flowers, and glue them to the vine.

Add colorful parrots to the room. Photocopy or enlarge the parrot patterns found on page 237 onto card stock, poster board or butcher paper. Paint parrots in various colors. Glue colored feathers on the wings and tails. Attach perched parrots to the trees on the walls. For flying parrots, decorate both sides of cutout. Use fishing line to hang flying parrots from the ceiling. Add cutouts of lizards and monkeys to the room or use plastic or stuffed toys. Play island sounds from a nature CD.

The Beach

Create a beach setting in one area. Place grass, straw or bamboo mats on the floor. Set out sand toys, boogie boards, beach umbrellas, beach towels, chairs and bags. Complete the scene by placing artificial palms and plants throughout the room.

Attach blue butcher paper to the lower half of one wall for the ocean. Enlarge the various island patterns found on pages 234-237 onto butcher paper, paint and cut out. Attach cutouts to walls, hang from the ceiling or place in butcher-paper ocean. Hang fishnets on the wall. Add shells and plastic or cutout fish and shellfish to the nets.

You may wish to cover one wall with an island backdrop to help kids catch the excitement of the island setting as they enter your assembly room each day.

For additional room decoration, attach a grass garland over the room entrance, or fringe strips of brown or green butcher paper to make roof thatching. Paint long strips of paper to look like bamboo supports and attach to either side of entrance.

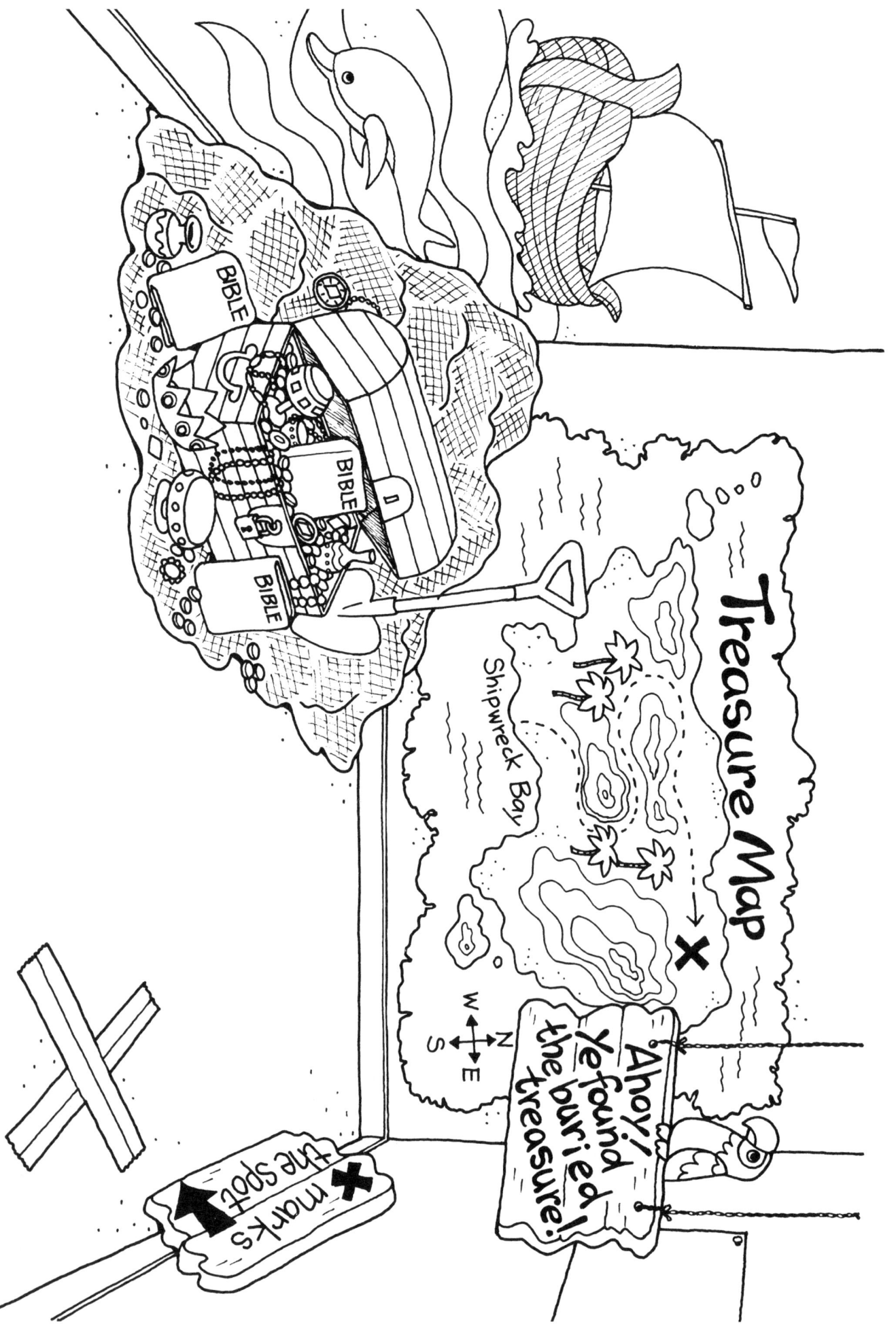

Theme Ideas

The Bonus Island Ideas offered in every session will add an unforgettable dimension to *Treasure Seekers*. Here are additional ways to fill your church with the sights and sounds of the Caribbean islands.

Scenery
Use the decorating ideas on pages 29-32 to decorate the classrooms and activity centers.

Sounds
The *Island Music* CD provides lively songs to help your students learn Bible truths. These memorable songs help students and adults alike discover who God is. Consider purchasing a CD of island sounds to add a fun atmosphere to your program! Play island sounds throughout your hallways and outdoor areas.

At the beginning and end of each Worship Center segment, ask a volunteer to dress in island clothing and blow on a large conch shell like a trumpet. You may also use this sound to signal transition times in your schedule.

Arrange for a brief musical performance using one or more steel drums or other Caribbean instruments (maracas, etc.). Musicians can describe the instruments and then perform songs.

Groups of children will enjoy creating their own chants or cheers to say while moving between centers or while entering the assembly area.

Special Days
Build interest and create enthusiasm for *Treasure Seekers* by asking students, teachers and helpers to bring in or wear items to enhance the fun. Consider doing one or more of the following:

- **Island Hat Day** Provide beach hats, straw hats or visors for everyone to decorate and wear.
- **Adventure Day** Give each participant a tropical-print bandana to wear along with other adventure-themed clothing (vest, hiking boots, sash, etc.).
- **Wacky Sunglasses Day** Encourage everyone involved in *Treasure Seekers* to wear sunglasses—the more colorful the better!
- **Island Clothing** Ask students and teachers to wear island-themed clothing one day—or every day, and give a prize for the day's best "island wear."
- **Tropical Bird or Animal Day** Students and team members wear something to represent an island bird or animal (fish, sea creature, etc.).

Invite someone who makes balloon animals to come in and demonstrate how to make several tropical birds and fish.

Invite a local zoo or the owner of a tropical bird(s) to bring animals and tell students about them.

Staff Names and Group Names
Captain: Director
Island Guides: Teachers and Helpers
Treasure Seekers: Students
Sea Life (starfish, octopi, crabs, etc.): Groups

Curriculum Resources
Familiarize yourself with the theme-related ideas provided throughout the curriculum. Each session includes a page of ideas for decorating, snacks, additional games, etc.

Bible Story Center Tips

Most of us can still remember a childhood story told by a good storyteller. What makes a good storyteller so memorable? A good storyteller draws listeners into the story, helping them imagine the story themselves and thus making it their own. You may not feel like one of the world's great storytellers, but fortunately, effective storytelling is a skill that you can develop by following the suggestions in this curriculum and by practicing a few simple principles. Here are some ideas and tips to help you become more confident and memorable!

A Good Beginning and Ending

A good beginning is essential, because it is much easier to capture an audience than it is to recapture them after their attention has wandered.

Bible Story Introduction

To help you make the most of the opening minutes of the Bible story, each story in *Treasure Seekers* begins with an introduction. In the introduction, you will find a question or comment that connects an element of the Bible story with a familiar childhood experience. In addition, to help you keep the interest of older children, a creative Bible storytelling technique is suggested for each lesson. As children are involved in making sound effects, roleplaying, using storytelling props, etc., they will be motivated to follow along with the story action.

Treasure Chest Activity

To enhance the treasure-hunting theme of this course, each Bible story also gives directions for an optional treasure chest activity. (If you do not have a chest, see directions on p. 234 for making a treasure chest.) In the Bible story for younger children, the object(s) in the treasure chest is (are) used as the basis for an interactive way of telling the Bible story.

The treasure chest activity for older children provides one or more creative clues that are removed from the chest at the end of the story. As you guide children to solve the clues (a rebus, a puzzle, a code, etc.), children will discover the attribute of God that is presented in the lesson.

Bible Story Conclusion

Each story also provides a conclusion—a brief summary of the basic focus of the story and how the Bible truth presented in the story connects with everyday life. This conclusion is called God's Word and Me. In the conclusion, one or more discussion questions are provided for you to use in helping children

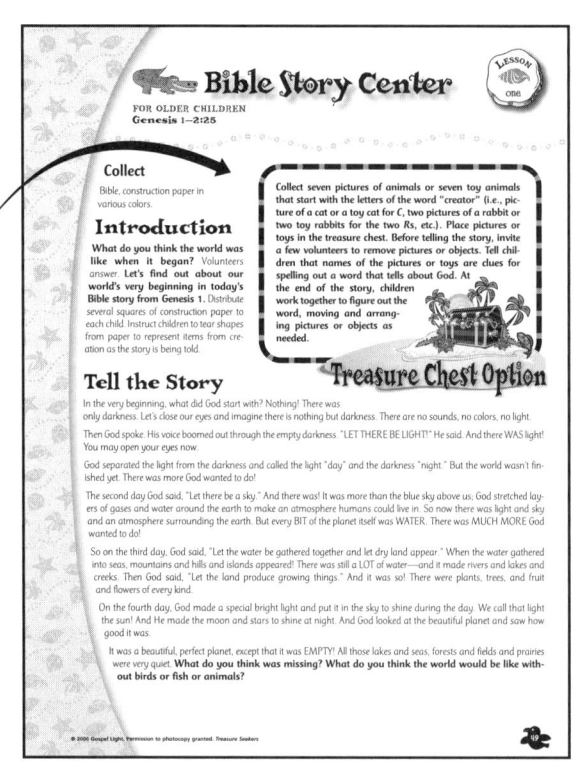

express their understanding of the lesson's focus and the Bible verse. A concluding prayer is suggested for elementary-age children. If the Bible story is told in a large group of 12 to 16 children, form small groups for the discussion time.

Storytelling Tips

- Practice telling the story aloud. Tell your story to yourself or someone in your family. Make notes or briefly outline the story.

- Have your open Bible at hand while you are telling the story. Occasionally referring to the Bible reinforces the idea that the Bible stories are true and are found in the Bible. With preschoolers, frequently repeat that the stories are true and are written in the Bible for us to read.

- While the Bible story is being told, other teachers and helpers sit separately among the children. Encourage them to fully participate with children, reacting appropriately and having fun! Their listening presence will encourage children to listen attentively as well, and they can help redirect children's attention back to the storyteller if needed.

- Use dramatic facial expressions and vary your tone of voice according to the story action.

- If students indicate a familiarity with the story, ask volunteers to tell some of the story action. Be sure to clarify and supplement information as needed.

- Keep your story brief. A good rule of thumb for a beginning teacher is to limit your story to one minute for each year of the children's age. If you have more than one age level in your group, target for the middle of the group, but be ready to shorten the story if the younger ones are restless.

- Work at maintaining eye contact with your children throughout the story. Know your story well enough that you can glance at your Bible and your notes and then look up.

Art Center Tips

The Art Center is a place where children can become absorbed in a creative activity as a way of expressing their understanding of how the lesson's focus relates to their lives. Each art activity incorporates discussion of a characteristic of God and/or the Bible story and the lesson's Bible verse. Some art activities may involve children in creating visual reminders of the Bible story action. In each art activity, the questions you ask and the comments you make will encourage students to apply Bible truth to everyday life. When students' hands are busy, they often talk freely!

Choose the Appropriate Activity

In each session, an art activity is provided for older children (elementary age) and for younger children (preschool age). Provide two centers, one for each age level. If you cannot provide two centers, choose the activity for which you have the most children. Each activity also includes a way to modify the activity (using the same or similar materials) for either younger or older children.

Before You Begin

Preparation is the key to making an art experience a joyful, creative one. No one enjoys a long stretch of waiting for a stapler or scissors. So make sure you have the following supplies on hand: newspaper (to protect surfaces), functional scissors, usable glue bottles and sticks, working markers, usable crayons and chalk, an adequate supply of tape, paint smocks (or men's old shirts) and butcher paper or newsprint end rolls (ask at your local newspaper office).

Before Every Activity

Before students arrive at your center, cover the work table(s) with newspaper or plastic table cover, securing it with masking tape, if needed. Set out materials in an orderly fashion, making sure you have enough materials for the number of children who will visit the Art Center.

If table space is limited, set out materials on a nearby shelf or supply table. Allow students to get and return materials to the appropriate places.

If most of your students are younger, use older students as helpers (for distributing supplies, stapling, etc.) during the Art Center time.

As Children Create

While children are working on their art creations, look for natural opportunities to use the Talk About suggestions on each Art Center page to help children relate the lesson focus to their daily lives. As children create, they are relaxed and eager to talk. Guided discussion will take the activity beyond art to discovery of Bible truth.

Avoid making value judgments as children create ("That's nice" or "How pretty!"). First, any child who then doesn't hear such a positive judgment will be crushed. Second and most important, focusing on the visual appeal of the artwork will not help children better understand the lesson. How a child's work *looks* is far less important than the child's *process* of creating that work and how the child can better understand the lesson. Comment on colors, lines and ideas you see represented. **Jenna, I see you used lots of colors on your project. Tell me about your work.** As you invite children to tell you about their work, many opportunities will arise for you to ask the discussion questions or to make comments that will help children understand the lesson focus.

Game Center Tips

The Game Center can be the perfect place for your students to let off steam, work out the wiggles and be open to guided discussion that relates the lesson focus to students' lives.

Choose the Appropriate Game

In each session, a game is provided for older children (elementary age) and for younger children (preschool age). Provide two centers, one for each age level. If you cannot provide two centers, choose the game for which you have the most children. Each game also includes a suggested modification (using the same or similar materials) for either younger or older children.

Creating a Play Area

Before leading a game, give yourself ample time to set up the play area. You may have little space in your classroom for a play area, so consider alternatives: outdoors, a gymnasium or a vacant area of the church from which sound will not carry to disturb other programs.

Once you have chosen the area, plan what you will need.

- Will you need to move furniture?

- Will you need to mark boundaries? Use chalk or rope outdoors; yarn or masking tape works indoors. (Remove masking tape from carpets after each session.)

- How much space will you need? Carefully review the game procedures to plan what amount and shape of space will be needed.

From time to time, take stock of your classroom area. Is it time to remove that large table or unused bookshelf? Should the chairs be rearranged or the rug put in a different place? Small changes in arrangement can result in more usable space!

Forming Groups or Teams

To keep students' interest high and to keep cliques from forming, use a variety of ways to determine teams or groups.

- Group teams by clothing color or other clothing features (wearing a sweater, wearing tennis shoes, etc.).

- Place equal numbers of two colors of paper squares in a bag. Students shake the bag and draw out a square to determine teams.

- Group teams by birthday month (for two teams, January through June and July through December); adjust as needed to make numbers even.

- Group teams by the alphabetical order of their first or last names.

- Group teams by telling them to stand on one foot: Those standing on a right foot form one team; those standing on a left foot form the other team.

© 2006 Gospel Light. Permission to photocopy granted. Treasure Seekers

After playing a round or two of a game, announce that the person on each team who is wearing the most (red) should rotate to another team. Then play the game again. As you repeat this rotation process, vary the method of rotation so that students play with several different students each time.

Leading the Game

Explain rules clearly and simply. It's helpful to write out the rules to the game. Make sure you explain rules step-by-step.

Offer a practice round. When playing a game for the first time with your group, play it a few times just for practice. Students will learn the game's structure and rules best by actually playing the game.

Guiding Conversation

Using guided conversation turns a game activity into discovery learning! Make use of the Talk About suggestions provided in the curriculum throughout the game time. You might ask a game's winners to answer questions or to consult with each other and answer as a group. You might discuss three questions between the rounds of a game or ask a question at the beginning of the round, inviting answers when the round is over.

Coloring/Puzzle Center Tips

The Bible story or verse coloring and puzzle pages provided for each lesson in *Treasure Seekers* provide an activity that you can use in several ways. These pages may be used as the basis of a separate activity center in which the youngest children (preschoolers) complete the coloring page and the older children (elementary age) work on the puzzle. The coloring and puzzle pages often directly connect with a lesson's Bible story or verse, or sometimes provide additional Bible information. In order to complete the puzzle pages, students need Bibles for reference.

Alternatively, these pages can be used to supplement an existing center. For example, a Bible story coloring page can be provided for younger children to extend their interest in the Bible story. Or children who complete an art activity before others can be challenged to complete the coloring or puzzle page. Coloring and puzzle pages can also be kept for use when an activity runs short.

The coloring and puzzle pages may also be sent home with children on a weekly basis as a way of extending their Bible learning into the home. In addition, the coloring pages can be copied onto transparencies, projected and traced onto butcher paper and used for wall murals or bulletin boards.

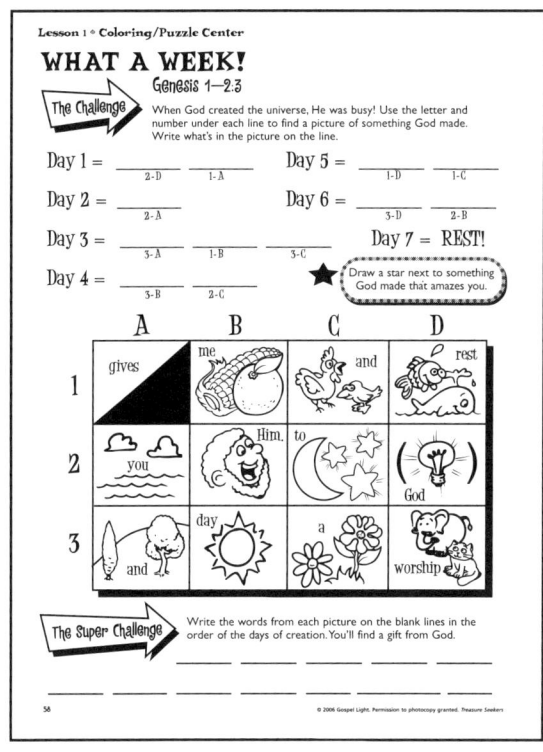

Preparation

- It's easiest to copy at one time all the pages needed rather than photocopying on a weekly basis. Store the pages in marked folders for easy use.

- If you plan to use markers for the coloring pages, photocopy those pages onto heavier stock to avoid marker bleed-through.

- Provide a variety of art materials for coloring; in addition to crayons and markers, colored pencils and watercolors add interest.

- Have the puzzle answer sheets (pp. 242-245) available for children who are working on the Bible puzzle pages.

Discussion Opportunities

While students are coloring or working on the puzzles, ask the questions suggested on the coloring or puzzle pages. Using these questions will help you connect the coloring or puzzle activity to the lesson focus. Encourage student participation by introducing each question with a statement such as **I'm looking for four students wearing red to answer this question.** Another way to attract the interest of students is to say, **Someone whose name begins with the letter J can answer this question.**

Consider storing each child's coloring and/or puzzle pages in a folder. As time permits, refer to these pages as a way of reviewing past lessons. At the end of *Treasure Seekers*, give pages to children to take home.

Worship Center Tips

The Worship Center is a large-group gathering time that is best scheduled at the beginning or the end of each session. The goal is to build enthusiasm for discovering the attributes of God and to help children participate in meaningful worship. Fun games, lesson-related music, saying or reading God's Word and prayer are all provided in the Worship Center.

Plan to have an enthusiastic youth-group-type leader guide the Worship Center activities. Ask him or her to dress in island clothing—perhaps with a unique hat or vest to help establish his or her character. Consider giving a name to the leader (Island Pete, Coco Bill, Island Queen, etc.) to catch kids' attention.

Games

Each week a wacky game is suggested that will catch everyone's attention and involve children in team-building camaraderie. Often the game requires representatives from two or more teams. The number of children on a team may vary, depending on group size. While not all children (especially preschoolers) will feel comfortable getting up in front to lead or participate in a game, they will enjoy being part of a team and cheering for their teammates.

Worship Times

Adults sometimes see children's worship time as occupying kids with frenzied repetitions of "Father Abraham" or as simply teaching children to worship in the same way as adults. But children need informal worship opportunities at their own level of understanding. Worship experiences designed to meet children's needs help them respond in love and praise to their heavenly Father.

Worship is indeed a time to show reverence and respect for God, but it doesn't mean always sitting still and being quiet. The activities offered in the Worship Center involve children and help them interact with each other and with teachers in singing praise to God and hearing His Word.

A Place of Worship

Worship is also enhanced by setting apart a place especially for praising Him. To create a space in your classroom for the Worship Center, prayerfully consider the ages and abilities of the children in your group, the kind of worship experience appropriate for them and the time and space available.

Consider ideas such as displaying a contemporary picture of Jesus, spreading a rug on the floor upon which children sit, and playing a theme-related song as a signal to begin worship.

If taking an offering, singing a particular response or placing candles on an altarpiece are part of your church's adult worship, occasionally add those elements to the Worship Center as well. Give a simple explanation to help children understand why each of these acts is part of worship.

Keep in mind that the Worship Center is not just a place for entertainment or observation; your goal is to see every child participate in a positive way that is in keeping with his or her development.

Music Just for You!

Consider making copies of the *Island Music* CD to help your students become familiar with the songs used during *Treasure Seekers*. A variety of musical styles are represented, making it easy for you to customize your worship time to include your students' favorites.

Leading Songs

Each of the upbeat songs on the *Island Music* CD is designed to relate to who God is or to the treasure-hunting theme of the course.

Children may participate by singing, clapping, playing rhythm instruments, holding up word charts, operating the overhead projector or adjusting the CD player. Help children understand that all these activities have one goal: to honor and praise God. Your example of sincere worship sets the tone—it is the strongest teaching about worship the children will receive.

Learning new songs can be difficult for some teachers. Listen to the song on the *Island Music* CD. Then play the song again and sing along. Practice it several times (listen to it while driving in the car, while you cook, etc.). You may want to choose three or four favorite songs from the *Island Music* CD and repeat them at each session, rather than teaching a variety of new songs. The younger the children are, the more repetition should be provided.

To teach a new song to children, print the words on a large chart or use the song charts in this book (pp. 246-254) to make a transparency to project on an overhead projector or to make PowerPoint slides. Project the words on a place where they may be seen easily by all the children.

As you play the song, sing along with the song, inviting children to join in with you. It is usually a good idea to sing only one stanza and/or chorus the first time through. If you are using an overhead, cover the entire transparency with a blank sheet of paper. As you sing, move the paper to reveal words one line at a time.

Choosing Additional Songs

If your church chooses to lead students in additional worship songs, select songs with the same prayer and sensitivity with which you'd plan adult worship. Utilizing simple worship choruses and hymns from among your own church's favorites will prepare children for the transition to adult-level worship in a gradual, age-appropriate manner. In this way, children will become familiar with a body of songs used in adult worship.

Whatever songs you use, if unfamiliar words are used, take the time to give a brief definition of the word. Use a children's Bible dictionary if needed. For example, **The word "holy" means to be chosen or set apart. When we sing that God is holy, it means that He is perfect and without sin.** If you cannot put the words or concepts of a song in terms a child can truly understand, recognize that the song is probably appropriate only for adult worship.

Bible Verse

The simple verse activity provided encourages students to hear and/or say the Scripture in a creative way that invites their participation. While children may often memorize the verse as part of this activity, Bible memory is not the primary goal. Instead, the goal is simply the interactive reading or hearing of God's Word.

If the reading abilities of children and the number of teachers permit, children may find and read the verse in Bibles as part of this activity.

Consider printing out each week's verse on a computer banner for easy reading.

Prayer Time

Prayer is an integral part of worship. Don't deny children this privilege because they seem unable to hold still with folded hands and bowed heads for long periods of time. Instead, involve children in prayer in ways that will help them understand that prayer is something they can do. Don't insist that students pray in a particular posture; keep prayer times short and make them times of high involvement. Remember that your prayers give the students in your class a model for prayer that they will follow. Keep your prayers brief and use simple words. Long sentences and long prayers make prayer seem boring and not something for a child.

Each Worship Center provides prayer activity ideas for a large-group prayer at the end of the Worship time. In addition to these ideas, you may also invite students to say sentence prayers, record requests and answers in a prayer journal, list prayer requests on a large sheet of paper, and allow children to pray with eyes open so that they are able to read and recall requests.

Treasure Seekers Lessons

In this section are each lesson's instructions. Before each session, photocopy and distribute the lesson to each teacher and leader.

BIBLE STORY ◆ Genesis 1—2:25

God Creates

LESSON one

Teacher's Devotional

It's been said that 10 of the most controversial words in the English language are "In the beginning God created the heavens and the earth" (Genesis 1:1). Certainly, few other sentences could have such a profound impact: These words declare a worldview that colors all we see, feel and think! Believing any other idea of Earth's origin produces a worldview that says we are random accidents with no meaning or purpose beyond our momentary self-gratification. But as God's creatures, we recognize the vastness and variety of His work. It fairly shouts to us that, although we are small and finite, our creator's love, wisdom and power are forever beyond our imagining! More than that, Jesus tells us in John 14 that He is preparing a place for those who are His that is beyond anything we can conceive. As beautiful as His physical creation is, His spiritual "new creation in Christ Jesus" within us and our future home in a place of His creating exceeds anything we have yet experienced. What joy, hope and genuine meaning that produces! We aren't accidents: We matter; we are loved; we have purpose for being!

Let those 10 controversial words spark your imagination. Take them as God's invitation to wide-eyed wonder! Teach part of the lesson outdoors or spend a few minutes together really looking at God's creation. As you really notice and genuinely express your joy and admiration, your kids will feel free to express wonder and thanks as well! If going outdoors isn't possible, look at your own hands. Notice the millions of intricate connections that are happening to make your eyes see and your fingers move right now. Breathe deeply and think of what it takes for hearts to beat and for lungs to transfer oxygen. Then use every bit of that wonder and joy to celebrate with your kids in praise for all God has made for us to enjoy!

God's Word

"I will praise you, O LORD, with all my heart; I will tell of all your wonders."
Psalm 9:1

For Younger Children:
"O LORD, . . . I will tell of all your wonders."

God's Word & Me

We can praise God for all the things He has made for us to enjoy.

© 2006 Gospel Light. Permission to photocopy granted. *Treasure Seekers*

Planning Page

Choose which centers you will provide and the order in which children will participate in them (see pp. 14-18 for schedule tips and pp. 24-25 for guidelines in combining older and younger children). Also plan who will lead each center (for staffing tips see pp. 19-21). Use the reproducible planning sheet (p. 238) to record your plans.

Bible Story Center

Bible Story
God Creates • Genesis 1—2:25

Younger Child Option
Hold up colored paper squares that help to tell the Bible story

Older Child Option
Use pictures and objects as clues to spell the word "Creator"

Art Center

Younger Child Option
Create 3-D balloon fish and talk about things God made for us to enjoy

Materials
Bible, Pattern Page (p. 56), white card stock, large balloons, ruler, string, scissors, crayons, hole punch, tape, large wiggle eyes, glue sticks, stickers

Older Child Option
Make sand-art pictures and praise God for His creation

Materials
Bible, sand or salt, small disposable cups, colored sidewalk chalk, dark-colored card stock or poster board, pencils, glue

Game Center

Younger Child Option
Play a game making animal sounds and thank God for making animals

Materials
Bible, *Island Music* CD and player

Older Child Option
Move through stations and talk about how God's creation gives us reasons to praise Him

Materials
Bible, two flashlights, several white and blue inflated balloons, two large containers, butcher paper, green play dough, yellow chenille wire, snorkel mask, binoculars

Coloring/Puzzle Center

Younger Child Option
Review the Bible story while completing coloring page

Materials
Lesson 1 Coloring Page (p. 57) for each student, crayons

Older Child Option
Review the Bible story while completing puzzle page

Materials
Lesson 1 Puzzle Page (p. 58) for each student, pencils

Worship Center

For the Younger and Older Child
Participate in large-group activities to review Bible verse and to worship God together

Materials
Bibles, *Island Music* CD and player, song charts (pp. 246-247)

Bonus Island Ideas

LESSON one

Bonus Island Ideas can be used at any time during this session: as an additional activity center, to extend the session for a longer time, or for added island excitement.

Palm Tree Display

Create a palm tree display that will remain in the classroom during the 13-week *Treasure Seekers* course. Cover bulletin board or wall with a length of blue butcher paper. Cut brown butcher paper or brown paper bags into the shape of a palm tree trunk and attach trunk to bulletin board or wall. Cut 13 large palm shapes from green poster board. Provide decorating materials (glitter paint, puffy paint, markers, etc.) for children to use to decorate palm leaves and trunk. Print "God is my creator!" on one decorated palm shape. Attach the palm at the top of the trunk. Collect other palms and place them in a large basket. Keep the basket near the palm tree display and add palms with attributes of God written on shapes at the end or beginning of each session.

Post a note alerting parents to the use of food. Also, check registration forms for possible food allergies.

Beach Bowling Fun

If you have a sand play area at your church, divide class into teams of six to eight players. Invite two to four volunteers from each team to fill 10 large paper or plastic cups with wet sand. Turn over and remove cups to form sand bowling pins. (Note: Create one bowling area for every team.) Teams line up opposite sand pins and team members take turns rolling a tennis ball at the sand pins. First team to knock over all the pins is the winner! Play additional rounds, inviting new volunteers to form pins.

A Fishin' Snack

In pitcher, mix 2 large packages of blue Jell-O according to printed directions for speed-set method. Allow children to take turns stirring ingredients. Help each child line a paper or plastic cup with a sandwich bag. Each child puts one or two Gummy Fish into lined cup and pours liquid into cup, filling cup three-fourths full. Keeping bags open, place cups in refrigerator for 30 minutes. When Jell-O has set, remove bags from cups and serve. Provide plastic spoons. Serves 12.

© 2006 Gospel Light. Permission to photocopy granted. *Treasure Seekers*

Bible Story Center

FOR YOUNGER CHILDREN
Genesis 1—2:25

Collect

Bible.

Introduction

Let's use our fingers to count to seven. Lead children in counting. **Listen to find out what God did in seven days!**

Treasure Chest Option

Place a variety of colored paper squares in a treasure chest to represent items God created (i.e., yellow square to represent daytime, black square to represent nighttime, light blue square to represent oceans, etc.). Hold up colored squares as you tell the story.

Tell the Story

God made our beautiful world! After God made daytime and nighttime, He filled the world with oceans and rivers and lakes. He made beautiful green plants grow everywhere. He made the yellow sun. He made the white moon and stars. God's world was good!

But God's world was VERY quiet. The lakes, rivers and oceans were empty! So God said, "Let the water be full of fish!" And there were FISH! Big fish and whales and dolphins jumped and swam in the oceans.

God made big gray fish and little green fish. God made yellow fish that look like stars and fish that have heads like tiny, tiny horses. God made crabs that crawled and clams that dug themselves into the sand.

Then God looked at the beautiful blue sky. Nothing was there but clouds. So God said, "Let birds fly in the sky." Soon, blue birds and yellow birds, big birds and little birds flew in the sky. They made nests in the trees.

The dry land was full of grass and flowers and trees. But nothing moved there. So God said, "Let there be all kinds of animals." And just as God said, there were animals everywhere! Horses and zebras ran and kicked. Monkeys swung in the trees. Black cows, brown goats and white sheep ate the grass. Big gray elephants stomped. Tiny gray mice hid. Big lions roared and tall kangaroos hopped. God looked at all the fish and birds and other animals He had made. God said, "It is good."

But God wasn't finished yet! Our Bible tells us that God made someone to talk to. God called this person Adam. God told Adam to name all the animals. So Adam gave just the right name to each one.

Adam was happy with the animals and the trees and flowers. But God knew that Adam needed someone to talk to and to love. So God made a woman. Adam called her Eve. God said to Adam and Eve, "Take care of the animals and birds and fish that I made. Use the plants for your food."

Adam and Eve lived in the beautiful garden God made. God loved them very much. And Adam and Eve loved God. After God made everything in the world, He rested! God saw that everything He had made was very good!

God's Word & Me

I'm glad that God made EVERYTHING in our world! The Bible says, "O Lord, . . . I will tell of all your wonders." God's wonders are all the good things He has made and done. What is something God has made that you are glad for? We can praise God for all the things He has made for us to enjoy!

© 2006 Gospel Light. Permission to photocopy granted. *Treasure Seekers*

Bible Story Center

FOR OLDER CHILDREN
Genesis 1—2:25

LESSON one

Collect

Bible, construction paper in various colors.

Introduction

What do you think the world was like when it began? Volunteers answer. **Let's find out about our world's very beginning in today's Bible story from Genesis 1.** Distribute several squares of construction paper to each child. Instruct children to tear shapes from paper to represent items from creation as the story is being told.

Treasure Chest Option

Collect seven pictures of animals or seven toy animals that start with the letters of the word "creator" (i.e., picture of a cat or a toy cat for C, two pictures of a rabbit or two toy rabbits for the two Rs, etc.). Place pictures or toys in the treasure chest. Before telling the story, invite a few volunteers to remove pictures or objects. Tell children that names of the pictures or toys are clues for spelling out a word that tells about God. At the end of the story, children work together to figure out the word, moving and arranging pictures or objects as needed.

Tell the Story

In the very beginning, what did God start with? Nothing! There was only darkness. Let's close our eyes and imagine there is nothing but darkness. There are no sounds, no colors, no light.

Then God spoke. His voice boomed out through the empty darkness. "LET THERE BE LIGHT!" He said. And there WAS light! You may open your eyes now.

God separated the light from the darkness and called the light "day" and the darkness "night." But the world wasn't finished yet. There was more God wanted to do!

The second day God said, "Let there be a sky." And there was! It was more than the blue sky above us; God stretched layers of gases and water around the earth to make an atmosphere humans could live in. So now there was light and sky and an atmosphere surrounding the earth. But every BIT of the planet itself was WATER. There was MUCH MORE God wanted to do!

So on the third day, God said, "Let the water be gathered together and let dry land appear." When the water gathered into seas, mountains and hills and islands appeared! There was still a LOT of water—and it made rivers and lakes and creeks. Then God said, "Let the land produce growing things." And it was so! There were plants, trees, and fruit and flowers of every kind.

On the fourth day, God made a special bright light and put it in the sky to shine during the day. We call that light the sun! And He made the moon and stars to shine at night. And God looked at the beautiful planet and saw how good it was.

It was a beautiful, perfect planet, except that it was EMPTY! All those lakes and seas, forests and fields and prairies were very quiet. **What do you think was missing? What do you think the world would be like without birds or fish or animals?**

© 2006 Gospel Light. Permission to photocopy granted. *Treasure Seekers*

Lesson one

So on the fifth day, God created fish and sea life in the rivers and oceans. He created birds, butterflies and every other creature with wings to fly in the sky. And on the sixth day God said, "Let there be all kinds of animals—big ones and little ones and all sizes in between. And let them roam all over the earth." And roam all over the earth they did—walruses and wallabies, iguanas and ibexes! **What are some unusual creatures you can think of that God made?**

Now this was all very wonderful—but there was something else God wanted to create. On the sixth day, God created people.

The first people, Adam and Eve, were different from everything else God had created. God lovingly created people to care for all that He had created. More than that, God created people to love Him and to be loved by Him. The Bible tells us that people were created in the image of God—that means we are like God in some important ways.

Best of all, the people God made would be able to talk with God and know Him. Day and night, people could pray and know that God would hear them. That's what made people the most amazing part of all of God's wonderful creation!

And what about the seventh day? Well, on the seventh day God rested from the work of creating the world. God was happy with His creation. The world was off to a perfect start!

God's Word & Me

God's creation is all around us. We can see it, taste it, touch it and hear it from the minute we wake up with birds chirping outside our windows until the minute we go to sleep with the glow of the moon and stars at night. Sometimes we don't even notice the amazing way God has made the world! But when we pay attention to what God has made, it reminds us of how wonderful God really is.

- **When was a time you saw something amazing in God's creation? What was the amazing creation you saw?** (A beautiful sunset. The Grand Canyon. Fifteen-foot waves in Hawaii. A unique fish at the aquarium.) **How did it make you feel?**

- Read Psalm 9:1 aloud. **What are some things God created that you praise Him for?** (People. Beaches. The sun.)

- **God is the creator of our world and of you and me! We can praise God for all the things He has made for us to enjoy.** Pray briefly, **Dear God, we love You and thank You for being our awesome creator.** Thank God for items mentioned by children. **In Jesus' name, amen.**

Game Center

FOR YOUNGER CHILDREN
Genesis 1—2:25

Collect

Bible, *Island Music* CD and player.

Do

1. **What is your favorite animal? What sound does that animal make?** Children make animal sounds. **Let's play a game making the sounds of some different kinds of animals that God has made.**

2. Children stand in a line. As you play "Before All Time," first child in line leads the others around the room. When you stop the music, children freeze in place. Call out the name of an animal. Children make the sounds of the named animal. (Optional: Children may also pantomime motions of the animal.)

3. Repeat game as time permits, inviting new volunteers to lead others around the room and calling out different animal names.

God's Word

"I will praise you, O LORD, with all my heart; I will tell of all your wonders."
Psalm 9:1
For Younger Children:
"O LORD, . . . I will tell of all your wonders."

God's Word & Me

We can praise God for all the things He has made for us to enjoy.

Talk About

- Our Bible says, "O Lord, . . . I will tell of all your wonders." God is amazing! God made our wonderful world and EVERYTHING in it—all the bugs, the fish, the animals, the birds—everything!

- If you have a pet, raise your hand. Katy, what kind of pet do you have? Who has a different kind of pet? We can be thankful for all the different kinds of pets God made.

- We're glad for all the animals and other wonderful things God has made in the world. Pray briefly, **Thank You, God, for the animals and all the wonderful things You have made.**

For Older Children

Secretly assign each child to be a monkey, crocodile or a parrot. As the music plays, children walk around the room. When the music stops, children call out the sounds and/or make motions that their assigned animal makes and gather together with others making the same sound and/or motion. When all members of a group have gathered, group calls out some or all of Psalm 9:1.

© 2006 Gospel Light. Permission to photocopy granted. *Treasure Seekers*

Game Center

FOR OLDER CHILDREN
Genesis 1—2:25

LESSON one

Collect

Bible, two flashlights, several white and blue inflated balloons, two large containers, green play dough, butcher paper, yellow chenille wire, snorkel mask, binoculars.

Prepare

Set up seven stations in an open area as described below. (Optional: Label stations, "Day 1," "Day 2," etc.)

Do

1. **What was the first thing God created?** (Light.) Walk to the first station and turn a flashlight on and off. **On the first day God said, "Let there be light."** Continue to review the creation story as you demonstrate what to do at each station. Station 2: Sort balloons by color, placing each color in separate containers and then remove balloons and place them on floor again. Station 3: Use green play dough to make a small shape and place on butcher paper. Station 4: Use chenille wire to make a moon shape. Station 5: Put on snorkel mask or look through binoculars and say, "Wow! Look what God made!" Station 6: Pantomime actions of any animal. Station 7: Sit in chair and give a thumbs up.

2. Divide the class into two teams. Teams line up by first station. At your signal, first child in each line completes task at the first station. Once a child moves to the next station, the next child in his or her line may begin. Players share materials at each station. Game continues until all team members have completed each station. When finished, teams sit down and call out some or all of Psalm 9:1.

God's Word

"I will praise you, O LORD, with all my heart; I will tell of all your wonders."
Psalm 9:1

For Younger Children:
"O LORD, . . . I will tell of all your wonders."

God's Word & Me

We can praise God for all the things He has made for us to enjoy.

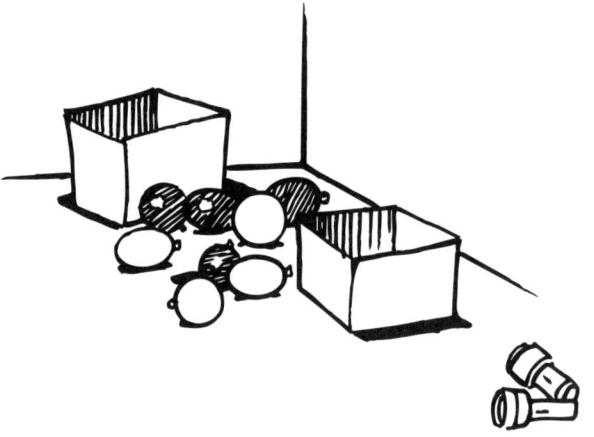

Talk About

- Why do you think God made light? Plants? Birds?
- What is one thing God created that amazes you? What do you enjoy seeing? Smelling?
- What is one powerful thing God created? What's one thing that you think really shows God's wisdom? Read Psalm 9:1. **How can God's creation help us to praise Him?** (Gives us reasons to thank God. Helps us see God's care and power.)

 ## For Younger Children

Divide class into small groups of four to six children. Groups move through stations, one station at a time.

© 2006 Gospel Light. Permission to photocopy granted. *Treasure Seekers*

Art Center

FOR YOUNGER CHILDREN
Genesis 1—2:25

Collect

Bible, Pattern Page (p. 56), white card stock, large balloons, scissors, ruler, string, crayons, hole punch, tape, glue sticks, large wiggle eyes, stickers (round, star, iridescent, etc.).

Prepare

For each child in the class: Photocopy the Pattern Page onto a sheet of card stock, inflate and tie one balloon and cut a 12-inch (30.5 cm) length of string.

Do

1. Child uses crayons to color tail and fin shapes and then cuts out tail and fin shapes from Pattern Page. (Note: Assist children with cutting as needed.)

2. Assist each child in punching a hole in the tail in the indicated area, folding tail on the fold line and pulling the knotted balloon neck through the hole in the tail. Secure with tape.

3. Child folds fins on fold lines and tapes fins to sides of the balloon. Child then glues wiggle eyes onto balloon in the face area and uses stickers to decorate the rest of the balloon.

4. Assist child in taping one end of the string to the top of the balloon to make a hanger for the fish. Hang 3-D fish from the classroom ceiling or invite children to take fish home to hang.

God's Word

"I will praise you, O L ORD, with all my heart; I will tell of all your wonders."
Psalm 9:1

For Younger Children:
"O L ORD, . . . I will tell of all your wonders."

God's Word & Me

We can praise God for all the things He has made for us to enjoy.

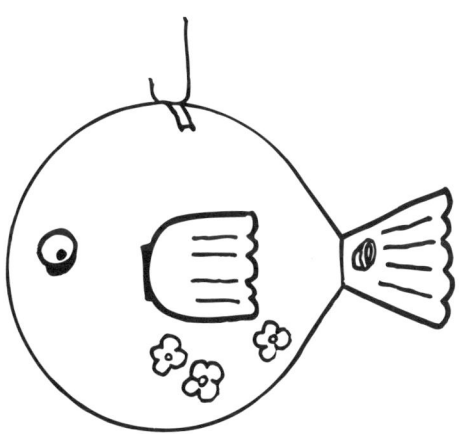

Talk About

- Today's Bible story is about how God made the world and everything in it. Joshua, what is something you would like to thank God for making?

- What is your favorite thing to do at the beach? I'm glad that God made the sand so that we can build sand castles at the beach. Where are some other places you see sand? (Backyard. Playground.)

- Our Bible says, "O Lord, . . . I will tell of all your wonders." We can thank God for all the wonderful things He made. Pray briefly, **Dear God, thank You for our wonderful world.**

 For Older Children

Children use inflated balloons to create any kind of animal face of their choice. Provide fun materials for children to create (tissue and construction paper, chenille wire, permanent markers, glitter glue, puff paint, etc.).

© 2006 Gospel Light. Permission to photocopy granted. *Treasure Seekers*

 # Art Center

FOR OLDER CHILDREN
Genesis 1—2:25

LESSON one

Collect

Bible, sand or salt, small disposable cups, colored sidewalk chalk, dark-colored card stock or poster board, pencils, glue.

Prepare

Pour sand or salt into several small disposable cups, filling cups one-quarter full. Add one stick of colored chalk to each cup.

Do

1. Invite children to use the chalk sticks to stir the sand or salt inside the cups. As color changes ask, **What is happening inside the cup?** Children continue stirring until sand or salt changes color.

2. Distribute dark-colored card stock or poster board to each child. Each child uses a pencil to draw a picture of God's creation. Child outlines the picture with white glue, then sprinkles colored sand onto glue, shaking off excess. (Note: For best results, sprinkle and shake off one color at a time.)

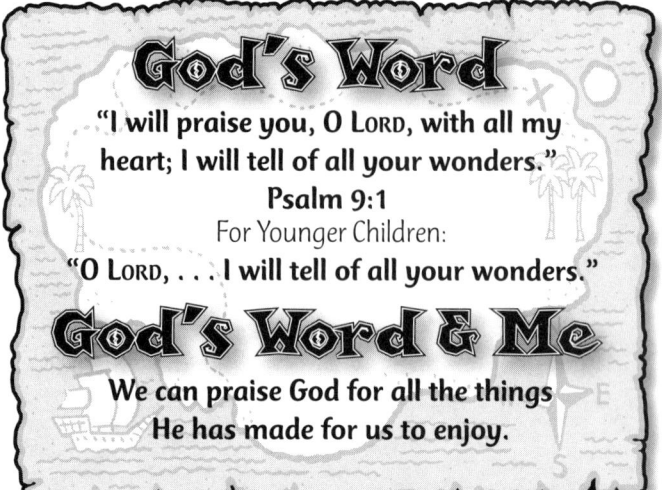

God's Word
"I will praise you, O LORD, with all my heart; I will tell of all your wonders."
Psalm 9:1
For Younger Children:
"O LORD, . . . I will tell of all your wonders."

God's Word & Me
We can praise God for all the things He has made for us to enjoy.

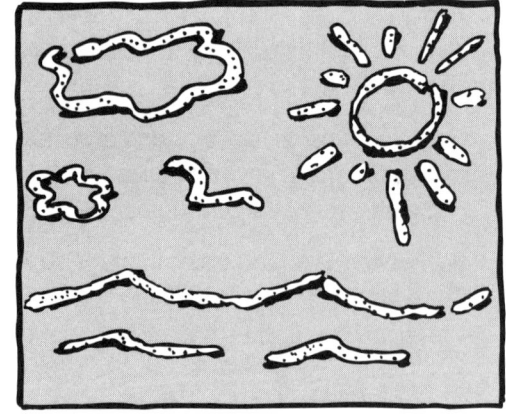

Talk About

🗝 **God's creation is all around us—in the sky, the sea, even in the mirror! How can God's creation help us learn about Him?** (Creation helps us to see God's care. It helps us to see God's power and greatness.)

🗝 **God used the word "good" to describe His creation. What words would you use to describe what God created?** ("Wonderful." "Amazing." "Awesome.") Read Psalm 9:1. Invite children to think about one of God's amazing creations. After several moments invite volunteers to complete the following prayer: **Dear God, I praise You for . . .**

 ## For Younger Children

Before class, collect a clear plastic or baby food jar for each child in your class. Children make sand-art creations by pouring colored sand or salt from cups into jars to create layers of different sand colors. Once jars are filled to the top, assist children in closing jars with lids.

Worship Center
Genesis 1—2:25

Collect
Bibles, *Island Music* CD and player, song charts (pp. 246-247).

Team Game
Divide group into two teams. Invite a volunteer from each team to come forward. Whisper the name of a different animal to each volunteer. At your signal, volunteers pantomime actions of the animal for their team members to guess. When a team member thinks he or she knows which animal is being pantomimed, he or she identifies the animal by calling out, "God created (elephants)!" First team to guess correctly is the winner of that round. Continue game with new volunteers after every round as time and interest allow. (Optional: Give animal crackers as a prize to the winning team.)

God's Word
"I will praise you, O Lord, with all my heart; I will tell of all your wonders."
Psalm 9:1
For Younger Children:
"O Lord, . . . I will tell of all your wonders."

God's Word & Me
We can praise God for all the things He has made for us to enjoy.

Bible Verse Game
Repeat Psalm 9:1 aloud with children. **Let's create supersized motions for the words of this verse that talks about praising the super works of our creator! What kind of motion can we make for the word "praise"?** (Jump up and cheer.) **"Heart"?** (Trace a large heart in the air.) After creating and practicing motions for four or five words, lead children in repeating verse while doing the motions.

Song
Lead children in singing "Before All Time," adding motions and/or clapping if desired.

Prayer
Let's praise God for His many wonders! Call out several praise starters (e.g., "I'm glad God made animals like . . ." "I'm glad God made foods like . . ." "I'm glad God made colors like . . ."). Children call out their responses.

Song
Play "Treasure Forever." Lead children in singing, adding motions and/or clapping if desired. Close by praying in unison the following prayer: **We praise You, Lord, for Your love and Your wonderful creation. We love You! Amen.**

Lesson 1 ⬥ Pattern Page

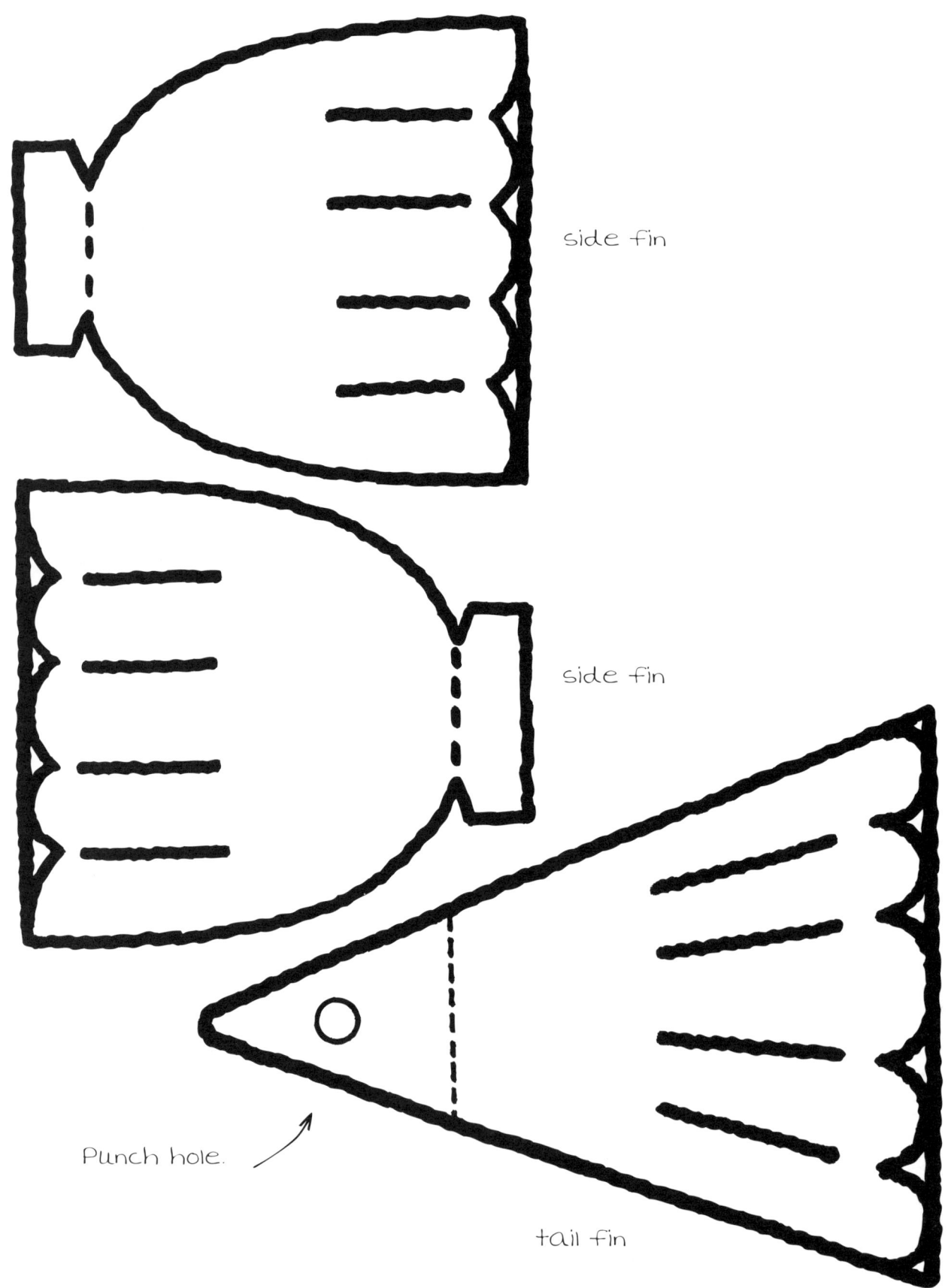

Fish Fin Patterns

Lesson 1 ◇ Coloring/Puzzle Center

God made the world.
Genesis 1—2:25

What is something God made that you are glad for?

© 2006 Gospel Light. Permission to photocopy granted. *Treasure Seekers*

Lesson 1 ◇ Coloring/Puzzle Center

WHAT A WEEK!
Genesis 1—2:3

 The Challenge

When God created the universe, He was busy! Use the letter and number under each line to find a picture of something God made. Write what's in the picture on the line.

Day 1 = _____ _____
         2-D   1-A

Day 2 = _____
         2-A

Day 3 = _____ _____ _____
         3-A   1-B   3-C

Day 4 = _____ _____
         3-B   2-C

Day 5 = _____ _____
         1-D   1-C

Day 6 = _____ _____
         3-D   2-B

Day 7 = REST!

★ Draw a star next to something God made that amazes you.

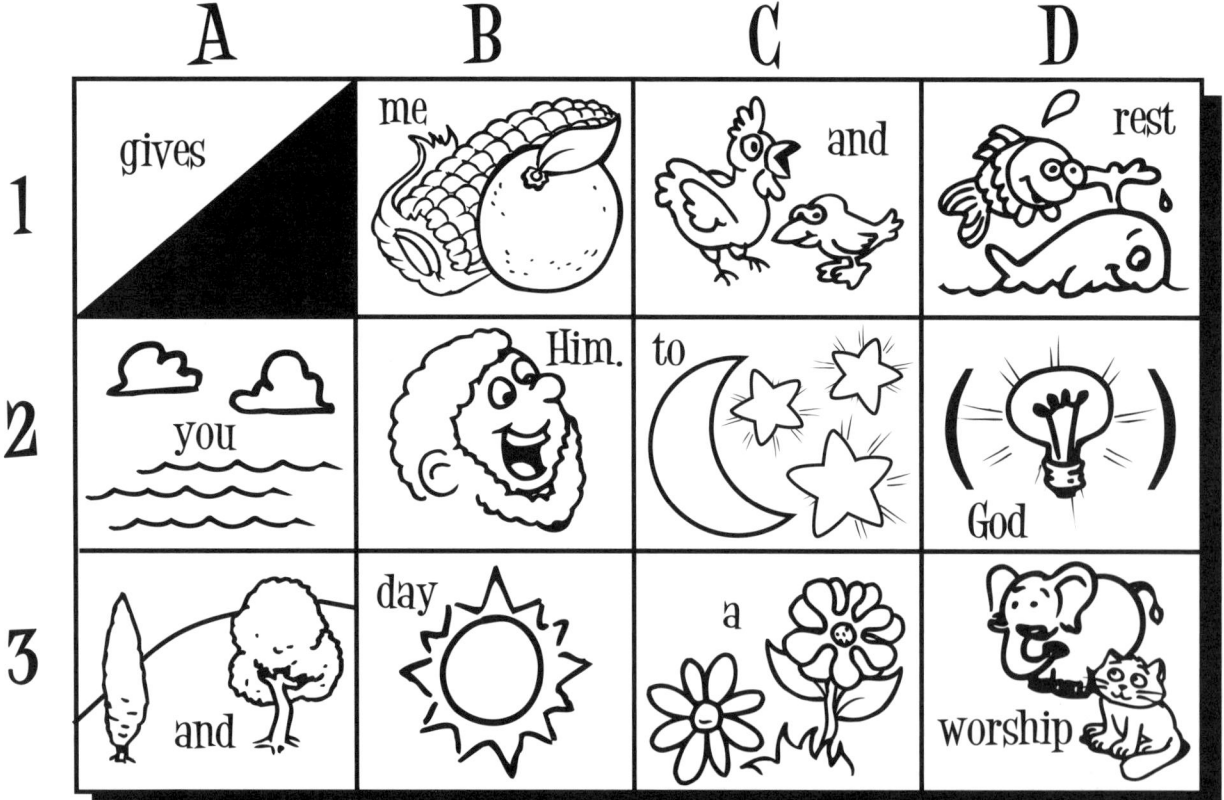

 The Super Challenge

Write the words from each picture on the blank lines in the order of the days of creation. You'll find a gift from God.

_____ _____ _____ _____

_____ _____ _____ _____

58 © 2006 Gospel Light. Permission to photocopy granted. Treasure Seekers

BIBLE STORY ◆ 1 Samuel 16:1-13

God Knows Me

LESSON two

Teacher's Devotional

"I know him inside and out." Such a comment reveals how well we think we know a person! We often assume that we know those with whom we work or live. But just as often, our "knowing" is simply a "management relationship" that replaces true knowledge. We know our spouse's favorite foods and habits, but we know nothing of his or her struggles and fears. Certainly the knowledge those spouses gained never yielded intimacy!

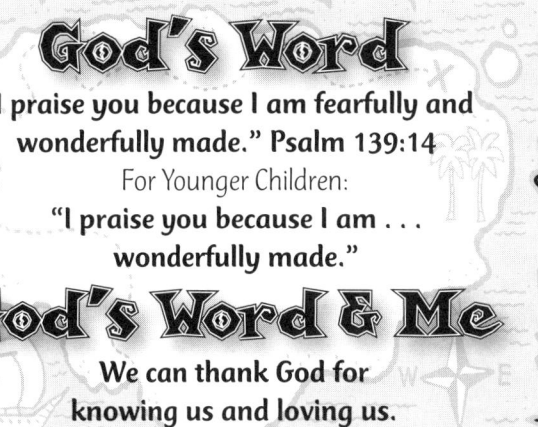

God's Word
"I praise you because I am fearfully and wonderfully made." Psalm 139:14
For Younger Children:
"I praise you because I am . . . wonderfully made."

God's Word & Me
We can thank God for knowing us and loving us.

We can live life at a "management" level of knowing others—even in our families or with our spouses. Because the administrative detail of life grows by leaps and bounds, we can become so preoccupied with synchronizing schedules that we begin to think that our time with another has value only when we are "on task." But knowing another goes beyond administrative detail—to the matters that *matter*. That's often perceived as too difficult or a waste of time!

The beauty of God our Father is that He always has time for the time-consuming business of knowing us intimately. He is completely aware of and part of all that goes on in our lives—physically, emotionally, mentally and spiritually! He sees the blockage in the artery, the fear in the back of the mind no one else knows, the secret smile that is only for Him at some new mercy revealed. And His knowing of every bit of us, inside and out, never drives Him away! With all He knows, He still loves us more than anyone else!

But by the same token, He longs for us to take time to truly know Him as well: instead of living at a management level of knowing Him (all that administrative detail of good works and church activities), Jesus calls us to be with Him, outside of our busyness. That yields knowing Him in an intimate way that will transform us from good managers into the intimate friends He longs for us to be (see John 15:13-15).

© 2006 Gospel Light. Permission to photocopy granted. *Treasure Seekers*

Planning Page

LESSON two

Choose which centers you will provide and the order in which children will participate in them (see pp. 14-18 for schedule tips and pp. 24-25 for guidelines in combining older and younger children). Also plan who will lead each center (for staffing tips see pp. 19-21). Use the reproducible planning sheet (p. 238) to record your plans.

Bible Story Center

Bible Story
God Knows Me • 1 Samuel 16:1-13

Younger Child Option
Draw stick figures to represent story characters

Older Child Option
Solve a message using rhyming clues

Art Center

Younger Child Option
Make face collages and talk about reasons to praise God for making us and knowing us

Materials
Bible, markers, paper, magazines, scissors, paper plates, glue sticks, lengths of hair-colored yarn (yellow, black, brown and orange), crayons

Older Child Option
Make macaroni skeleton shapes and talk about wonderful ways God has made us

Materials
Bible, black card stock or construction paper, lima beans, various types of dried macaroni, glue, white chalk or gel pens

Game Center

Younger Child Option
Make faces to show different feelings and talk about ways God knows us and loves us

Materials
Bible, *Island Music* CD and player, large mirror or small hand mirror

Older Child Option
Play a game like Steal the Bacon to help find team members' shoes and talk about ways God knows us

Materials
Bible

Coloring/Puzzle Center

Younger Child Option
Review the Bible story while completing coloring page

Materials
Lesson 2 Coloring Page (p. 71) for each student, crayons

Older Child Option
Review the Bible story while completing puzzle page

Materials
Lesson 2 Puzzle Page (p. 72) for each student, pencils

Worship Center

For the Younger and Older Child
Participate in large-group activities to review Bible verse and to worship God together

Materials
Bibles, *Island Music* CD and player, song charts (pp. 246-247), butcher paper, marker

© 2006 Gospel Light. Permission to photocopy granted. *Treasure Seekers*

Bonus Island Ideas

Bonus Island Ideas can be used at any time during this session: as an additional activity center, to extend the session for a longer time, or for added island excitement.

Beach Packin' Relay

Get ready for the beach! Fill two suitcases with beach items (sunglasses, visor, beach sandals, swim trunks, etc.), placing same items in each suitcase. (Optional: Use duffel bags instead of suitcases.) Place suitcases on one side of the playing area. Divide class into two teams. Teams line up opposite suitcases on the other side of the playing area. Members of each team take turns running to the suitcase, taking out and putting on all items in the suitcase, removing items and running back to their teams. First team to finish the relay is the winner! **For Younger Children:** Children put on only one item, remove item and run back to their teams.

Post a note alerting parents to the use of food. Also, check registration forms for possible food allergies.

Snacks Ahoy!

Distribute small paper bowls or clear plastic cups to each child. Child places several vanilla wafers in resealable plastic bags and uses rolling pin to crush wafers inside sealed bag. Next, children help prepare instant vanilla pudding following package directions. Add blue food coloring to pudding and mix well. (Optional: Use premade pudding.) Spoon blue pudding into half of each bowl or cup, and then add finely crushed vanilla wafers to the other half for "sand." Place chocolate treasure chest or chocolate coin(s) in the sand. (Optional: On the sand, add a small paper drink umbrella.)

Sandy Shore Designs

Fill large shallow containers (baking pans, plastic storage box lids or heavy cardboard-box lids) with 1 to 2 inches (2.5 to 5 cm) of sand. Add water to dampen. (Optional: Dampen sand in outdoor play area.) Children press pebbles, sea shells and starfish into the sand to make designs. Children smooth sand again with hands or putty knives before making new designs.

© 2006 Gospel Light. Permission to photocopy granted. *Treasure Seekers*

Bible Story Center

FOR YOUNGER CHILDREN
1 Samuel 16:1-13

Collect

Bible.

Introduction

Do you have brothers or sisters? What are their names? *Children respond.* **Today we're going to hear about a boy who had seven brothers.**

Treasure Chest Option

Place paper and markers inside a treasure chest. Invite a volunteer to remove materials at the beginning of the story. As you tell the story, draw (or invite volunteers to draw) stick figures to represent Bible characters, using different colored markers to draw each figure.

Tell the Story

Our Bible tells about a boy named Samuel. Samuel grew up to be a leader of God's people. Samuel loved God. Because Samuel loved God, he obeyed Him and did what was right.

One day God said to Samuel, "I have chosen a new king. I want you to show the people their new king." Samuel listened carefully to all God said to him.

"Take a little animal horn full of olive oil and go find a man named Jesse," God told Samuel. "I have chosen one of Jesse's sons to be the king. When you get to Jesse's home, talk to Jesse and his sons. I will show you which son I have chosen."

So Samuel obeyed God. Step, step, step. Samuel walked to Jesse's home. Samuel looked at each of Jesse's sons. The oldest one was tall and strong. *Surely this is the one God wants to be king,* Samuel thought. But God said, "No, he is not the one. You can only see how he looks on the outside. But I have chosen a man who loves Me and will obey Me. That doesn't always show on the outside."

Samuel looked at the next son and the next one. One, two, three, four, five, six, seven sons walked by Samuel. Each time God said, "No, I have not chosen this one to be king."

Samuel asked Jesse, "Do you have any more sons?"

"Yes," Jesse answered, "I have one more son. David is the youngest one. He is out in the hills taking care of our sheep."

"Tell David to come here to me," Samuel said. When David walked in, Samuel looked at David. David loved God very much. God said, "This is the one I have chosen to be king."

So Samuel took out the little animal horn filled with olive oil. He poured the oil on David's head to show that David was special—chosen by God to be king.

God's Word & Me

God chose David to be the new king because He loved David and knew that David loved Him. God knows us and loves us, too. The Bible says, "I praise you because I am . . . wonderfully made." What can we do to show that we are glad that God knows and loves us? **We can show our love for God by thanking Him for knowing and loving us.**

© 2006 Gospel Light. Permission to photocopy granted. *Treasure Seekers*

Bible Story Center

LESSON two

FOR OLDER CHILDREN
1 Samuel 16:1-13

Collect

Bible, index cards, marker, tape.

Prepare

Write each of the following on separate index cards: "Samuel," "Jesse," "Brother 1," "Brother 2," "Brother 3," "Brother 4," "Brother 5," "Brother 6," "Brother 7" and "David." Put a masking-tape loop on the back of each card to make 10 name tags.

Treasure Chest Option

Before class, collect a picture of a nose and a knee. Draw a line on a large sheet of paper to make two vertical columns. Glue each picture at the top of a column. Place paper in a treasure chest. After telling the story, remove paper from the treasure chest. Tell children that the two pictures are clues to find a message that tells a reason for which we can praise God. Brainstorm with children words that sound like "nose" and "knee." List the words on the paper until they guess the words "knows" and "me."

Introduction

If you could choose any person to be the leader of our country, who would it be? Why? In today's Bible story we'll hear about the reason God chose a most surprising candidate to be the new king of Israel. Before telling the story, invite 10 volunteers to wear prepared name tags. Volunteers stand in front of group and act out motions of the Bible story characters as the story is being told.

Tell the Story

Saul, the first king of Israel, did not always obey God's commands. King Saul seemed to want to do everything his own way, instead of God's way. God was patient with him, but Saul kept on disobeying God and making excuses. Finally God's prophet Samuel had to tell Saul, "Because you no longer obey God, you will no longer be king. The Lord wants a man who loves and obeys Him to be king!" Samuel probably hoped Saul would change and live the way God wanted him to. But Saul continued to disobey God's commands. Samuel eventually grew tired of Saul's excuses and lies. He was very upset that Saul had turned out to be such a disobedient king.

However, God had a plan. God sent Samuel to Bethlehem to the home of a man named Jesse so that God could show Samuel the next king. When Samuel arrived in Bethlehem, he did not mention to Jesse that his mission was to find the new king. Instead, Samuel invited Jesse's family to a celebration to worship God.

When everyone was ready, they came together for the celebration. Jesse introduced his sons one at a time to Samuel. When Samuel saw Eliab who was tall and handsome, he thought, *Surely this is the one the Lord has chosen!* But God told Samuel not to focus on outward appearances. Eliab may have had the physical characteristics of what a king might look like, but he was not the one that God had chosen. God said to Samuel, "The Lord does not look at the things man looks at. Man looks at the outward appearance, but the Lord looks at the heart." **What characteristics might God have been looking for?** Samuel was introduced to all seven of the sons that Jesse had brought to the celebration, but not one of them was God's choice! "Don't you have any other sons?" Samuel asked Jesse. Samuel knew God could not have made a mistake, so he assumed that Jesse *must* have more sons! And sure enough, there was one more son—David, the youngest brother, who was usually out in the fields taking care of the family's sheep.

© 2006 Gospel Light. Permission to photocopy granted. *Treasure Seekers*

When David was brought before Samuel, God told Samuel that David was the one God had chosen. So Samuel took a horn of oil and poured some of the oil on David's head, anointing David to be the next king of Israel. God chose David because he was a man after His own heart (see 1 Samuel 13:14). **Why do you think David is considered a man after God's own heart?** David loved God more than anything and followed His ways. Because of David's love for God, God promised that a descendant of David's would have a kingdom that would last forever. When God's Son, Jesus, was born many years later, He was called the Son of David because Jesus was from David's family.

God's Word & Me

Samuel was looking for the one God had chosen to be the new king of Israel. But the things he was looking for in a king were different from what God was looking for! God chose David to be king because He loved David and knew that David loved and obeyed Him. The Bible tells us that God chose us even before He created the world (see Ephesians 1:4)—not to be kings or queens but to be His children! Because we are God's children, He knows us and loves us!

- How do you think David felt when he was chosen to be king?

- How was Samuel's choice of the king different from God's? (He wanted to choose a king based on outward appearance. God chose a king based on his love and obedience for Him.)

- What did God know about David that Samuel could not see? (David loved and obeyed God.)

- What is something God knows about you that others may not know? Share with children your own answer, and let children know they do not have to answer the question aloud.

- Read Psalm 139:14. **King David wrote Psalm 139, praising God for making and knowing him. God knows everything about you and still loves you! What do you think it means that God knows everything about you?** Pray, **Dear God, You know us best because You made us! We love You and thank You for always loving us. In Jesus' name, amen.**

Game Center

FOR YOUNGER CHILDREN
1 Samuel 16:1-13

LESSON two

Collect

Bible, *Island Music* CD and player, large mirror or small hand mirror.

Do

1. **What does someone look like who is happy? Sad? Sleepy? Grumpy?** Hold mirror so that each child can take a turn to show facial expressions.

2. Play "Before All Time." Children walk in a circle as music plays. After 10-15 seconds, stop the music. Children stop walking. Count down from three and then say, **Show me a (happy) face.** Children respond. Continue as time and interest allow, asking children to make a variety of expressions (happy faces, sleepy faces, goofy faces, etc.).

God's Word

"I praise you because I am fearfully and wonderfully made." Psalm 139:14

For Younger Children:
"I praise you because I am . . . wonderfully made."

God's Word & Me

We can thank God for knowing us and loving us.

Talk About

🔑 **Sammy, what makes you happy? Natalie, what makes you sad? God knows when you feel sad and when you feel happy. No matter how you feel, God loves you!**

🔑 **Jessica, when you feel (sad) what can you remember about God?** (God loves me. God knows me.) Repeat with other feelings. **We can remember that God always loves us, no matter how we feel.**

🔑 **Our Bible says, "I praise you because I am . . . wonderfully made." We can be glad that God knows us and loves us.** Pray briefly, **Thank You, God, for knowing and loving (Tanya).** Repeat prayer, naming each child in the class.

 ## For Older Children

Instead of making faces when you stop the music, children quickly form pairs. Pairs stand facing each other. One child in each pair pantomimes one of the words from Psalm 139:14 for the other child to guess. Once all the words of the verse are pantomimed, children say the verse together.

© 2006 Gospel Light. Permission to photocopy granted. *Treasure Seekers*

Game Center

FOR OLDER CHILDREN
1 Samuel 16:1-13

Collect

Bible.

Do

1. Children take off one of their shoes and pile shoes in the middle of the playing area. Leader(s) helps mix up the pile of shoes. Divide class into two teams. Teams line up shoulder-to-shoulder on opposite sides of the playing area. Assign numbers to students as in the game Steal the Bacon (see sketch).

2. Call out two numbers. Students with those numbers from each team run to the shoe pile and collect as many shoes from their team as possible within three seconds. Call "Stop" when time is up. Students return to teams with the shoes and distribute shoes to correct owners. Students return unmatched shoes to the pile. Game continues until each team member has his or her shoe.

God's Word

"I praise you because I am fearfully and wonderfully made." Psalm 139:14

For Younger Children:
"I praise you because I am . . . wonderfully made."

God's Word & Me

We can thank God for knowing us and loving us.

Talk About

- In our game today, we tried to know which shoes belonged to the people on our teams. Was it hard or easy?

- What are some things that are easy to know about a person? (What color eyes they have. How tall they are.) What are some things that are more difficult to know about a person? (Their thoughts. What they like or dislike. Their age.)

- Who is someone that knows you very well? How does it make you feel that he or she knows you so well? Some of our friends or family members may know us well enough to finish our sentences! But there is someone who even knows what we're thinking before we speak—God! The Bible says that God knew us even before we were born! (See Psalm 139:15-16.)

- God not only knows us, He also loves us very much. How does it make you feel to know that God knows and loves you? Read Psalm 139:14. We can praise our maker for knowing and loving us.

For Younger Children

Instead of playing a game like Steal the Bacon, teams line up facing the pile of shoes and play a relay game. At your signal, first child in each line runs to the pile of shoes. Each one finds his or her shoe, and then returns to his or her team to put on the shoe. Then the next team member repeats action. Game continues until each team member has found and put on his or her shoe.

© 2006 Gospel Light. Permission to photocopy granted. *Treasure Seekers*

Art Center

FOR YOUNGER CHILDREN
1 Samuel 16:1-13

LESSON two

Collect

Bible, markers, paper, magazines, scissors, paper plates, glue sticks, lengths of hair-colored yarn (yellow, black, brown and orange), crayons.

Prepare

Draw faces on paper or collect large pictures of people's faces from magazines. Cut pictures into three horizontal strips so that different facial parts (pair of eyes, nose, and mouth) are on separate strips.

Do

1. Distribute a paper plate to each child. Place picture strips on floor. Invite children to choose eye, nose and mouth strips. Encourage children to find and choose eye strips that have the same color as their own eyes. Children arrange and glue strips onto paper plates to create faces. (Note: Trim ends of strips as needed to fit inner circles of paper plates.)

2. Children glue colored yarn around faces to represent hair. Provide crayons for children to draw ears and decorate their paper-plate faces.

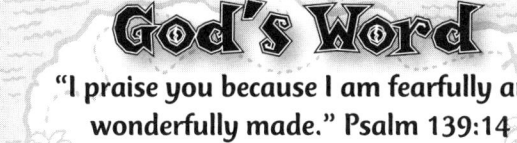

God's Word

"I praise you because I am fearfully and wonderfully made." Psalm 139:14

For Younger Children:
"I praise you because I am . . . wonderfully made."

God's Word & Me

We can thank God for knowing us and loving us.

Talk About

- Nathan, what is your favorite color? I'm glad that God made our eyes so that we can see colors. Samantha, what is your favorite snack? I'm glad that God made our mouths, too, so that we can eat our favorite foods. Our Bible says, "I praise you because I am . . . wonderfully made."

- Sara, what color are Justin's eyes? What else do you know about Justin? (He has brown hair. He likes dogs.) **God knows and loves each one of us.**

- **We can thank God for knowing and loving us.** Invite children to name others in the class to complete the following prayer: **Thank You, God, for (Laura).** Continue until each child has been named.

For Older Children

Children look through magazines to find large pictures of faces. They cut out features (eyes, hair, nose and mouth) that look similar to their own. Children glue the features onto construction paper to create portrait collages. They may fill in empty parts of the collage by coloring or with pieces of skin-tone pictures. They may also find words in magazines that describe themselves and glue words to the collages.

© 2006 Gospel Light. Permission to photocopy granted. *Treasure Seekers*

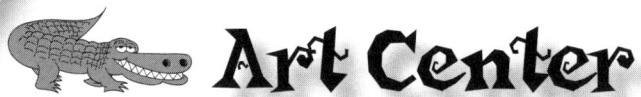

Art Center

FOR OLDER CHILDREN
1 Samuel 16:1-13

Collect

Bible, black card stock or construction paper, lima beans, various types of dried macaroni (tubes, spirals, elbow noodles, spaghetti, small shells, etc.), glue, white chalk or gel pens.

Do

Distribute a sheet of black card stock or construction paper and a handful of beans and macaroni shapes to each child. Children arrange beans and macaroni pieces to make human skeleton shapes. Children glue macaroni shapes in place. (Optional: Show a picture or diagram of the human skeleton from an encyclopedia or the Internet.) Children use white chalk or gel pens to write fun facts around the skeleton about themselves that others may not know.

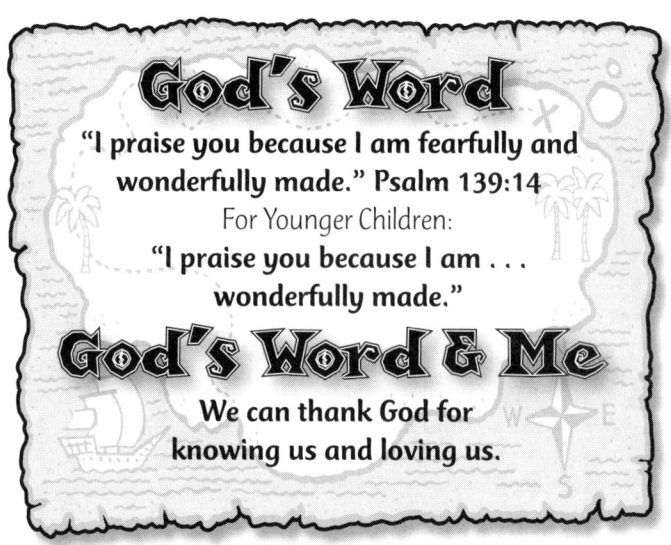

God's Word

"I praise you because I am fearfully and wonderfully made." Psalm 139:14

For Younger Children:
"I praise you because I am . . . wonderfully made."

God's Word & Me

We can thank God for knowing us and loving us.

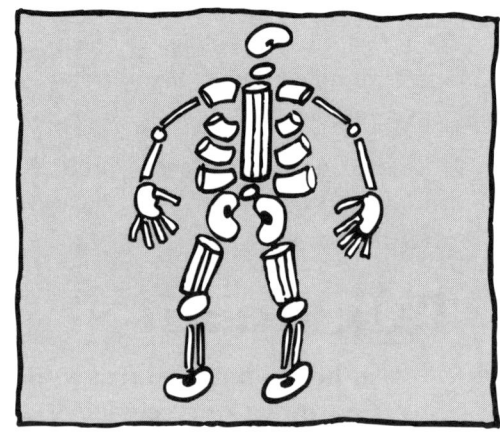

Talk About

- Who has ever been X-rayed? What was the reason for it? What do X-rays help to see? (The location of a broken bone. A tooth cavity. Things that we can't see with our eyes alone.)

- Share with students a fun fact about yourself that they might not know. Then ask, **What is something about yourself that others may not know or see right away?** Children may name their hobbies, share a surprising personality trait or perform a hidden talent. **Each of us have unique things about ourselves that might not be so apparent to others.**

- Read Psalm 139:14. **What do you think it means to be fearfully made? Another way of saying "I am fearfully made" is "I am in awe of how I am made." King David wrote Psalm 139 and he wrote verse 14 not to praise himself or to say how great he is but to say how great God, his maker, is! Let's praise our maker, too!** Lead children in saying Psalm 139:14 as a prayer.

For Younger Children

Photocopy Lesson 2 Pattern Page (p. 70) onto several sheets of card stock. Children glue macaroni shapes inside the body shape.

© 2006 Gospel Light. Permission to photocopy granted. *Treasure Seekers*

Worship Center
1 Samuel 16:1-13

LESSON two

Collect
Bibles, *Island Music* CD and player, song charts (pp. 246-247), butcher paper, marker.

Prepare
On a large piece of butcher paper, write the praise litany from the Prayer activity below.

Team Game
Divide group into teams of five or six students. At your signal, team members quickly arrange themselves in a line according to birth month order. Quickest team to arrange themselves in the correct birth month order wins! (Note: Have everyone sing "Happy Birthday" to the children who have birthdays in the current month.)

God's Word
"I praise you because I am fearfully and wonderfully made." Psalm 139:14

For Younger Children:
"I praise you because I am . . . wonderfully made."

God's Word & Me
We can thank God for knowing us and loving us.

Bible Verse Game
Lead children in repeating Psalm 139:14 several times, naming different body parts in place of the words "I am" in Psalm 139:14: "I praise you because (my ears are) fearfully and wonderfully made." Children move the body part that is named. Challenge children to be creative in moving body parts.

Song
Lead children in singing "Before All Time," adding motions and/or clapping if desired.

Prayer
Display prepared butcher paper. Lead children in reciting lines of the praise litany, inviting children to say the sentences that are marked "All."

Leader: We praise You, Lord, for making us with everything we need: a brain, a heart, hands and feet, eyes, ears and a mouth to eat!

All: We are fearfully and wonderfully made.

Leader: We praise You, Lord, for knowing us: our thoughts, our fears, and even our tears!

All: We are fearfully and wonderfully made.

Leader: We praise You, Lord, for loving us: You know us each by name; You love us all the same.

All: We are fearfully and wonderfully made! Amen.

Song
Play "Treasure Forever." Lead children in singing, adding motions and/or clapping if desired.

© 2006 Gospel Light. Permission to photocopy granted. *Treasure Seekers*

Lesson 2 ⬥ Pattern Page

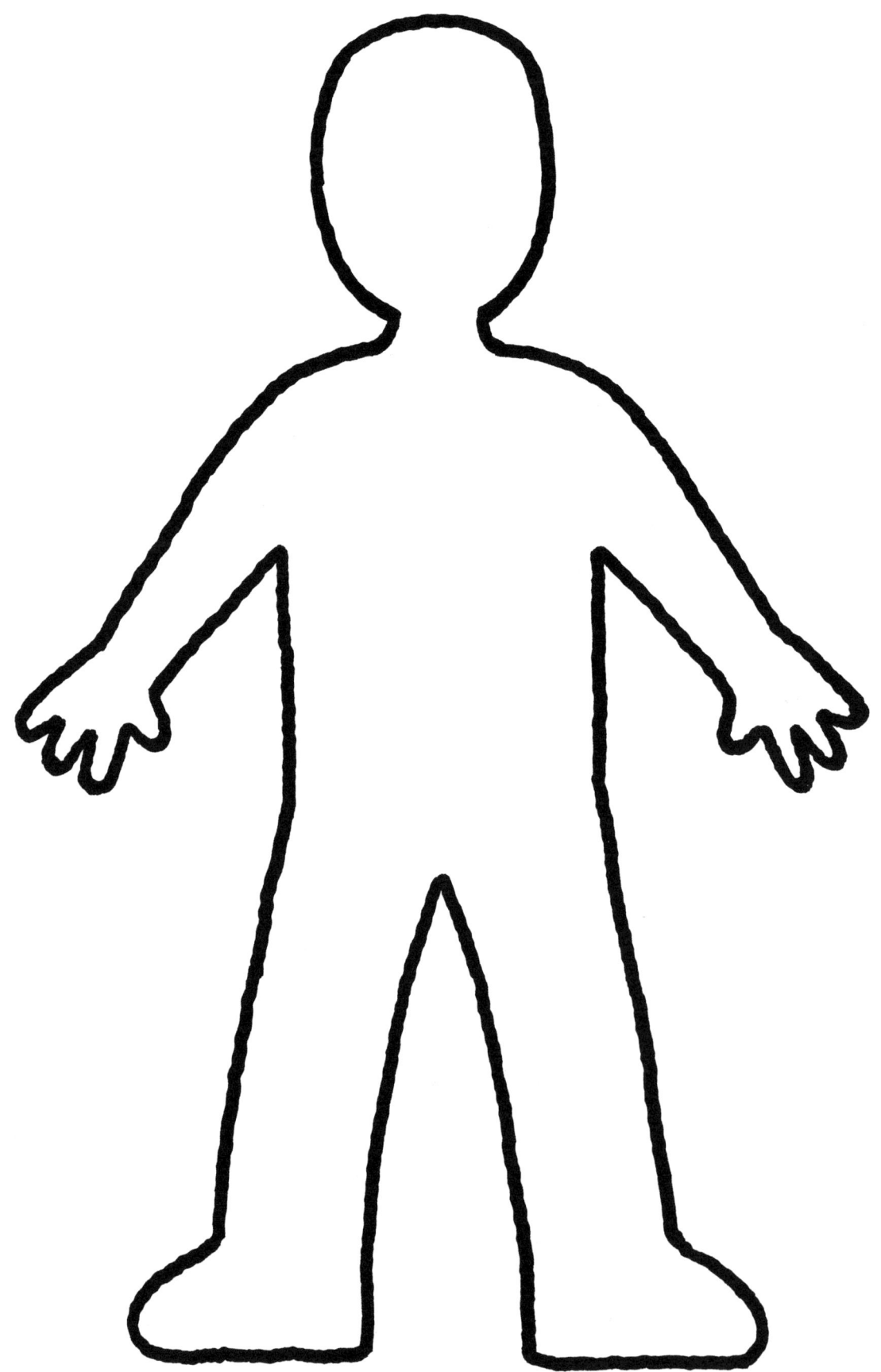

Body Pattern

Lesson 2 ⋄ **Coloring/Puzzle Center**

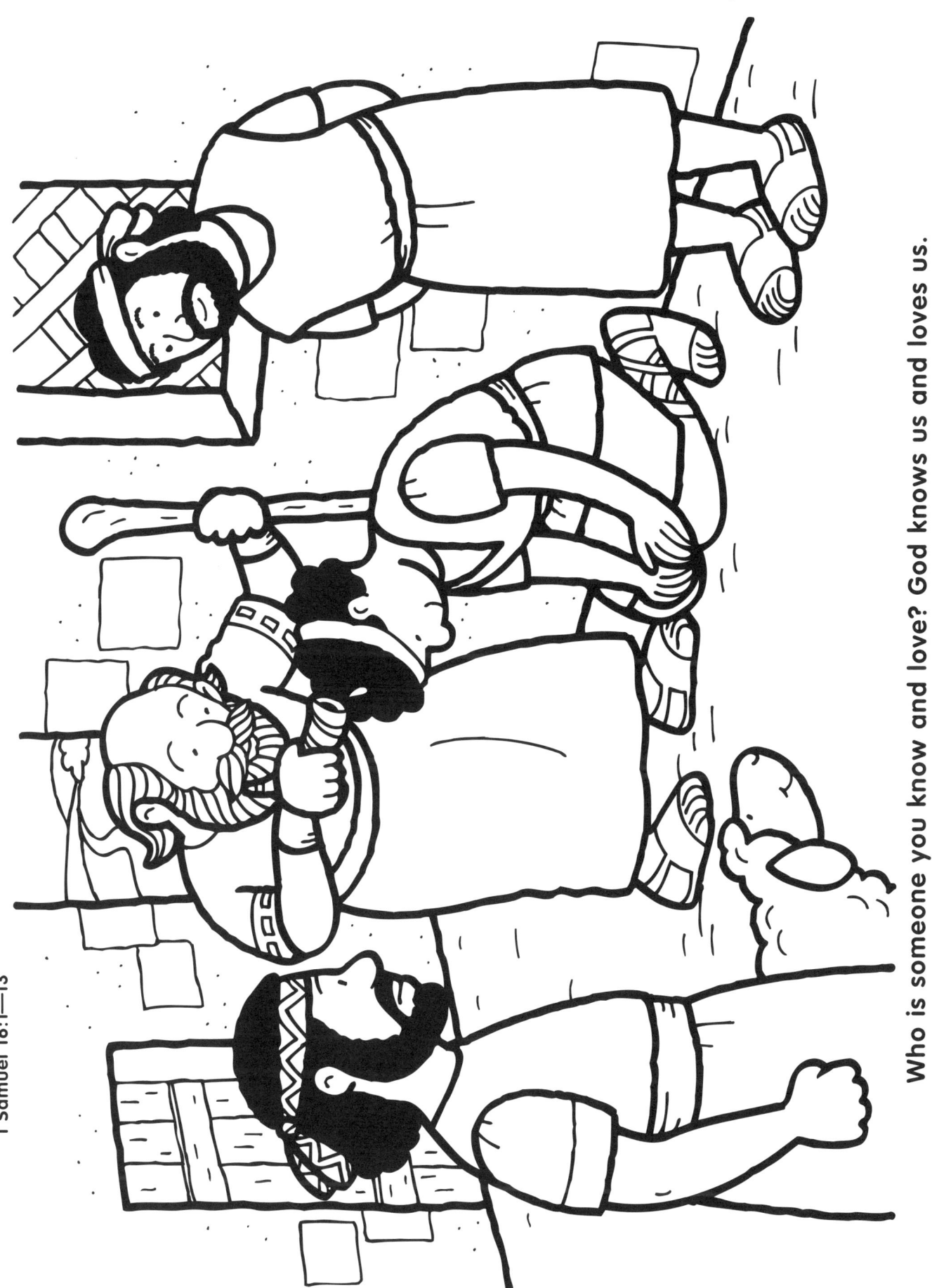

David is chosen as king.
1 Samuel 16:1—13

Who is someone you know and love? God knows us and loves us.

© 2006 Gospel Light. Permission to photocopy granted. *Treasure Seekers*

Lesson 2 ◆ Coloring/Puzzle Center

KING QUIZ

Read the Bible verses to find the missing letters in the names of some of the most famous Bible kings. Then find the names of all these kings in the word search. Why did God choose David to be a king? Draw a heart next to David's name to show that he loved God.

These men were kings between 930 BC and 415 BC.

Ah__ __ (1 Kings 16:33)
Ahaz
Amaziah
Asa
Baasha
__a__id (2 Samuel 2:4)
He__ek__ __h (2 Kings 18:16)
Hoshea
Jehoahaz
Jehoash
Jehoiakim
Jehoram
Jehoshaphat

J__ __u (2 Kings 9:5,6)
__er__b__am (1 Kings 12:20)
Jo__i__h (2 Kings 23:23)
Jotham
M__na__ __eh (2 Kings 21:1)
Menahem
Omri
Pekah
__eh__b__am (1 Kings 11:43)
S__u__ (1 Samuel 11:15)
S__lo__o__ (1 Kings 1:39)
Uzziah
Zedekiah

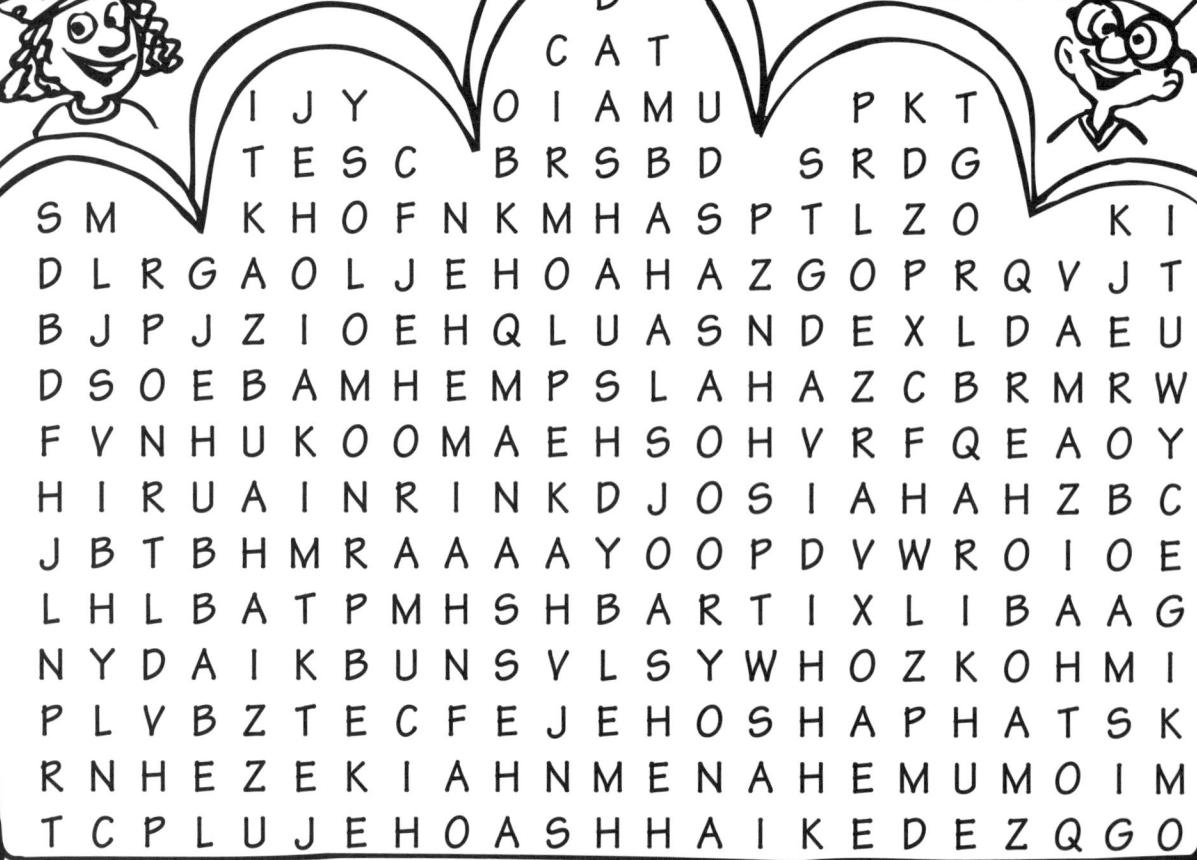

BIBLE STORY ◆ Genesis 37; 39—45

God Is Wise and Good

LESSON three

Teacher's Devotional

Most Christians, and many non-Christians as well, agree that God is wise and good, especially when their lives are going along as expected. Many others, however, when confronted with tragic circumstances express doubt that a wise and good God even exists. But however well or poorly we understand God's goodness, wisdom and sovereignty, certainly one man might have seemed justified to question it: Joseph!

God's Word

"The LORD is good, a refuge in times of trouble. He cares for those who trust in him." Nahum 1:7

For Younger Children:
"The LORD is good."

God's Word & Me

We can trust in God's wisdom and goodness, even in difficult times.

Born the favorite son of the favorite wife, Joseph was the obvious heir to his father's fortune. God sent him dreams that revealed a plan for his life. But Joseph's expected easy life took an unexpected turn: His brothers sold him to slave traders, telling his father he had been violently killed. From slavery to unjust accusation to jail to being forgotten there after showing kindness, Joseph spent most of his life in situations that seemed to declare that God is not good or wise! But Joseph made a deliberate choice to trust God's goodness and wisdom—so much so, that when his still-guilt-ridden brothers stood before him years later, he cried in delighted forgiveness, "You meant it for evil but God meant it for good!" (See Genesis 50:20.) Choosing every day to believe that God is good and wise prepared Joseph for the "rest of the story"!

What is unexpected or unwelcome in your life today? Stop to make this choice: Believe that God is good no matter what the circumstances are (see Romans 8:28). Choose to believe that He is wise and will freely share that wisdom with you, according to James 1:5. Choosing, in unexpected circumstances, to believe He is good and wise both expresses and exercises our faith. Made daily, those choices will make you stronger and stronger, until God reveals "the rest of" your story!

© 2006 Gospel Light. Permission to photocopy granted. *Treasure Seekers*

Planning Page

Choose which centers you will provide and the order in which children will participate in them (see pp. 14-18 for schedule tips and pp. 24-25 for guidelines in combining older and younger children). Also plan who will lead each center (for staffing tips see pp. 19-21). Use the reproducible planning sheet (p. 238) to record your plans.

Bible Story Center

Bible Story
God Is Wise and Good • Genesis 37; 39—45

Younger Child Option
Use tongue depressors or paper plates as puppets to act out story events

Older Child Option
Play a guessing game to discover missing letters of a message that tells God is wise and good

Art Center

Younger Child Option
Create a coat of colors and talk about people whom God has given to help us

Materials
Bible, large sheets of construction paper, marker, scissors, several plastic spray bottles, powdered or liquid tempera paint, clothesline or rope, clothespins

Older Child Option
Make an easel frame and write words on cards to place on frames as reminders of God's wisdom and goodness

Materials
Bible, Pattern Page (p. 84), card stock, scissors, measuring stick, thin ribbon or raffia, sticks or precut wooden dowels about ½ inch (1.3 cm) in diameter and 12 to 15 inches (30.5 to 38 cm) in length, 3-inch (7.5-cm) rubber bands, glue, decorating materials

Game Center

Younger Child Option
Play a tossing game and talk about good things God helps us have

Materials
Bible, scissors, red and blue sheets of construction paper, glue, butcher paper, beanbag

Older Child Option
Play a game doing things backward and talk about reasons to trust in God's wisdom and goodness in difficult times

Materials
Bible, two large coats with buttons or two oversized shirts with buttons

Coloring/Puzzle Center

Younger Child Option
Review the Bible story while completing coloring page

Materials
Lesson 3 Coloring Page (p. 85) for each student, crayons

Older Child Option
Review the Bible story while completing puzzle page

Materials
Lesson 3 Puzzle Page (p. 86) for each student, pencils

Worship Center

For the Younger and Older Child
Participate in large-group activities to review Bible verse and to worship God together

Materials
Bibles, *Island Music* CD and player, song charts (pp. 246, 248, masking tape, butcher paper, markers, large swim trunks, inflated beach ball

Bonus Island Ideas

LESSON three

Bonus Island Ideas can be used at any time during this session: as an additional activity center, to extend the session for a longer time, or for added island excitement.

BEACH FANS

Children make decorative fans to mark cups used at snack time. Cut construction paper into 3x12-inch (7.5x30.5-cm) strips. Distribute to children. Each child accordion-folds the strip widthwise with ½-inch (1.3-cm) folds and staples the folded piece across the width of the center. Child glues the ends of two craft sticks onto each side of the staple. Child glues together the other ends of paper, forming a semicircle (see sketch a). Child then brings the two craft sticks together, sandwiching the folded paper between them and wraps a rubber band around sticks (see sketch b). When the glue is dry, child removes the rubber bands and opens the craft sticks outward in opposite directions to open the fan. Child wraps the rubber band at the base of the fan and slips fan onto the rim of his or her drinking cup (see sketch c). **For younger children:** Assist children in assembling fans.

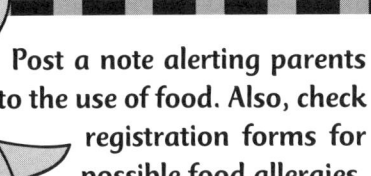

Post a note alerting parents to the use of food. Also, check registration forms for possible food allergies.

TROPICAL DRESS-UP DAY

Send flyers home announcing a Tropical Dress-up Day. Invite leaders, parents and students to come dressed in their best tropical get-up on a selected date. For additional fun, plan to have a fashion show on that day. Set up a platform or runway and invite dressed-up volunteers to participate in the fashion show. Choose three judges to award the participants according to various categories (Most Creative, Most Colorful, Best Effort, etc.) and give a small prize to everyone who participates

Freeze several flavors of fruit juice (fruit punch, grape, orange, etc.) in separate ice-cube trays. Place fruity ice cubes in separate bowls with ice tongs or spoons by each bowl. Children add ice cubes to a glass of clear soda or seltzer water and ENJOY!

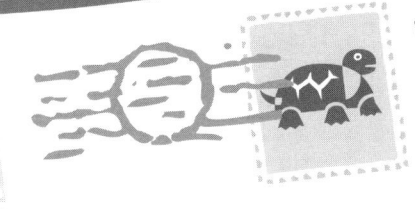

FRUITY FLOATERS

© 2006 Gospel Light. Permission to photocopy granted. *Treasure Seekers*

Bible Story Center

FOR YOUNGER CHILDREN
Genesis 37; 39—45

LESSON three

Collect

Bible.

Introduction

Who is someone who helps you? Children respond. **Today we're going to hear a story about someone who needed God's help.**

Tell the Story

Joseph had 11 brothers and a father named Jacob. Jacob loved Joseph the best of all his sons. To show that he loved Joseph, Jacob gave him a beautiful coat. But the beautiful coat made his brothers angry!

Treasure Chest Option

Before class, draw happy faces on one side of 12 large tongue depressors or paper plates and draw angry faces on the other side of depressors or plates. Color one depressor or plate with multi-colored stripes to represent Joseph. Place depressors or plates in a treasure chest. Show the appropriate faces to act out the story as it is being told.

Then one day Joseph told his family about two dreams that he had. Both dreams were about his family bowing down to Joseph, their leader. The dreams made his brothers REALLY angry! The brothers made a plan to take Joseph's coat and KILL Joseph! But instead, they threw him in a deep hole in the ground. Then they sold Joseph to some traders who were coming down the road.

Joseph was taken to Egypt, far from his home. He was sold as a slave to Potiphar (Pot-ih-fuhr), but still Joseph did his best work. Soon, Potiphar put Joseph in charge of his house. But then, Joseph was put in jail, even though he had not done anything wrong. Joseph stayed in jail for a long, long time. But Joseph knew that God was good and would help him.

One night, when Joseph was still in jail, the king of Egypt, called Pharaoh, had a very strange dream. He had heard that Joseph could tell him what his dream meant, so he called Joseph to come and see him. God helped Joseph tell Pharaoh what the dream meant. The dream was about a time when there would be no food to eat. Pharaoh put Joseph in charge of saving food. For seven years, Pharaoh's helpers kept extra food in big barns that Joseph had told them to build.

After seven years, no food grew at all. So Joseph opened the barns. He sold the food to the people. Soon there was no food growing where Jacob and his family lived. Two times, Jacob sent his sons to Egypt to buy grain. Each time, they went to Joseph who was selling the grain. They didn't know it was Joseph! The last time they came, Joseph told them, "I am your brother Joseph." The brothers were so surprised—then afraid! They had been very mean to Joseph. But Joseph hugged each of them. He sent them back home with lots of grain and asked them to come back to Egypt with their father, Jacob, to live with him. And they did!

God's Word & Me

Even when sad things happened to Joseph, he knew that God would always help him. Our Bible says, "The Lord is good." Some days we might feel sad. Who is someone who helps you when you feel sad? Every day we know that God is good and that He will always help us.

© 2006 Gospel Light. Permission to photocopy granted. *Treasure Seekers*

Bible Story Center

FOR OLDER CHILDREN
Genesis 37; 39—45

Collect

Bible.

Introduction

Who has a story about a really bad day? What happened? Invite volunteers to tell stories. **In today's Bible story, we'll find out how one person handled some pretty bad days.** At appropriate times as you tell the story, lead children in calling out "Yea!" when you show a thumbs up and "Boo!" when you show a thumbs down.

Treasure Chest Option

On a large sheet of paper, draw four blank lines on each side of the word "and," representing the letters of the words "wise" and "good." Place paper in a treasure chest. After the story is told, invite a volunteer to remove the paper from the chest. Lead children in a guessing game like Hangman to discover the missing letters. Draw parts of a palm tree (trunk and no more than eight leaves) each time a letter is guessed incorrectly.

Tell the Story

Four hundred years before God's people were slaves in Egypt, there lived a man named Jacob. He had 12 sons and one daughter. Joseph was his eleventh son. And Joseph was Jacob's FAVORITE son. This made the other brothers jealous!

Joseph also had some dreams when he was young. These dreams seemed to say that his family would one day bow down to him. Well, when he told his family his dreams, his brothers became even MORE jealous! And if that weren't enough, Jacob made a special coat for Joseph. The special coat showed everyone that Joseph was Jacob's favorite son. Now his brothers were REALLY jealous!

One day, Jacob sent Joseph to check on his brothers, who were taking care of the family's animals far away from home. When the brothers saw Joseph coming, they wanted to kill him. But they decided to take his coat from him and throw him into a nearby pit. Then the brothers sold Joseph to some traders (people who buy and sell things) who were on their way to Egypt.

Joseph's brothers told their father that Joseph was dead. But really Joseph was now a SLAVE in Egypt. Even though he was a slave, Joseph trusted in God's wisdom and goodness and kept on doing his best work. Soon he became his Egyptian owner's most trusted servant.

But the wife of the man who owned Joseph told lies about Joseph to get him in trouble. She got Joseph put in JAIL! But once again, Joseph trusted in God's wisdom and goodness. Joseph did his best and helped other prisoners. Soon he was put in CHARGE of the jail! He even helped two prisoners by telling them the meaning of dreams they had.

Some time later, Pharaoh, the ruler of all Egypt, had a STRANGE dream. No one could tell him what it meant! But one of the men Joseph had helped in jail told Pharaoh that Joseph understood dreams. So Pharaoh called for Joseph.

Joseph told Pharaoh, "I cannot interpret your dream. But, God can." Joseph listened to Pharaoh's dream and then told Pharaoh that his dream meant that there was going to be a famine—years when there wouldn't be any rain and very little food.

© 2006 Gospel Light. Permission to photocopy granted. *Treasure Seekers*

Lesson three

Pharaoh thought about what Joseph had told him. He realized that Joseph was a VERY wise man. So he made Joseph second ruler of the whole country of Egypt! He gave Joseph his ring so Joseph could make laws. He gave Joseph a royal necklace to wear around his neck so people would know Joseph was a ruler. Joseph had big barns built to store food so people could eat during the coming famine. He was in charge of everybody except Pharaoh!

After seven years, the famine DID come, as Joseph had said it would. There was also a famine where Jacob and all of Joseph's brothers lived. Soon the brothers came to Egypt in search of food. They came right to Joseph! But they didn't recognize him. They bowed low before Joseph, just as he had seen in his dream! They BEGGED Joseph to sell them food! Joseph didn't tell them who he was just yet. But he gave them lots of grain and sent them home. He also kept one brother with him, just to be sure they would come back!

Joseph's brothers DID come back. Finally, Joseph told them who he was! His brothers were afraid. *Will Joseph punish us?* they wondered. Joseph did not. Instead, he FORGAVE them! He loved his brothers, even though they had been so cruel to him. He told them that even though they had meant to hurt him, God had used it for good! Joseph invited them to come and live in Egypt, where there was plenty of food for them and all their families!

God's Word & Me

Joseph had some pretty hard times. But even in the troubles he faced, Joseph trusted in God's wisdom and goodness. Like Joseph, hard times will come our way, too. But, even when things happen to us or others that we may not understand, we can trust that God is good and that He is with us. God never forgets where we are or what we need. In good or bad times, we can know that God is wise and good.

- **What did Joseph do in today's Bible story to show that He depended on God's wisdom and goodness?** (Joseph always did his best work wherever he was. Joseph trusted in God's help to interpret Pharaoh's dream. Joseph was not angry with his brothers and forgave his brothers, even when they had done wrong to him.)

- **What are some troubles kids your age might face today?** (Parents getting a divorce. Parent loses his or her job. Friend from school dies.) **When someone is in a difficult situation, why might it be hard for that person to trust in God's wisdom and goodness? Why does God want us to trust in His wisdom and goodness?** (Because God's plans are always good. Because God loves us and cares for us. Because God promises to help us.)

- Read Nahum 1:7. **What promise does this verse give to us?** (God is good. God cares for us in times of trouble.) **We can remember this promise and trust in God's wisdom and goodness even in the most difficult times.** Lead children in prayer, thanking God for His wisdom and goodness.

# Game Center

FOR YOUNGER CHILDREN
Genesis 37; 39—45

LESSON three

Collect

Bible, scissors, red and blue sheets of construction paper, glue, butcher paper, beanbag.

Prepare

Cut circles from the red and blue sheets of construction paper, making sure to cut an equal number of red and blue circles. Glue circles randomly onto butcher paper, allowing several inches between each circle. (Note: If you have more than eight to ten children, prepare an additional butcher paper sheet.)

Do

Place prepared butcher paper on the floor or on a long table. Children line up and stand a few feet away from the paper. Each child takes a turn tossing a beanbag onto the paper. If the beanbag lands on a red circle, child recites Nahum 1:7: "The Lord is good." If the beanbag lands on a blue circle, child tells something good that God helps him or her have.

God's Word

"The LORD is good, a refuge in times of trouble. He cares for those who trust in him." Nahum 1:7

For Younger Children:
"The LORD is good."

God's Word & Me

We can trust in God's wisdom and goodness, even in difficult times.

Talk About

- Alex, who helps you when you feel sad or afraid? (Mom. Dad. Grandma.) **God has given us people who love us and help us. What are some of the other good things God helps us have?** (A sunny day to play outside. Food to eat. Friends to play with.)

- **What can we do to show that we are thankful for the good things God helps us have?** (Say "Thank You" to God before we eat. Give Grandma and Grandpa big hugs. Be kind to our friends.)

- **Our Bible says, "The Lord is good." Another name for God is "Lord." Even when bad things happen and we might feel sad, we know that God is good because He helps us in so many ways! Let's say a prayer thanking God for helping us.** Pray with children, **Thank You, God, that You are so good. Thank You for helping us. Amen.**

 For Older Children

Cut smaller circles in various colors and glue onto butcher paper, or cover a long table with a polka dot tablecloth or wrapping paper. Assign points to each of the colors. Divide the class into teams. Children take turns tossing pennies instead of beanbags. A volunteer, from the first team to collect 20 points, tells a situation in which someone might need to remember God's wisdom and goodness.

© 2006 Gospel Light. Permission to photocopy granted. *Treasure Seekers*

Game Center

LESSON three

FOR OLDER CHILDREN
Genesis 37; 39—45

Collect
Bible, two large coats with buttons or two oversized shirts with buttons.

Do
1. Divide the class into two teams. Teams line up. Give a coat or shirt to the first child in each line. Children put on coats or shirts backward.

2. At your signal, child standing behind first child in line buttons one or two buttons on the coat or shirt the first child in line is wearing. The child wearing the coat unbuttons the coat or shirt and passes it to the second child in line. That child then puts the coat on backward, and the third child in line buttons one or two buttons on the coat and so on. Game continues until each child has worn coat or shirt. First team to get the coat or shirt to the end of the line wins.

God's Word
"The LORD is good, a refuge in times of trouble. He cares for those who trust in him." Nahum 1:7

For Younger Children:
"The LORD is good."

God's Word & Me
We can trust in God's wisdom and goodness, even in difficult times.

Talk About

- In today's Bible story, when Joseph's dad gave him a special coat, Joseph probably thought nothing could go wrong in his life. But even when something wrong did happen, Joseph remembered that God is wise and good.

- **When is a time something turned out differently from what you expected?** (Studied hard for a test and didn't get the grade that I wanted. Wanted a snowboard for Christmas but got a sweater instead. Parents got divorced.)

- **When kids are having hard times or are in difficult situations, how might they feel about God?** (God doesn't love them anymore. Nothing good will ever happen to them again.) Even in those times, we can remember that God will always help us. God is wise and good, and when we have trouble or difficulty, He still provides good things for us. **When is a time someone your age might need to remember God's wisdom and goodness?**

- Read Nahum 1:7. **Why can we trust in God's wisdom and goodness in difficult times?** (He loves us. He has shown His care in the past. God is good.) Pray briefly, thanking God for His wisdom and goodness.

 For Younger Children
Place coats or shirts on floor. Teams line up next to coats or shirts. Place a chair on the other side of the playing area. At your signal, first child in each line puts on coat, runs to chair and back to his or her team, takes off coat and gives it to next child in line. Next child in line repeats action. Continue until all children have had a turn.

© 2006 Gospel Light. Permission to photocopy granted. *Treasure Seekers*

 # Art Center

FOR YOUNGER CHILDREN
Genesis 37; 39—45

LESSON three

Collect

Bible, large sheets of construction paper, marker, scissors, several plastic spray bottles, powdered or liquid tempera paint, clothesline or rope, clothespins.

Prepare

Draw large shirt outlines on separate sheets of construction paper, making one for each child in your class. Cut shirts from paper. Fill plastic spray bottles ¾ full of water and drop a small amount of paint into the water. Shake well. In an open area outdoors, tie ends of a clothesline or rope to low chairs placed several feet apart or to a fence so that clothesline or rope is hanging taut at children's eye-level.

God's Word

"The LORD is good, a refuge in times of trouble. He cares for those who trust in him." Nahum 1:7

For Younger Children:
"The LORD is good."

God's Word & Me

We can trust in God's wisdom and goodness, even in difficult times.

Do

Distribute a shirt and two clothespins to each child. Each child uses clothespins to hang shirts from the clothesline or rope. Children take turns lightly spraying paint from spray bottles onto hanging shirts. Allow to dry. (Optional: If you are unable to go outdoors for this activity, children may paint shirts with brushes, laying shirts on newspaper-covered tables indoors.)

Talk About

- In today's Bible story, a boy named Joseph was given a special coat of many colors. Joseph's father, Jacob, gave Joseph the coat to show that he loved Joseph very much. Who are the people in your family who love and help you? What do they do when you feel sad? God is good and gives us people who help us.

- Who gives you a big hug when you feel sad? Cooks you soup when you feel sick? Reads you stories when you can't sleep? Our Bible says, "The Lord is good." He has given us all these people to help us. We can thank God that He is good and always helps us.

 ## For Older Children

Divide the class into two teams. Distribute large sheets of construction paper or newspaper sections, scissors, crayons or markers and a roll of masking tape to each team. Teams use materials to design their own coat of many colors. Invite two leaders to judge coat creations. Award prizes to the winning team.

© 2006 Gospel Light. Permission to photocopy granted. *Treasure Seekers*

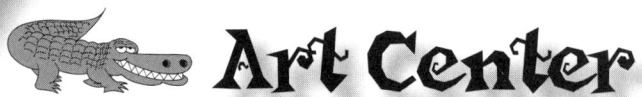 # Art Center

FOR OLDER CHILDREN
Genesis 37; 39—45

Collect

Bible, Pattern Page (p. 84), card stock, scissors, measuring stick, thin ribbon or raffia, sticks or precut wooden dowels about ½ inch (1.3 cm) in diameter and 12 to 15 inches (30.5 to 38 cm) in length, 3-inch (7.5 cm) rubber bands, glue, decorating materials (markers, colored pencils, glitter glue, etc.).

Prepare

Photocopy the Pattern Page onto card stock for each child. Cut three 2-foot (0.6-m) lengths of ribbon or raffia for each child.

God's Word

"The LORD is good, a refuge in times of trouble. He cares for those who trust in him." Nahum 1:7

For Younger Children: **"The LORD is good."**

God's Word & Me

We can trust in God's wisdom and goodness, even in difficult times.

Do

1. To make an easel cardholder, each child makes an A shape with three sticks (sketch a) and then tightly wraps a rubber band around each point where the sticks cross. Child uses another rubber band to attach a fourth stick to the top of the A, sticking out behind to form a stand (sketch b). Child adds a small amount of glue at each connecting point for reinforcement.

2. Child firmly wraps and ties a length of ribbon or raffia around each connecting point to ensure stability and hide rubber bands. Child sets easel aside to dry.

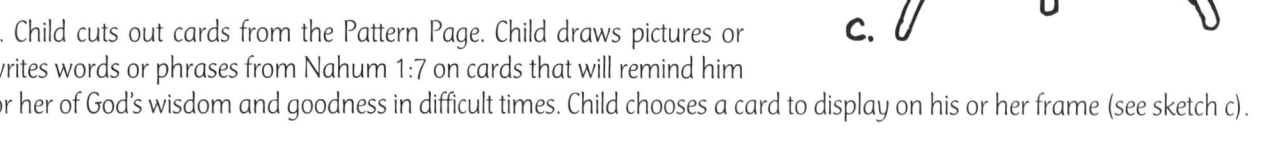

3. Child cuts out cards from the Pattern Page. Child draws pictures or writes words or phrases from Nahum 1:7 on cards that will remind him or her of God's wisdom and goodness in difficult times. Child chooses a card to display on his or her frame (see sketch c).

Talk About

- Read Nahum 1:7. **What is a refuge?** (A place where one is safe from danger. A shelter.) **What comes to mind when you think of God as a refuge? When is a time you might need God's protection and help?**

- **What are some ways God shows His goodness?** (Helps us know what to do. Gives wisdom when we ask.) **When are some times we need to trust in God's goodness?** Volunteers complete the following sentence prayer: **Dear God, help me to trust in Your goodness when . . .**

 ## For Younger Children

Children cut out, decorate and draw pictures of themselves on Pattern Page cards. Write "God cares for me!" on the cards. Children glue cards to the front and back of a sheet of construction paper or card stock.

Worship Center

Genesis 37; 39—45

Collect

Bibles, *Island Music* CD and player, song charts (pp. 246, 248), masking tape, butcher paper, markers, large swim trunks, inflated beach ball.

Prepare

Place strips of masking tape on the floor to designate a start and finish line for use in the Team Game. Print the word "good" in large letters at the top of a butcher paper sheet for use in the Prayer activity below. Tape paper to a wall.

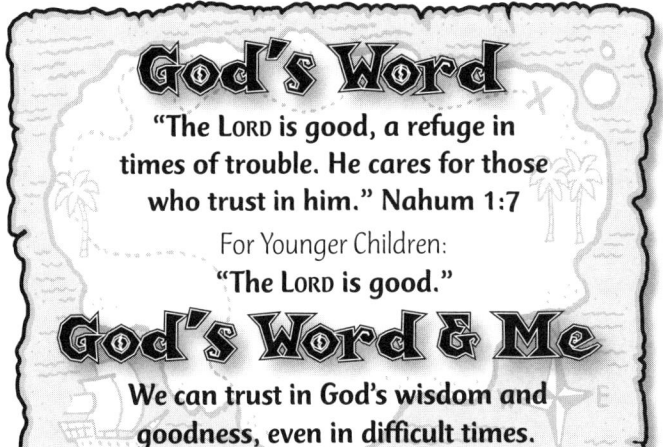

God's Word

"The LORD is good, a refuge in times of trouble. He cares for those who trust in him." Nahum 1:7

For Younger Children: "The LORD is good."

God's Word & Me

We can trust in God's wisdom and goodness, even in difficult times.

Team Game

Divide group into three or four teams. Invite a pair of leaders or older children to represent each team. Each person in the pair places a leg through the leg hole of a pair of swim trunks for a three-legged race. Pairs line up behind the start line. At your signal, pairs race to the finish line. Invite children to cheer for their team representatives.

Bible Verse Game

Everyone says the first word of Nahum 1:7 as you tap the beach ball to any child in the room. Everyone says the next word of the verse as child taps ball to someone else in the room. (Option: Children may catch ball before tapping it.) Children continue tapping ball around the room until all the words of the verse are said or until the ball hits the ground. If the beach ball hits the ground, start the verse again.

Song

You, or another leader, lead children in singing "You, O Lord," adding motions and/or clapping if desired.

Prayer

Point to the prepared paper. **God has shown His wisdom and goodness in many ways. Let's see how many words we can list that tell the good things that God has done for us or the ways He helps us.** Use different colored markers and add phrases using one of the letters in "good" or in a new phrase. Continue until butcher paper is almost filled or as time and interest allow. Invite children to choose one of the good things listed on the paper. Invite volunteers to complete the prayer starter **Thank You, God, for . . . ,** mentioning phrases from the paper.

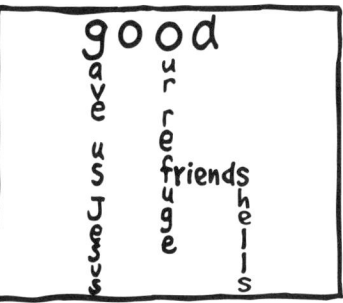

Song

Play "Treasure Forever." Lead children in singing, adding motions and/or clapping if desired. Close with the following prayer: **Thank You, God, for being good and wise! Help us to remember Your goodness and help. Amen.**

Lesson 3 ◆ Pattern Page

Lesson 3 ◇ **Coloring/Puzzle Center**

Joseph helps his family.
Genesis 42—45

Who in your family helps you? We can thank God for giving us people who help us.

Lesson 3 ◆ Coloring/Puzzle Center
OH, BROTHER!

Genesis 37; 41—45

The Challenge

Unscramble the names of Joseph's brothers. (Hint: Read Genesis 35:23-26.) Then choose one brother and draw a line to link him with the brother with the same ID number. Link all the brothers, being careful not to cross any lines when forming your links!

④ Ⓞ H J S E P

_ _ _ _ _ _

④

Ⓘ E L V

_ _ _ _

② A D Ⓝ

_ _ _

④

A H S A Ⓒ R I Ⓢ

_ _ _ _ _ _ _ _

⑤ Ⓐ D G

_ _ _

②

B U L Z U N E

_ _ _ _ _ _ _

①

H A Ⓢ R E

_ _ _ _ _

③ E Ⓞ S I N M

_ _ _ _ _ _

⑥

H A U J D

_ _ _ _ _

③

E I J Ⓜ N B N A

_ _ _ _ _ _ _ _

⑥

B E R E N U

_ _ _ _ _ _

⑤

H Ⓟ A I N L T A

_ _ _ _ _ _ _ _

The Super Challenge

Take the circled letters in the names to spell out the important trait that Joseph showed when dealing with his brothers.

_____ = _____

❓ What did Joseph know about God that made him able to show this trait to his brothers? ❓

86 © 2006 Gospel Light. Permission to photocopy granted. *Treasure Seekers*

BIBLE STORY ◆ Genesis 12:1-7; 15:1-7; 18:1-19; 21:1-7

God Keeps His Promises

LESSON four

Teacher's Devotional

We can probably recall a time when our faith and trust in the people around us was complete, whole and undamaged. But invariably, that breaking of faith, that tearing of trust do come: The loss of faith and trust is a foundational feature of living in a fallen world. Along with the loss comes the worry and uncertainty that result from broken trust. We worry that every stranger is a danger, that no one is safe and that we must be constantly on guard against the designs of those who would harm us in any number of ways. Sometimes it may feel as though the only wise way to live is not to trust anyone—which is a common attitude in our culture. But what an exhausting way to live!

God's Word

"The LORD is faithful to all his promises and loving toward all he has made."
Psalm 145:13

For Younger Children:
"The LORD is faithful to all his promises."

God's Word & Me

We can thank God for keeping His promises.

How reassuring it is that God, who loves us and wants us to *rest* in Him, makes it a point to reveal Himself as the faithful One. He never breaks His Word. He keeps His promises, no matter how quickly those whom He loves break theirs. He is the same yesterday, today, forever! (See Hebrews 13:6.) Breathe a sigh of relief—there is someone we can trust! One reason God gave us His Word is to show us just how trustworthy He is! So no matter the fearfulness of the situation, God can be trusted. He will prove Himself faithful in that frightening time. But it is only when we *know* God that we can trust Him: His ability to be faithful is perfect, but our ability to trust is damaged and needs repair! Until we take the time to *see* the ways He has revealed Himself in His Word, we tend to be disbelieving of a God who is *that* good, *that* kind, *that* merciful.

Thank God that He is not only trustworthy but also the healer of our damaged faith and trust! All we need to do is to depend on Him day-by-day and He will prove Himself, over and over, to be faithful to heal our trust, fix our faith, and find true rest—in Him!

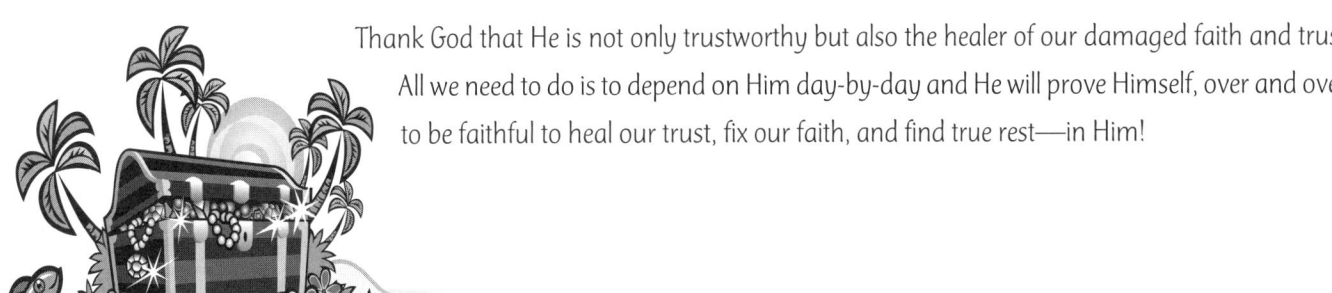

© 2006 Gospel Light. Permission to photocopy granted. *Treasure Seekers*

Planning Page

Choose which centers you will provide and the order in which children will participate in them (see pp. 14-18 for schedule tips and pp. 24-25 for guidelines in combining older and younger children). Also plan who will lead each center (for staffing tips see pp. 19-21). Use the reproducible planning sheet (p. 238) to record your plans.

LESSON four

Bible Story Center

Bible Story
God Keeps His Promises • Genesis 12:1-7; 15:1-7; 18:1-19; 21:1-7

Younger Child Option
Remove baby items from a bag to introduce a promise God made about a baby in the story

Older Child Option
Unscramble letters of a word that tells something God gives and keeps

Art Center

Younger Child Option
Make wristbands with heart beads as reminders of God's love and thank God for His promise to love us

Materials
Bible, plastic straws, ruler, scissors, chenille wire, heart-shaped pony beads

Older Child Option
Make promise cardholders as reminders of God's promises and discuss times when God's promises can help us

Materials
Bible, 19 tongue depressors and 2 craft sticks for each child, craft glue, index cards, decorating materials, tape, yarn, scissors

Game Center

Younger Child Option
Play a game to thank God for keeping His promises and talk about what a promise is

Materials
Bible

Older Child Option
Toss paper balls through a hula hoop and tell promises God has made

Materials
Bible, scratch paper in two different colors, masking tape, hula hoop

Coloring/Puzzle Center

Younger Child Option
Review the Bible story while completing coloring page

Materials
Lesson 4 Coloring Page (p. 99) for each student, crayons

Older Child Option
Review the Bible story while completing puzzle page

Materials
Lesson 4 Puzzle Page (p. 100) for each student, pencils

Worship Center

For the Younger and Older Child
Participate in large-group activities to review Bible verse and to worship God together

Materials
Bibles, *Island Music* CD and player, song charts (pp. 249-250), 16 inflated balloons, permanent marker, large bath towels or beach towels, large sheet of paper

Bonus Island Ideas

LESSON four

Bonus Island Ideas can be used at any time during this session: as an additional activity center, to extend the session for a longer time, or for added island excitement.

Island Pizzas

Before class, bake 10-inch (25.5-cm) round sugar cookies and allow to cool (bake one cookie for each group of 8 to 10 students). (Optional: Use 10-inch [25.5-cm] pizza pans to shape the cookie dough.) Mix one 8-ounce package of softened cream cheese, 1 cup of sugar, and an 8-ounce container of whipped topping. Prepare several bowls of sliced fruit (strawberries, blueberries, bananas, pineapples, etc.). In class, children help to spread the cream cheese mixture on cookies and then arrange sliced fruit as toppings. Sprinkle coconut flakes on island pizza creation to top it off! Cut pizza into slices and serve. (Optional: Bake or purchase 4-inch [10-cm] sugar cookies for children to make individual pizzas with fruit toppings of their choice.)

Post a note alerting parents to the use of food. Also, check registration forms for possible food allergies.

Stylin' Island Seats

For each chair in the classroom, cut a large sheet of butcher paper to fold over both sides of chair backs, stapling left and right edges of paper together to create a chair slipcover. Before class, cut tropical island shapes (palm trees, sun, shells, fish, waves, etc.) from colored card stock or fun foam, or have children cut shapes during class. Children choose and glue island shapes onto backs of slipcovers.

Invite a member from your church who owns a tropical bird to visit your class to show and share information about the bird and how to care for it. Or arrange with a local pet store for someone to give a brief talk about the birds in the store. If either option is not possible, bring to class various pictures of tropical birds and share with children the information you've researched about them.

Tropical Bird Show-n-Tell

© 2006 Gospel Light. Permission to photocopy granted. *Treasure Seekers*

Bible Story Center

FOR YOUNGER CHILDREN

Genesis 12:1-7; 15:1-7; 18:1-19; 21:1-7

LESSON four

Collect

Bible.

Introduction

A promise is something someone tells you he or she will do and then the person does it! When has someone promised something to you? Listen to find out about a promise God made to Abraham.

> **Treasure Chest Option**
>
> Place bag filled with baby items (rattle, toy, bottle, pacifier, blanket) in a treasure chest. When God's promise to send a baby is mentioned in the story, remove bag from the treasure chest and remove items from the bag, one at a time, inviting children to identify each item. (Optional: Children take turns feeling objects in the bag and trying to identify an item before it is shown to others.)

Tell the Story

Abraham was a very old man. His wife, Sarah, was very old, too. They had no children. One day Abraham heard God's voice speaking to him. He was surprised! "Abraham," God said, "I am going to send a baby boy to you and Sarah." Abraham laughed to himself. *A baby boy?* he thought. God said, "Yes! You and Sarah will have a son. You will name your baby Isaac."

One day Abraham saw one, two, three men coming to his tent. These visitors looked like men, but one was really God! The other two were angels. Abraham hurried to invite them in. "Please stay awhile," Abraham said. "Come and rest in the shade! I'll bring water and food."

Abraham said to Sarah, "Please make some bread—quickly!" Sarah baked loaves of bread. Abraham got meat and a helper cooked it. Abraham served the food to his visitors in the shade of his trees.

The visitors ate. And God said to Abraham, "Next year, your wife, Sarah, will have a baby boy." Sarah was behind the tent door. She was listening. *A baby?* she thought. *How can two old people have a baby?* She laughed!

God heard Sarah laugh. "Abraham," He asked, "why did Sarah laugh? Doesn't she know that I can do anything? Nothing in the whole world is too hard for Me to do. You and Sarah will have a son!"

Even though Abraham and Sarah had to wait a LONG time, they DID have their own baby boy—just as God promised! Abraham and Sarah were very happy. They named their baby Isaac. Abraham and Sarah had a big party to celebrate! Many, many times Abraham and Sarah must have thanked God for Isaac. God had done just what He promised!

God's Word & Me

What did God promise to give to Abraham and Sarah? God did what He promised. Our Bible says, "The Lord is faithful to all his promises." Some people might forget to keep a promise, but this Bible verse tells us that God always keeps His promises. God has promised to love us and help us do what is right. We can thank God for keeping His promises.

© 2006 Gospel Light. Permission to photocopy granted. *Treasure Seekers*

Bible Story Center

FOR OLDER CHILDREN
Genesis 12:1-7; 15:1-7; 18:1-19; 21:1-7

Collect
Bible.

Introduction
Who has a really good laugh? Let's hear it! Invite several volunteers to demonstrate their laughs. Volunteers laugh each time the word "laugh" is said in the Bible story. Everyone laughs when the name "Isaac" is mentioned. (Warning: Laughter is contagious!)

Treasure Chest Option
Photocopy Pattern Page (p. 98), enlarging star. Place cut-out star, a penny, a large sheet of paper and a marker in a treasure chest. At the end of the story, volunteer removes materials from chest. Place star on floor. Another volunteer pitches penny onto the star and writes the letter the penny lands nearest to on large sheet of paper, and then crosses out the letter on the star. Volunteers continue until all letters are written on the sheet. Class works together to unscramble letters to find out something God gives and always keeps.

Tell the Story

Abraham had lived in a city called Ur for many years. Abraham loved God and God loved him. One day, God told Abraham to leave Ur. God promised to lead Abraham to a new country. So Abraham packed up his family and followed where God led him. For many years, he and his family lived in tents as they traveled.

Many years passed, but during that time God made another promise to Abraham: Abraham would be a father. God said that Abraham would have many grandchildren and great-grandchildren. But Abraham and his wife, Sarah, were old—even OLDER than most grandparents. And they didn't have ANY children yet!

But God hadn't forgotten His promise. He told Abraham again, "You WILL have a baby boy. From that baby will come more grandchildren and great-grandchildren than you can imagine!"

God said, "Look at the stars, Abraham. Can you count them? You'll have more grandchildren than there are stars in the sky!" Abraham believed God. He trusted that God would keep His promise.

More years went by and Abraham grew even older. But STILL he and Sarah did not have a baby. Surely it was too late for Abraham and Sarah to become parents. But God hadn't forgotten His promise about a son. Abraham still believed God would give them a son, even though by this time Abraham was 100 years old and Sarah was 90!

Then one day, three visitors came to Abraham's tent. And even though the visitors looked like men, one of them was really GOD! Abraham invited his guests to eat and rest. He asked Sarah and a helper to get some food ready. Abraham served a good meal to these important guests.

As the visitors ate out under a tree, Sarah stood at the opening of the tent listening to the things God and Abraham were talking about. Guess what she heard? She heard God say that within a year she and Abraham would have a SON!

Now what do you think Sarah did? Sarah LAUGHED to herself! *What an impossible thing!* she thought to herself. *I'm so OLD! Will I really have a child NOW?*

God knew what Sarah had said to herself. He said to Abraham, "Why did Sarah laugh? Don't you know? NOTHING is too hard for the Lord! When I come back here next year, Sarah really WILL have a son!"

© 2006 Gospel Light. Permission to photocopy granted. *Treasure Seekers*

Lesson three

Later, at the EXACT time God had promised, Abraham and Sarah DID have their own baby boy! They named him Isaac. The name means "laughter"!

Sarah looked down at the beautiful baby in her arms. She said, "God has made me laugh! Everyone who hears about this baby will laugh, too. Who would have BELIEVED that old Abraham and Sarah would have a baby?"

Abraham and Sarah were VERY happy to have little Isaac. He must have made them laugh many, many times. And every time they laughed, Abraham and Sarah must have remembered that God ALWAYS keeps His promises!

God's Word & Me

God has made great promises to love and help us, too. Sometimes things happen that might make us feel that God has forgotten all about us. But God shows us in the Bible that He never forgets us. And He never, EVER forgets to keep His promises! That's why the Bible says God is faithful. Read Psalm 145:13. **God always keeps His promises.**

- **What did Abraham and Sarah learn about God?** (He keeps promises, even when it seems impossible. He is faithful.)

- **What are some reasons it may have been difficult for Abraham and Sarah to believe in God's promise that they would have a child?** (Abraham and Sarah were very old. They waited for a very long time and nothing happened.) **How do you think Abraham felt when God pointed to the stars in the night sky and promised Abraham many sons and grandsons?** (Hopeful. Excited. Thankful.) **How do you think Abraham and Sarah felt when their son, Isaac, was born?**

- **One of God's promises is to help us make wise choices.** (See Proverbs 3:5-6.) **What are some choices kids your age have to make?** (To tell the truth or to lie. To make fun or not to make fun of others.) **You can pray to God and ask His help in doing what is right.** Pray with children.

 # Game Center

FOR YOUNGER CHILDREN
Genesis 12:1-7; 15:1-7; 18:1-19; 21:1-7

LESSON four

Collect

Bible.

Do

1. Lead children in saying the following sentence, clapping once for each word: "Thank You, God, for keeping Your promises." Repeat sentence several times, each time doing a different motion (stomping, tapping knees, etc.) while saying each word of the sentence.

2. Children sit in a circle. One child walks around the outside of the circle, tapping each child's head while group slowly says, "Thank You, God, for keeping Your promises to," completing the sentence by saying the name of the child whose head is tapped last. Repeat with different children doing the tapping, until each child's name has been said.

God's Word

"The LORD is faithful to all his promises and loving toward all he has made."
Psalm 145:13

For Younger Children:
"The LORD is faithful to all his promises."

God's Word & Me

We can thank God for keeping His promises.

Talk About

- Patty, what is a promise? **A promise is something you say you will do and then you do it!**

- In today's Bible story, God promised Abraham and Sarah a baby boy. God did what He promised. God always keeps His promises!

- Justin, what is something you told your mom you would do and then you did it? (Put toys away.) **You know how to keep a promise!**

- Our Bible says, "The Lord is faithful to all his promises." God always keeps His promises. *Pray briefly,* Thank You, God, for keeping Your promises. Help us to keep our promises, too.

 ## For Older Children

Divide into two equal groups. Group 1 forms a circle with everyone facing out. Group 2 forms an outer circle facing Group 1. Players give a high-five to the person in the other circle whom they are facing and become partners for the game. Then those in inner circle march, skip or slide counterclockwise while outer circle moves clockwise around the circle. When leader shouts "God keeps His promises!" each player must run to find his or her partner, give partner a high-five and then sit down.

© 2006 Gospel Light. Permission to photocopy granted. *Treasure Seekers*

 # Game Center

FOR OLDER CHILDREN

Genesis 12:1-7; 15:1-7; 18:1-19; 21:1-7

LESSON four

Collect

Bible, scratch paper in two different colors, masking tape, hula hoop.

Prepare

Crumple papers to make an equal number of balls of each color. Place a masking-tape line in the middle of an open playing area.

Do

1. Divide the class into two teams. Teams kneel in a line facing each other on either side of the masking tape line, approximately 3 feet (0.9 m) from the line. Teams choose a paper color. Distribute the appropriate colored paper balls to members of each team.

2. Stand at one end of the masking tape line with hula hoop. Count down from three and then roll the hula hoop along the line. Team members from each side attempt to throw paper balls through hoop as it rolls past them. Team members count aloud the number of their paper balls that make it through the hoop as it passes. Play several rounds, keeping a tally of each team's successful throws.

3. After each round of game, team with highest tally tells a promise that God has made. (Optional: Lead children in reading the following verses in the Bible: Proverbs 2:6, Isaiah 41:10, Matthew 28:20 and Philippians 4:19.)

God's Word

"The LORD is faithful to all his promises and loving toward all he has made."
Psalm 145:13

For Younger Children:
"The LORD is faithful to all his promises."

God's Word & Me

We can thank God for keeping His promises.

Talk About

- **What are some promises God has made?** (To hear and answer our prayers. To give us courage to do right. To help us know what to do when we need help.) **How can we find out more about God's promises?** (Read the Bible. Listen to what other Christians say about God.)

- Read Psalm 145:13. **What does it mean to be faithful?** (To always do what you say you are going to do.) **How does God show He is faithful? Let's thank God for His love and faithfulness.** Pray with children.

 ## For Younger Children

Place hula hoop on floor. Children take turns standing around the hoop and throwing a beanbag toward hoop. Everyone says, "God keeps His promises" each time beanbag lands in hula hoop.

© 2006 Gospel Light. Permission to photocopy granted. *Treasure Seekers*

Art Center

FOR YOUNGER CHILDREN
Genesis 12:1-7; 15:1-7; 18:1-19; 21:1-7

LESSON four

Collect

Bible, plastic straws, ruler, scissors, chenille wire, heart-shaped pony beads.

Prepare

Cut straws into 1-inch (2.5-cm) pieces.

Do

Distribute beads and chenille wire to each child. Children string heart-shaped beads and straw pieces onto wires. Assist children in twisting ends of wire to form wristbands that can easily be taken on and off children's wrists. Trim wires as needed.

God's Word

"The LORD is faithful to all his promises and loving toward all he has made."
Psalm 145:13

For Younger Children:
"The LORD is faithful to all his promises."

God's Word & Me

We can thank God for keeping His promises.

Talk About

- In today's Bible story, God showed His love for Abraham and his wife, Sarah, by keeping His promises. God promised that Abraham and Sarah would have a baby. And they did!

- Holding your Bible open to Psalm 145:13, say verse aloud. **We can read about God's promises in God's Word, the Bible. One promise that God gives in the Bible is that He will always love us. I'm glad God keeps His promises!**

- **Natalie, which beads on your bracelet remind you of God's promise to always love you?**

- Pray briefly, **Dear God, thank You for Your promise to love us. Thank You for loving (Madison).** Repeat last sentence once for each child in your class. If you have a large class, name more than one child each time you repeat the sentence.

 ## For Older Children

Children use alphabet beads (available at craft stores) to string onto yarn or ribbon, spelling words that remind them of God's promises, such as "love," "care," "help," "courage," etc.

Art Center

FOR OLDER CHILDREN
Genesis 12:1-7; 15:1-7; 18:1-19; 21:1-7

LESSON four

Collect

Bible, 19 tongue depressors and 2 craft sticks for each child, craft glue, index cards, decorating materials (stickers, stamps, colored pencils, markers, glitter glue, etc.), tape, yarn, scissors.

Prepare

Make a sample promise cardholder following the procedure below.

Do

1. Distribute tongue depressors and craft sticks to each child. Child glues three tongue depressors together into a U shape (see sketch a). Child then glues seven tongue depressors across the piece (see sketch b). Child then carefully turns piece over and stacks and glues two more tongue depressors on each side of the U shape (see sketch c).

2. Child stacks and glues two craft sticks onto the bottom of the U (see sketch c). Child glues five tongue depressors across the piece (see sketch d).

3. Distribute several index cards to each child. Child writes on separate cards words that will remind him or her of God's promises or Bible verses that tell God's promises (Proverbs 2:6; Isaiah 41:10; Matthew 28:20; Philippians 4:19). Child then decorates holder using decorating materials and tapes ends of a short yarn or ribbon length to back of holder to create a hanger.

God's Word

"The LORD is faithful to all his promises and loving toward all he has made."
Psalm 145:13

For Younger Children:
"The LORD is faithful to all his promises."

God's Word & Me

We can thank God for keeping His promises.

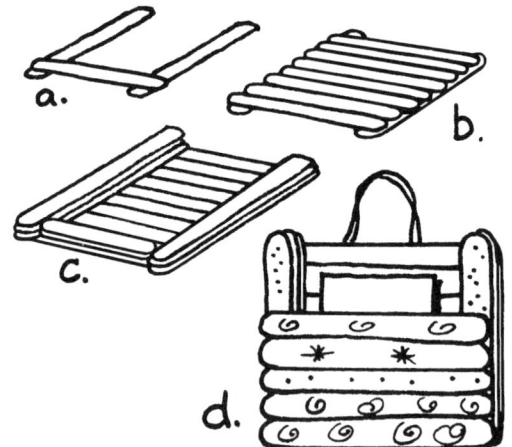

Talk About

- How does it feel when someone keeps his or her promise to you? What was the best-kept promise you've been given?

- Read Psalm 145:13. **What has God done to show that we can trust Him to always keep His promises?** (God kept His promises to people in the Bible. God promised to send Jesus, His only Son, into the world and He did.) **When are some times God's promises can help us?** (When my grandmother is sick. When I feel lonely. When I want to make a good decision.)

For Younger Children

Make holders before class. Write "God promises to love (Emily)." on index cards, one for each child. Children decorate holders and promise cards using markers and stickers and place promise cards in holder.

© 2006 Gospel Light. Permission to photocopy granted. *Treasure Seekers*

Worship Center
Genesis 12:1-7; 15:1-7; 18:1-19; 21:1-7

LESSON four

Collect

Bibles, *Island Music* CD and player, song charts (pp. 249-250), 16 inflated balloons (plus several extras), permanent marker, large bath towels or beach towels, large sheet of paper.

Prepare

Use permanent marker to write each word of Psalm 145:13 and the reference on a separate balloon.

God's Word

"The LORD is faithful to all his promises and loving toward all he has made."
Psalm 145:13

For Younger Children:
"The LORD is faithful to all his promises."

God's Word & Me

We can thank God for keeping His promises.

Team Game

Divide group into two or three teams. Distribute one or two towels to each team. Several volunteers from each team race to form each letter of the word "promises" using towels, rolling them up and forming them into letter shapes. After each letter shape is made, team calls out the letter. First team to complete the word shouts, "God keeps His promises!"

Bible Verse Game

Tap prepared balloons to children around the room. Invite children to continue tapping balloons around the room. After 10 or 15 seconds, say, "Catch!" Children try to grab the nearest balloon. Children holding balloons run to the front of the room and quickly arrange themselves in verse order. Read Psalm 145:13 aloud all together.

Song

You, or another leader, lead children in singing "Promises," adding motions and/or clapping if desired.

Prayer

One way God shows He is faithful to His promises is by listening to our prayers. Across the top of a large sheet of paper, write the following headings: "Prayer Requests" and "Praises." Invite volunteers to share prayer requests and praises. List children's responses on the paper under the appropriate category heading. Close in prayer, mentioning requests and praises.

Song

Play "The Only One." Lead children in singing, adding motions and/or clapping if desired. Close with the following prayer: **Thank You, God, for Your love and faithfulness. We love You! In Jesus' name, amen.**

© 2006 Gospel Light. Permission to photocopy granted. *Treasure Seekers*

Lesson 4 ◆ **Pattern Page**

Star Pattern

Lesson 4 ◇ Coloring/Puzzle Center

God keeps His promises to Abraham.
Genesis 12:1-7; 15:1-7; 18:1-19; 21:1-7

What is a promise that God has made to you? God promises to always love you. God keeps His promises!

© 2006 Gospel Light. Permission to photocopy granted. Treasure Seekers

Lesson 4 ◆ Coloring/Puzzle Center

PROMISES, PROMISES!

Genesis 12:1-9;13

Write the first letter of each item in the blank box below it. When you are done, you can read what Abraham learned about God.

The Super Challenge — On the blanks, write the letters from the numbered boxes to find a three-word message.

___ ___ ___ ___ ___ ___ ___ ___
 3   4   5   6   7   1   8   5

Write one of your favorite promises from the Bible here:
When is a time you might need to remember this promise?

100   © 2006 Gospel Light. Permission to photocopy granted. *Treasure Seekers*

BIBLE STORY ◆ Exodus 19:1—24:18

God Is Holy and Perfect

LESSON five

Teacher's Devotional

Scripture reveals that God is holy. But like so many other "big ideas," this one is difficult to grasp. One definition of "holy" is "perfect." Since Scripture says God is without sin, the word "perfect" helps us to imagine something that has no flaws or mistakes, that brings us closer to the reality of God's holiness! He has never had a flawed thought; He has never made a mistake. He has never spoken a word or done a deed that is not completely perfect in love, in righteousness and in justice. It's easy to see how we unholy folk have trouble grasping a word whose meaning is so far beyond our experience!

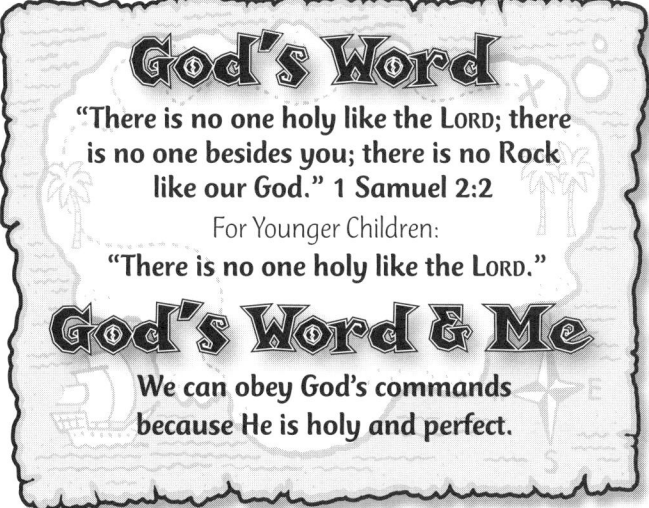

God's Word

"There is no one holy like the LORD; there is no one besides you; there is no Rock like our God." 1 Samuel 2:2

For Younger Children:
"There is no one holy like the LORD."

God's Word & Me

We can obey God's commands because He is holy and perfect.

But God's holiness is more than distant perfection; it acts in perfect compassion. He doesn't draw away from unholy sinners but reaches out to touch them—in Jesus Christ! Jesus lived a perfect, holy (sinless), human life (never done before or since). In His death and resurrection, He took all the punishment for our unholy state and our unholy, sinful deeds. He paid the price so that when we receive His holy (perfect) righteousness by faith in what He has done, God declares us to be holy in Jesus! That is a big idea—one that should shake our foundations, stomp our self-satisfaction and stir us to praise Him!

Taking the time to help your children understand God's holiness gives you a marvelous opportunity to "set the stage" for salvation, the next lesson's focus. Help your kids see that because God is perfect and holy, His commands are good ones, designed to make us the happiest people on Earth! But for those of us who cannot keep from breaking God's perfect law (that's all of us), we can point to the perfect hope we receive in Jesus Christ!

© 2006 Gospel Light. Permission to photocopy granted. *Treasure Seekers*

Planning Page

LESSON five

Choose which centers you will provide and the order in which children will participate in them (see pp. 14-18 for schedule tips and pp. 24-25 for guidelines in combining older and younger children). Also plan who will lead each center (for staffing tips see pp. 19-21). Use the reproducible planning sheet (p. 238) to record your plans.

Bible Story Center

Bible Story
God Is Holy and Perfect • Exodus 19:1—24:18

Younger Child Option
Hold up red and green papers as the story is told

Older Child Option
Decode a text message that says God is holy and perfect

Art Center

Younger Child Option
Use nature items to paint and talk about obeying God

Materials
Bible, tempera paint, shallow baking pans, nature objects to use as painting tools, large sheets of paper

Older Child Option
Make verse plaques and talk about what it means to say that God is holy and perfect

Materials
Bible, Pattern Page (p. 112), materials for making play dough, card stock, coffee grounds, large bowl, scissors, decorating materials, glue, small twigs or toothpicks

Game Center

Younger Child Option
Play Red Light, Green Light and ask for God's help to love and obey Him

Materials
Bible, red and green construction paper, marker, scissors

Older Child Option
Play a game on a life-sized game board and discuss why God gave His commands

Materials
Bible, masking tape, construction paper in various colors, marker, number cube

Coloring/Puzzle Center

Younger Child Option
Review the Bible story while completing coloring page

Materials
Lesson 5 Coloring Page (p. 113) for each student, crayons

Older Child Option
Review the Bible story while completing puzzle page

Materials
Lesson 5 Puzzle Page (p. 114) for each student, pencils

Worship Center

For the Younger and Older Child
Participate in large-group activities to review Bible verse and to worship God together

Materials
Bibles, *Island Music* CD and player, song charts (pp. 246, 250), marker, index cards of two different colors, 12 clear (and empty) water bottles with labels removed, paper bowls, fish-shaped crackers

102

© 2006 Gospel Light. Permission to photocopy granted. *Treasure Seekers*

Bonus Island Ideas

Bonus Island Ideas can be used at any time during this session: as an additional activity center, to extend the session for a longer time, or for added island excitement.

Gone Banana Snacks

Children wash hands (or wipe hands with premoistened cloths) and then make one of the following banana snacks:

Banana Bugs: Students poke pretzel sticks into peeled bananas to make legs and antennae. Make a spine and eyes by using peanut butter or cream cheese to attach chocolate chips. Place each banana bug on a plate.

Frozen Bananas: Cut peeled bananas in half. Insert a popsicle stick into each cut end. Wrap bananas with plastic wrap and freeze. Place flavored yogurt, chopped nuts, flaked coconut or granola on separate paper plates. Children roll their bananas in yogurt, and then in chopped nuts, coconut or granola. (Optional: Melt chocolate bars and place in shallow bowls. Children dip bananas into chocolate.)

Post a note alerting parents to the use of food. Also, check registration forms for possible food allergies.

Secret Treasures

Place wrapped candies in a treasure chest and lock the chest. Place the lock's key in an envelope and seal envelope (if using a combination lock, draw a picture of a key on an index card and place card in envelope). Hide envelope and other empty envelopes in an outdoor play area for children to find. Child who finds envelope with key, opens chest with key and distributes candy to children. (Optional: Hide various metal objects [coins, metal utensils, etc.] in your church's sand play area. Use a metal detector to search for objects.)

Beach Party Day

Send flyers home ahead of time, inviting families to join in on some beach party fun after a *Treasure Seekers* lesson! Bring out the beach chairs and umbrellas, lay out beach towels and soda-filled coolers on the church lawn or in a large gathering area or room in the church. Serve fruit snacks and smoothies. Play beach music and/or show a movie that the whole family will enjoy!

© 2006 Gospel Light. Permission to photocopy granted. *Treasure Seekers*

Bible Story Center

FOR YOUNGER CHILDREN
Exodus 19:1—24:18

LESSON five

Collect
Bible.

Introduction
What is one rule your mom or dad asks you to follow (at dinnertime)? Children answer. **Listen to find out about a time when God gave 10 rules for His people. Hold up your fingers when I hold up mine!**

Treasure Chest Option
Place one red and one green sheet of construction paper in a treasure chest. Invite two volunteers to remove papers from treasure chest. As the story is being told, show the red paper to children when a "Do not" command is mentioned and show the green paper when other commands are mentioned.

Tell the Story

The Israelites walked, walked and walked in the desert for many, many days. Finally, they came to a mountain. God told them to camp by the mountain. All the people set up tents. They gathered sticks and made fires so they could cook food. They found places for their animals to rest and eat.

God told Moses to come up to the top of the mountain. Up, up and up Moses climbed the mountain. God wanted to talk with Moses. God told Moses many important things while Moses was on the mountain. God gave Moses two stone tablets that God wrote His laws on. **Hold up two fingers.** These laws were God's rules and they were called the Ten Commandments. **Hold up 10 fingers.** God gave these 10 rules to help the Israelites know the best way to live.

Hold up four fingers. The first four rules were about ways to show love to God. One of these rules was, "Show you love God more than anything or anyone." Another rule said, "Don't use God's name in wrong ways." **Hold up six fingers.** The other six rules told ways to show love to others. One of these rules said, "Show respect to your mom and dad." Another rule said, "Don't take what isn't yours." God told Moses other rules for the people to follow.

Moses went down from the mountain. He carried with him the two stone tablets with God's laws written on them. Down, down, down he went. Moses then told the Israelites everything God had told him. God's rules helped the people know what God wanted. The people promised to show love for God and obey God's rules.

God's Word & Me

Our Bible says, "There is no one holy like the Lord." This means that God is perfect! He can never do wrong things. Because God is perfect and He loves us, He gives us rules to help us know the best way to live. When we obey God's rules, we show that we love God!

© 2006 Gospel Light. Permission to photocopy granted. *Treasure Seekers*

Bible Story Center

FOR OLDER CHILDREN
Exodus 19:1—24:18

Collect

Bible.

Introduction

What kinds of special events do you and your family spend a lot of time getting ready for? (First day of school. Christmas. Visit from grandparents.) **What do you do to get ready for these events?** A long time ago in Bible times, Moses and the Israelites had to get ready for a VERY special event. We'll find out what the event was and how they got ready for it. Divide class into several groups. Assign each group one or two words for which to plan and practice sound effects (sheep, climb, lightning, thunder, trumpet, earthquake). Give students a few moments to practice sound effects. At your signal, students make sounds during the story when these objects or events are mentioned (see keywords). (Optional: Provide items for students to use in making sound effects, such as wooden blocks, kazoos, cellophane paper, baking pans.)

Treasure Chest Option

Place a phone with text messaging capability in a treasure chest. Arrange with another leader before class who also has a cell phone to send the following text message to your phone: "GDZ HLY and GDZ PRFKT," after the Bible story is told. A volunteer removes phone from treasure chest, reads and writes the message on a large sheet of paper. Class works together to decode the message: "God is holy and God is perfect."

Tell the Story

For three months after the Israelites escaped from Egypt, they walked through the desert. They were on their way to the land God had promised to give them. God guided them with a cloud during the day and a fire by night. One day, the cloud that guided them stopped at the base of steep, rocky Mount Sinai. As the Israelites set up their tents and put their **sheep** out to graze, they had no idea what was about to take place!

Moses **climbed** the mountain to talk to God. Somewhere, WAY UP among the rocks and boulders, the Lord told Moses how He wanted the Israelites to be His special people, a nation that belonged to Him. Moses listened carefully and then **climbed** back down the mountain to the Israelite camp. He told all the leaders what God had said. The people all responded, "We will do everything the Lord has said!"

For the second time, Moses **climbed** up Mount Sinai and told the Lord that the people wanted to obey. God answered, "I am going to visit the people. When I speak with you, everyone will hear the sound of My voice. Then they will always believe you. Have the people get ready." And once again Moses listened carefully to God's instructions and then hurried down the mountain to call the people together.

"The day after tomorrow the Lord is going to visit us in a special way," Moses said. "Get ready for His visit!" So the people did the things God had told them to do to get ready for His visit—including washing all their clothes. Moses also told the people to set up a boundary around the mountain. NO ONE was to go up on the mountain—or even touch it! The whole mountain would become holy because of God's holy and perfect presence.

Everyone got busy and prepared for the visit. Finally, the day of the Lord's visit arrived. **Thunder** and **lightning** came over the mountain. A LOUD **trumpet** blast rang out. The people trembled as the trumpet **thundered**

© 2006 Gospel Light. Permission to photocopy granted. *Treasure Seekers*

and billows of smoke rose from the mountain. The Lord CERTAINLY had their attention now! And that was just what He wanted, for God had some VERY important things for Moses to tell them!

God called Moses up to the top of the mountain and began to speak. He gave Moses 10 commandments written on two stone tablets. The first four commandments that God gave were about how to worship and respect Him. He said the people were not to make or worship any idols (false gods) like the people around them did. They were not to misuse God's name in any way. And they were to keep the Sabbath (the seventh day of the week) holy and special by resting on that day and not doing any work.

Then God gave six commandments about how people should treat each other. God said children should treat parents with respect. God told Moses that the people should never murder, take each other's wives or husbands or steal anything from each other. God also commanded not to give false testimony against a neighbor, which means we should not lie about others. Finally, God warned against wanting what others have.

Then God was quiet. But the smoke rose and the **thunder** and **trumpeting** continued. The people stayed far away. They were all terrified! They said to Moses, "YOU listen to God and then tell us God's message! Don't let God speak to us or we will die!"

"Don't be afraid," Moses told them. "God has shown you His mighty power so that you will have respect for Him and won't sin against Him." But the people stayed at a distance from the mountain. Moses returned to the mountain to talk more with God. He listened carefully as God gave him more instructions for the Israelites so that they would be His special people.

God's Word & Me

The commandments God gave the Israelites are called the Ten Commandments. God thought these commands were so important that He sent earthquakes, thunder and lightning to get the people's attention. God didn't give these commands just so we would have a bunch of rules to follow. He gave these commands and all the other wise instructions in the Bible because He wants us to know the best way to live.

- Name one commandment that tells a way to love God. Name another that tells a way to love others.

- Why is it important to obey God's commands? (God made us and loves us, so He knows what is best for us. Following His commands helps us show that we love Him. God's commands help us know how to treat others in good ways.)

- Read 1 Samuel 2:2. **What does this verse tell us about God?** (God is holy. No one can compare to what God is like. God is like a rock, strong and dependable.) **Because God is holy and perfect, we know that all of His commands are holy and perfect, too!** Pray, Dear God, You are holy and perfect and so is everything You do. Help us know how to follow and obey Your commands. In Jesus' name, amen.

© 2006 Gospel Light. Permission to photocopy granted. *Treasure Seekers*

Game Center

FOR YOUNGER CHILDREN
Exodus 19:1—24:18

Collect
Bible, red and green construction paper, marker, scissors.

Prepare
Use red and green construction paper to make a Stop sign and a Go sign.

Do

1. Children line up across one side of the playing area. Stand on the opposite side of the playing area. **When I hold this Go sign, everyone may walk towards me. But when I hold up the Stop sign, everyone must freeze in place.**

2. Begin the activity by holding up the Go sign, and then after a few seconds hold up the Stop sign. If children do not freeze when you hold up the Stop sign, gently remind them that the Stop sign is up. Do not make children start over. Continue activity until children reach you. Play again as time and interest allow. (Optional: Vary the way children move towards you [hop, crawl, skip, etc.] each round.)

God's Word
"There is no one holy like the LORD; there is no one besides you; there is no Rock like our God." 1 Samuel 2:2

For Younger Children:
"There is no one holy like the LORD."

God's Word & Me
We can obey God's commands because He is holy and perfect.

Talk About

- When you saw the green sign what did you do? When you saw the red sign what did you do? These signs helped us know what to do!

- God helps us know what to do, too. Because God is perfect, He always helps us know what is right and wrong. **Sheri, what is a good thing to say to your mom and dad?** (Thank you. I love you. Excuse me.) **Curtis, what is a good thing to do when you want to use a crayon that Kelly has?** (Ask if you can have a turn using the crayon. Wait until she is finished using it.)

- Our Bible says, "There is no one holy like the Lord." God never does wrong things. God is perfect. We can ask for God's help to love and obey Him by saying and doing what is right. Pray, Dear God, help us to love and obey You in all that we say and do. In Jesus' name, amen.

For Older Children

Play the game as described above with a tagging variation: Stand with your back turned to children who are standing on the other side of the playing area. Hold up red and green signs indicating when children should move toward you or freeze in place. When you feel that children are close enough, turn around and try to tag one of the children. Child who is tagged recites 1 Samuel 2:2 and is the leader for the next round.

© 2006 Gospel Light. Permission to photocopy granted. *Treasure Seekers*

 # Game Center

FOR OLDER CHILDREN
Exodus 19:1—24:18

LESSON five

Collect

Bible, masking tape, construction paper in various colors, marker, number cube.

Prepare

Tape construction paper onto floor as shown in sketch to make a game path. Make one game path for each group of six to eight students. Draw a palm tree on any two or three of the papers on the path. (Optional: If number cube is not available, print numbers one to six on separate slips of paper and place in a paper bag.)

God's Word

"There is no one holy like the LORD; there is no one besides you; there is no Rock like our God." 1 Samuel 2:2

For Younger Children:
"There is no one holy like the LORD."

God's Word & Me

We can obey God's commands because He is holy and perfect.

Do

Children stand on game path, one child on each paper. Roll the number cube (or choose a slip of paper from bag). All players move that number of papers on the path, each player choosing to move clockwise or counterclockwise on path. (Note: More than one student may stand on or near the same paper.) Any child who ends up standing on a paper marked with a palm tree recites 1 Samuel 2:2 or answers one of the questions below. Repeat game as time permits.

Talk About

- Which way did you choose to go on the game path? What was it like when everyone chose to go their own direction? Why did God give the Ten Commandments? (To teach us the best way to live.) **We don't have to figure out the best way to live all by ourselves. God is perfect and will help us know what to do if we ask Him.**

- Read 1 Samuel 2:2. What does "there is no Rock like our God" mean? (We can depend on God. We can trust Him.) **Because God is holy and perfect and never does anything wrong, we know that obeying His commands will help us do what is best for us.**

- What are some other commands God gives us in the Bible? **Let's pray, asking for God's help in obeying His commands.** Pray with children.

 ## For Younger Children

Children use game path to play a game like Cake Walk. Play "The Only One" from *Island Music* CD. Children walk around the path as music plays. When the music stops, children standing on or near papers marked with a palm tree say, "There is no one holy like the Lord" or "I can love and obey God!"

© 2006 Gospel Light. Permission to photocopy granted. *Treasure Seekers*

Art Center

FOR YOUNGER CHILDREN
Exodus 19:1—24:18

Collect

Bible, tempera paint, shallow baking pans, nature objects to use as painting tools (feathers, twigs, flower petals, bark, stones, leaves, etc.), large sheets of paper.

Prepare

Pour a ½ inch (1.3 cm) of paint into several baking pans. (Optional: Set up painting area outdoors. Lead children on a nature walk to collect nature objects before painting.)

Do

Children dip nature objects into paint and then paint designs on paper. Invite children to experiment with all the nature objects but help them to choose and use one object to paint with at a time.

God's Word

"There is no one holy like the LORD; there is no one besides you; there is no Rock like our God." 1 Samuel 2:2

For Younger Children:
"There is no one holy like the LORD."

God's Word & Me

We can obey God's commands because He is holy and perfect.

Talk About

- In today's Bible story, God gave Moses and the Israelites special rules for them to follow. These rules helped them to know the best way to live.

- When we paint, what are some rules we follow? (Take turns. Share paint. Don't paint on others' papers.) **These are good rules to follow because they help each one of us to use and enjoy the paint!**

- Our Bible says, "There is no one holy like the Lord." "Lord" is another name for God. This verse means that God is perfect. He can never do wrong things. God gives us good rules to follow.

- We can ask God's help to obey His rules. Pray briefly, **Dear God, help us obey Your rules and do good things. We love You. In Jesus' name, amen.**

 ## For Older Children

Children use markers to write words of 1 Samuel 2:2 on their individual papers or on one large sheet of butcher paper before using nature items to paint designs.

© 2006 Gospel Light. Permission to photocopy granted. *Treasure Seekers*

 # Art Center

FOR OLDER CHILDREN
Exodus 19:1—24:18

LESSON five

Collect

Bible, Pattern Page (p. 112), materials for making play dough (see recipe below), card stock, coffee grounds, large bowl, scissors, decorating materials (markers, glitter, gold and silver paint pens, foil stickers, etc.), glue, small twigs or toothpicks.

Prepare

Make play dough using the following recipe: Mix 1½ cups flour, 1 cup cornstarch, 1 cup salt and 1 cup warm water. If dough is sticky, dust with flour. If dough is stiff, add water. Store dough in airtight container. Copy Pattern Page onto card stock, making one copy for each child.

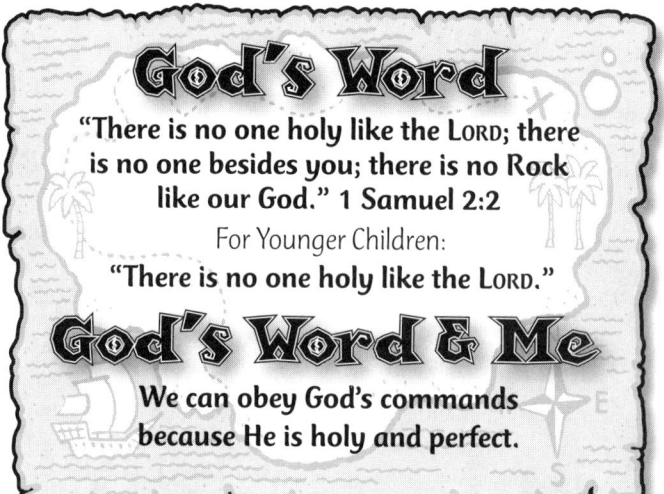

God's Word
"There is no one holy like the LORD; there is no one besides you; there is no Rock like our God." 1 Samuel 2:2

For Younger Children:
"There is no one holy like the LORD."

God's Word & Me
We can obey God's commands because He is holy and perfect.

Do

1. Children take turns mixing coffee grounds and play dough in a large bowl. Each child takes a fist-sized lump of dough to create a flat rock shape. Child then chooses and cuts out one of the plaque borders or draws his or her own border on a blank rectangle from the Pattern Page. Child writes a phrase of 1 Samuel 2:2 on the plaque and decorates the plaque with the given materials.

2. Child glues plaque onto the dough "rock." Child then glues twigs or toothpicks to create a border for the plaque (see sketch).

Talk About

- Read 1 Samuel 2:2. **What does it mean to be holy?** (Set apart. Pure. Belonging to God.) **When this verse says that "there is no one holy like the Lord," it means that God is perfect and without sin. In today's story, God showed His holiness and power when He gave the Ten Commandments.**

- **Why did God give the Ten Commandments?** (To help us live in ways that show love and respect for God and others. To help us know that we need God's help to love and obey Him.) **Later, God sent His one and only Son, Jesus, to die on the cross to take the punishment for our sins so that by His power we can obey His commands.**

- **What are some words to describe a rock?** (Solid. Strong. Sturdy.) **How is a rock similar to what God is like?** (God is strong. We can always depend on God's love and help to obey Him.) Pray with children.

 ## For Younger Children

Children play with dough and use twigs to draw numbers or marks on dough. Talk about God's rules.

Worship Center
Exodus 19:1—24:18

LESSON five

Collect
Bibles, *Island Music* CD and player, song charts (pp. 246, 250), marker, index cards of two different colors, 12 clear (and empty) water bottles with labels removed, paper bowls, fish-shaped crackers.

Prepare
Divide 1 Samuel 2:2 into six phrases and write each phrase on separate index cards of the same color. Make another set of verse cards on index cards of another color. Roll each index card so that the words are facing outward. Insert rolled index cards into separate water bottles.

God's Word
"There is no one holy like the LORD; there is no one besides you; there is no Rock like our God." 1 Samuel 2:2

For Younger Children:
"There is no one holy like the LORD."

God's Word & Me
We can obey God's commands because He is holy and perfect.

Team Game
Divide group into four to six teams. Invite one volunteer from each team to be his or her team's "seal." Seals line up and kneel on one side of the room (and act like seals during the game). Place a masking-tape line 2 to 4 feet away (.6 to 1.2 m) from seals. Each seal holds a paper bowl in his or her mouth and keeps hands behind back. Team members line up on the other side of the playing area. Team members run to the masking-tape line and take turns tossing fish-shaped crackers toward the bowl their team seal is holding in his or her mouth, "feeding" the seal. Each time a cracker lands in the bowl, the seal's team barks. Team who gets most fish in their seal's bowl wins!

Bible Verse Game
Toss out prepared water bottles to children around the room. Children with bottles run to the front of the room and quickly group themselves with others whose bottles hold the same colored index cards. Each group works together to arrange verse cards in order. Once cards are in correct order, group calls out verse.

Song
You, or another leader, lead children in singing "The Only One," adding motions and/or clapping if desired.

Prayer
How many of God's commands did we learn about today? (10) Invite children to hold up one hand in the air. **Let's see if we can think of four ways to show love and obedience to God.** Children call out responses. **Now hold up your other hand. Let's see if we can think of six ways to show love to others.** Say a brief prayer asking God's help to show love to God and others, mentioning children's responses.

Song
Play "Treasure Forever." Lead children in singing, adding motions and/or clapping if desired.

© 2006 Gospel Light. Permission to photocopy granted. *Treasure Seekers*

Lesson 5 ◇ Pattern Page

Lesson 5 ◇ Coloring/Puzzle Center

God gives the Ten Commandments.
Exodus 19:1—24:18

What is one rule that you follow every day? God gave us rules to help us know the best way to live. These rules are called the Ten Commandments.

Lesson 5 ◇ Coloring/Puzzle Center

TAKE TWO TABLETS...
Exodus 20:1-21

The Challenge → Fill in the words from the word list to finish the Ten Commandments.

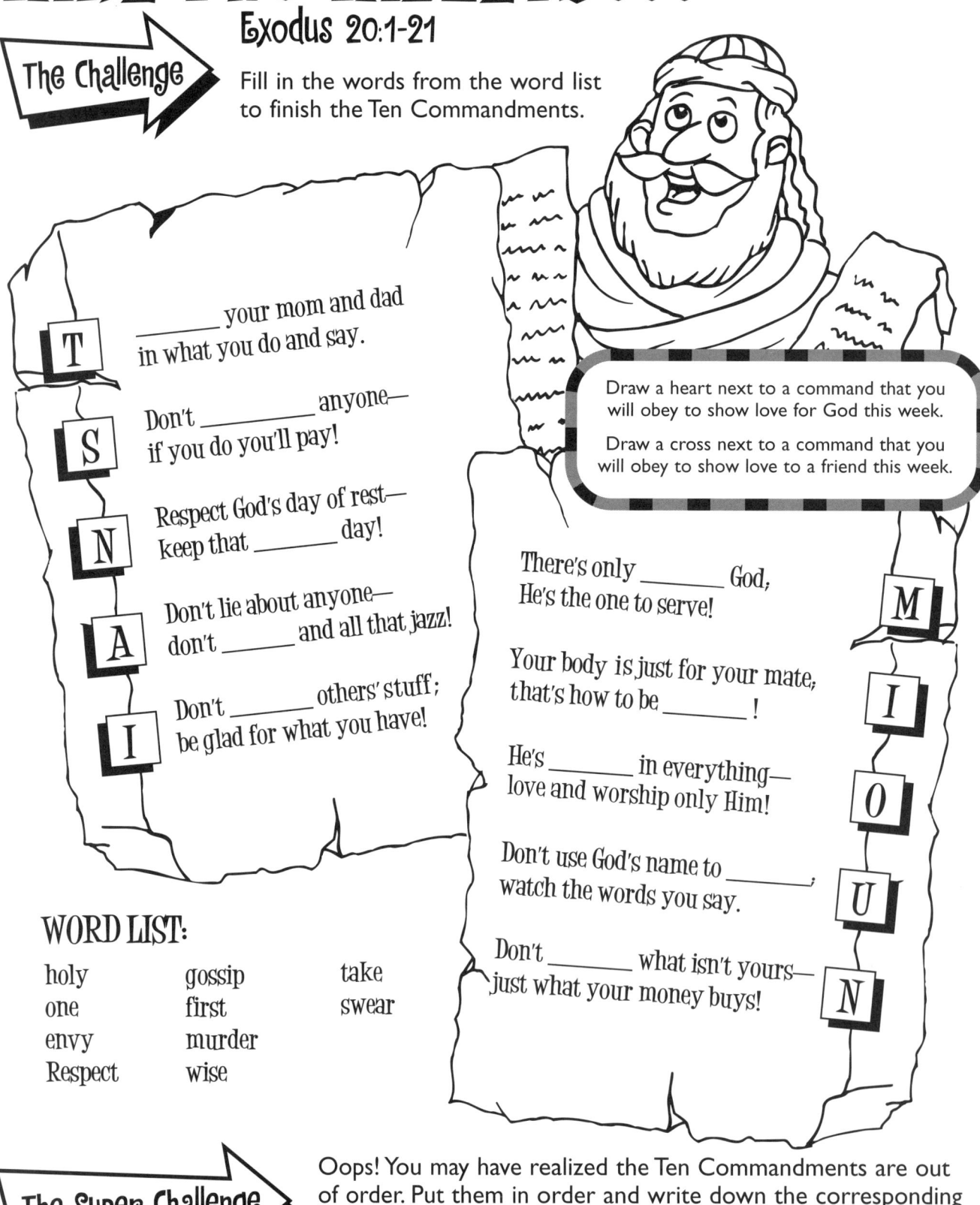

[T] _____ your mom and dad in what you do and say.

[S] Don't _____ anyone— if you do you'll pay!

[N] Respect God's day of rest— keep that _____ day!

[A] Don't lie about anyone— don't _____ and all that jazz!

[I] Don't _____ others' stuff; be glad for what you have!

There's only _____ God, He's the one to serve! [M]

Your body is just for your mate; that's how to be _____ ! [I]

He's _____ in everything— love and worship only Him! [O]

Don't use God's name to _____ ; watch the words you say. [U]

Don't _____ what isn't yours— just what your money buys! [N]

> Draw a heart next to a command that you will obey to show love for God this week.
>
> Draw a cross next to a command that you will obey to show love to a friend this week.

WORD LIST:

holy	gossip	take
one	first	swear
envy	murder	
Respect	wise	

The Super Challenge → Oops! You may have realized the Ten Commandments are out of order. Put them in order and write down the corresponding letter to discover where Moses was when God gave him the commandments.

M _ _ _ _ _ _   _ _ _ _ _

114 © 2006 Gospel Light. Permission to photocopy granted. *Treasure Seekers*

BIBLE STORY ◆ **Selections from the Gospels**

God Loves and Forgives Me

LESSON six

Teacher's Devotional

Love is probably the most talked-about subject on the planet. It is one thing we all seem to believe we cannot live without! But love is a little-understood concept: We say that we love Sam or Susie, that we love chocolate, the flag, our mothers, our Chihuahuas and that new color of lipstick. Clearly, those don't all merit the same kind of love. To increase the confusion, Scripture tells us that God is love!

God's Word

"For God so loved the world that he gave his one and only Son, that whoever believes in him shall not perish but have eternal life." John 3:16

For Younger Children:
"God so loved the world that he gave his one and only Son."

God's Word & Me

We can be a part of God's family because of God's love and forgiveness through Jesus.

In Greek, there are several words we freely translate as "love." One word is for brotherly love and affection (dogs and chocolate might fall into this category); one is for sexual attraction ("love" in the sense of lusting after another); the third is *agape*: This is the kind of love God shows. This love considers what is best for the other person and sacrifices for his or her good. This love is completely unselfish; it is a love that gives. In God's case, the giving is so complete that it wasn't too much to send His Son to be born as a baby, live as a human on Earth and then die on the cross. Jesus articulated the essence of this love in John 15:13: "Greater love has no one than this, that he lay down his life for his friends." However, Jesus not only articulated it, but He also lived it—and died it. Then, He rose again to prove He could beat death, the final enemy!

As you talk about the astounding love God offers us in Jesus, share your awe and delight. God loves us—that much! As Paul exults in Romans 8:32: "He who did not spare his own Son, but gave him up for us all—how will he not also, along with him, graciously give us all things?" His love is real: He did it all so that He could enfold us in a love so pure and complete that it will not only carry us through this life but also will sweep us on into His presence to love us face to face, forever!

© 2006 Gospel Light. Permission to photocopy granted. *Treasure Seekers*

Planning Page

Choose which centers you will provide and the order in which children will participate in them (see pp. 14-18 for schedule tips and pp. 24-25 for guidelines in combining older and younger children). Also plan who will lead each center (for staffing tips see pp. 19-21). Use the reproducible planning sheet (p. 238) to record your plans.

Lesson six

Bible Story Center

Bible Story
God Loves and Forgives Me
• Selections from the Gospels

Younger Child Option
Show happy or sad paper-plate faces while story is being told

Older Child Option
Hear some clues to solve words from the message "God loves and forgives"

Art Center

Younger Child Option
Make heart-shaped pockets and thank God for Jesus

Materials
Bible, Pattern Page (p. 126), card stock, scissors, markers, index cards, various decorative stickers, tape or stapler, hole punch, one 36-inch (91.5-cm) length of yarn or ribbon for each child

Older Child Option
Make cross mobiles and discuss God's love and forgiveness for all people

Materials
Bible, scissors, measuring stick, 20 or 24 gauge spool of wire, small beads, chenille wires, short lengths of ribbon or string

Game Center

Younger Child Option
Play a ball-rolling game to say the words of John 3:16

Materials
Bible, beach ball

Older Child Option
Play a game like HORSE and tell reasons God sent Jesus

Materials
Bible, markers, construction paper, large container, tape, two large sheets of paper, two beach balls

Coloring/Puzzle Center

Younger Child Option
Review the Bible story while completing coloring page

Materials
Lesson 6 Coloring Page (p. 127) for each student, crayons

Older Child Option
Review the Bible story while completing puzzle page

Materials
Lesson 6 Puzzle Page (p. 128) for each student, pencils

Worship Center

For the Younger and Older Child
Participate in large-group activities to review Bible verse and to worship God together

Materials
Bibles, *Island Music* CD and player, song charts (pp. 250-251), marker, large sheet of butcher paper, wrapped candies, two beach chairs, colored strips of paper, pencils, tape

© 2006 Gospel Light. Permission to photocopy granted. *Treasure Seekers*

Bonus Island Ideas

Bonus Island Ideas can be used at any time during this session: as an additional activity center, to extend the session for a longer time, or for added island excitement.

Creative Juices

Pour each of several kinds of fruit juices into a separate pitcher. Distribute small paper cups to children. Children experiment with adding two or more different types of juices together to create their own unique fruit-juice flavor. Invite volunteers to submit their creative concoctions to a judging panel. Leaders choose the tastiest and most creative fruit juices and give small awards to children. (Optional: Freeze grapes and strawberries. Children add frozen fruits to their drinks.)

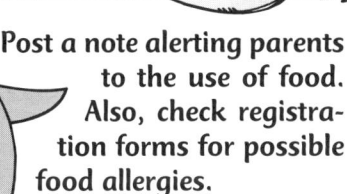

Post a note alerting parents to the use of food. Also, check registration forms for possible food allergies.

Island Ball

Assemble children in a large outdoor play area. Divide group into two teams. Place sheets of cardboard or carpet on the ground in a baseball-diamond layout. Children play Island Ball, following regular baseball rules but using a beach ball and long cardboard tube or plastic bat. **For younger children:** Children play a game of kickball with the beach ball.

Using sidewalk chalk, children draw large underwater scenes on sidewalk or blacktop area in church playground area. If going outdoors is not an option, children may draw scenes on butcher paper. Display underwater scenes around the room.

Under-the-Sea Mural

© 2006 Gospel Light. Permission to photocopy granted. *Treasure Seekers*

Bible Story Center

FOR YOUNGER CHILDREN
Selections from the Gospels

LESSON six

Collect
Bible.

Introduction
Who is someone that you love? Volunteers answer. **Listen to find out about someone who loves us very much!**

Treasure Chest Option
Collect a paper plate for each child. On each plate, draw a happy face on one side and a sad face on the other side. Place plates in a treasure chest. Invite a volunteer to remove plates from treasure chest and distribute plates. Lead children in showing happy or sad faces at appropriate times in the story.

Tell the Story

A long, long time ago, God promised He would send His special Son. God's people waited and waited and waited.

Many years later, the day finally came when Jesus, God's Son, was born! God chose two people named Mary and Joseph to help care for this special baby.

When Jesus was older, He began His important work. He taught people about God and made many sick people well again. Many people loved Jesus because of the wonderful things He had done for them. But some people did not like what Jesus said and did. They were angry that so many people loved Jesus.

One day Jesus told 12 of His friends, "In a few days, some people are going to take Me away. I'm going to be killed." Jesus' friends were very sad. But Jesus was not afraid. Jesus knew this was part of God's good plan. Jesus knew He wouldn't STAY dead!

When the people who wanted to kill Jesus came to get Him, Jesus let them take Him. And Jesus let them kill Him on a cross. Jesus' friends were very sad that Jesus had died. They took Jesus' body and put it into a tomb. (This tomb was a little room made in the side of a hill.) Some men put a huge rock in front of the doorway of the tomb. It was a very sad and scary time, but it didn't STAY sad and scary!

On the third morning, one of Jesus' friends named Mary came to the tomb. Mary saw that the tomb was EMPTY! She cried and cried. But then she looked into the tomb and saw two angels. One angel asked, "Why are you crying?" Mary said, "Because Jesus is gone, and I don't know where He is."

Just then, Mary turned around. She almost bumped into someone. "Mary!" the person said. Mary knew that voice—it was JESUS! Mary was so happy to know that Jesus is alive! Jesus told Mary to go and tell His friends that He is alive.

Later that night, Jesus came to the place where His friends were. Now Jesus' friends SAW Jesus alive. They were very excited! The very SAD day had turned into a very GLAD day—because Jesus is alive!

God's Word & Me

Jesus' friends were very glad when they saw that Jesus is alive. Jesus' friends knew how much Jesus loved them. Jesus loves us, too. Our Bible says, "God so loved the world that he gave his one and only Son." What can you do to show that you're glad God sent Jesus?

© 2006 Gospel Light. Permission to photocopy granted. *Treasure Seekers*

Bible Story Center

FOR OLDER CHILDREN
Selections from the Gospels

Collect

Bible, five large sheets of paper, marker.

Introduction

What are some famous love stories you know? (Romeo and Juliet. Cinderella.) **Listen to find out about the world's greatest love story.** Place five large sheets of paper around the room. Label papers "Who?" "What?" "When?" "Where?" "Why?" Invite students to tell what they remember about the life of Jesus. Record information on the appropriate sheet of paper.

Treasure Chest Option

Write these clues on an index card: (1) Has four letters; (2) Is a noun and a verb; (3) Sounds like the word "dove." Write these clues on another card: (1) Has eight letters; (2) Is made up of two words, one beginning with *f* and one beginning with *g*; (3) Tells what to do when someone says "I'm sorry." Place cards in a treasure chest. At the end of the story, invite a volunteer to read aloud clues on cards for others to guess the words "loves" and "forgives."

Tell The Story

Jesus and His disciples traveled for three years, talking with people about God's love, healing sick people and doing all kinds of miracles. (Miracles are things done by God's power that no one else can do.) Many, many people followed Jesus. But most of them didn't really understand who Jesus is or why He was there.

Because of Jesus' popularity, the religious leaders were jealous of Jesus. They were afraid that the people who followed Jesus wouldn't listen to them anymore! So they decided to get rid of Jesus. The leaders paid one of Jesus' disciples to betray Him. This disciple, Judas Iscariot, led soldiers through the dark to where Jesus was praying. They arrested Jesus and pressured the Roman governor to order Jesus to die on a cross!

As Jesus hung on the cross, He looked at the people around Him. There were people making fun of Him and yelling angrily at Him. Jesus didn't say anything to them. Instead He prayed, "Father, forgive them, for they do not know what they are doing." Jesus is much more powerful than the ropes and nails that the soldiers used to put Him on the cross. He could have broken free at any moment! Jesus chose to stay on the cross because of His love for us. He knew He was there to pay the penalty for sin so all people everywhere would have the chance to be forgiven and live forever with Him.

Jesus hung on the cross for six hours. Some of Jesus' friends and followers watched from a distance. *This wasn't supposed to happen!* they must have thought. *We thought Jesus was the One who would set us free and give us a new life.* Even though they were afraid they would be killed, they loved Jesus and wanted to be near Him. All these people must have heard Jesus when He cried, "It is finished." They didn't understand then but Jesus meant that when He died, all the sins of all the people in the world were paid for. Jesus had done what He came to do.

After Jesus died, His body was buried in a tomb cut into a rock. A large stone was rolled across the opening of the tomb. But this wasn't the end. It was just the beginning! Something exciting was about to happen! Early Sunday morning, on the third day after He died, some of Jesus' friends went to the tomb. As these women walked to the tomb, they wondered who would help them move the stone from the entrance to the tomb.

© 2006 Gospel Light. Permission to photocopy granted. *Treasure Seekers*

When the women got to the tomb, they found that the stone had been rolled away from the tomb, and when they looked inside, Jesus' body was not there! As the women were wondering what had happened, two angels suddenly appeared! The angels said, "Why do you look for the living among the dead? He is not here; He has risen! Remember what He told you while He was still with you in Galilee." The women remembered Jesus' words. They knew it was true! Jesus had come back to life! They ran to tell the disciples, but the disciples didn't believe them!

Later that day, two of Jesus' friends were walking from Jerusalem to Emmaus. As they walked, they sadly talked about all that had happened to Jesus.

Jesus came along and began to walk with them but they didn't recognize Him. "What are you talking about?" Jesus asked. The two stopped. They stood still for a moment, looking at the ground.

One of them, named Cleopas, asked "Are you only a visitor to Jerusalem that you don't know what has happened in these past few days?" Of COURSE Jesus knew what had happened! But Jesus wanted to help His two friends understand. So He said, "What things?"

The friends explained all the things that had happened to Jesus. Then Jesus began to teach His friends. He started with the very first books in the Old Testament written by Moses and continued all the way through the Old Testament prophets. He explained that the same Jesus they were talking about was the One God had promised to send. He would take the punishment for the sins of the whole world.

The friends talked and listened to Jesus all the way to Emmaus. When they got to Emmaus, they invited Jesus to stay with them for the night. As they sat down to eat, Jesus took the bread and thanked God for it. Then all of sudden, they could see—it was Jesus! They were amazed! JESUS had been talking with them. They were so excited, they got up and hurried right back to Jerusalem! In fact, they probably RAN! They had to tell the others that they had seen Jesus. He IS alive!

God's Word & Me

God showed His great love to all of us when He sent His Son, Jesus, to die on the cross for our sins. Jesus loves and forgives us today just like He loved and forgave the people who nailed Him to the cross. Jesus was willing to go through the pain of dying on the cross because He knew it was the only way to make it possible for us to become a part of God's family and live forever with Him. Let's thank God for His love! (Talk with interested students about salvation. See "Leading a Child to Christ" on p. 12.)

- **If you were hearing this story for the first time, how would you describe Jesus?**

- **Why is Jesus' death and resurrection so important?** (Jesus took the punishment for all the wrong things everyone in the world has done. Because of Jesus we can be forgiven, be a part of God's family and live forever with God when we trust in Him.)

- Read John 3:16. **Who is this important message for according to John 3:16?** (Everybody.) **Why is it important for all people to know the reason God sent Jesus?** (To know about God's love. To receive forgiveness.)

- Lead children in saying the following prayer: **Dear God, thank You for Your amazing love for me shown through Jesus' death and resurrection. Thank You for forgiving me. In Jesus' name, amen.**

 # Game Center

FOR YOUNGER CHILDREN
Selections from the Gospels

Collect

Bible, beach ball.

Do

Sit with children in a circle. Roll the ball to a child in the circle while saying, **"God so loved (Tami) that he gave his one and only Son,"** naming the child to whom the ball is being rolled. Child rolls ball back to you. Continue until each child has been named. (Optional: Vary the way the ball is rolled to each child—with one bounce, under legs, tapping with elbow or knee, etc. Invite children to return the ball to you in the same manner.)

God's Word

"For God so loved the world that he gave his one and only Son, that whoever believes in him shall not perish but have eternal life." John 3:16

For Younger Children:
"God so loved the world that he gave his one and only Son."

God's Word & Me

We can be a part of God's family because of God's love and forgiveness through Jesus.

Talk About

- Our Bible says, "God so loved the world that he gave his one and only Son." God has shown His love to us by sending His Son, Jesus, to Earth.

- Whose birthday do we celebrate at Christmastime? What do we celebrate at Easter? (That Jesus is alive.)

- Kaitlyn, what is one way your family celebrates Jesus' birth at Christmas? Harrison, what is one way your family celebrates Easter?

- Let's thank God for Jesus. Pray, **Dear God, thank You for sending Jesus. We love You. In Jesus' name, amen.**

 ## For Older Children

Divide the class into two teams. Invite two pairs from each team to play game. Each pair holds opposite ends of a towel and stands the towel's length apart. Pairs use towels to toss and catch the beach ball while saying words of John 3:16. Continue with new pairs from each team.

© 2006 Gospel Light. Permission to photocopy granted. *Treasure Seekers*

 # Game Center

LESSON six

FOR OLDER CHILDREN
Selections from the Gospels

Collect
Bible, markers, construction paper, large container (cardboard box, inflated kiddie pool, etc.), tape, two large sheets of paper, two beach balls.

Prepare
Print each letter of the words "love" and "forgive" on a separate sheet of paper. Set container in the center of an open area in the classroom. Arrange papers that spell out "love" at varying distances from the container. Tape large sheets of paper to wall nearby, labeling sheets "Team 1" and "Team 2."

God's Word
"For God so loved the world that he gave his one and only Son, that whoever believes in him shall not perish but have eternal life." John 3:16

For Younger Children:
"God so loved the world that he gave his one and only Son."

God's Word & Me
We can be a part of God's family because of God's love and forgiveness through Jesus.

Do
1. Divide class into two teams. Teams stand in two lines. First child in each line stands next to the paper lettered L. Give each player a ball. At your signal, children take turns tossing ball towards the container. If the ball lands in the container, write the letter L on the appropriate team's paper.

2. Next two children in line stand next to the paper lettered O. Game quickly continues, with teams trying to collect each letter of the word "love" in order. Repeat throws for missing letters. First team to collect all the letters for "love" repeats John 3:16 or tells a reason God sent Jesus. Repeat game, collecting letters for the word "forgive."

Talk About
- Who is someone you love? When is a time you needed to forgive this person or needed to ask for his or her forgiveness?
- How could you use the words "love" and "forgive" in a sentence to tell about Jesus?
- Read John 3:16. **What reason does this verse say that God sent Jesus to Earth?** (God loved the world.) **What was God's purpose in sending Jesus?** (To die on the cross to take the punishment for our sins. To show God's love.) Pray, **Thank You, God, that You love us so much that You sent Your Son, Jesus, to suffer and die for us and take the punishment for our sins. We love You, too. In Jesus' name, amen.**

 ## For Younger Children
Before class, write the name of each child in your class on a separate index card. Place cards in a bag. During class, children line up a few feet away from container. Children take turns tossing ball. After each toss, draw a name card from bag and show children. Everybody says, "God loves (Amy)." Repeat for each child.

© 2006 Gospel Light. Permission to photocopy granted. *Treasure Seekers*

Art Center

FOR YOUNGER CHILDREN
Selections from the Gospels

LESSON six

Collect
Bible, Pattern Page (p. 126), card stock, scissors, markers, index cards, various decorative stickers, tape or stapler, hole punch, one 36-inch (91.5-cm) length of yarn or ribbon for each child.

Prepare
Copy Pattern Page onto card stock, making one copy for each child in your class. Cut out heart shapes.

Do
1. Children decorate heart shapes. Each child then writes his or her name on an index card and decorates card with stickers.

2. Assist children in folding hearts and taping or stapling right side of hearts to make a pocket as shown in the sketch. Children place decorated name cards in heart pockets. Hole punch left and right top of heart shapes and tie yarn or ribbon ends through holes for children to wear as necklaces or to hang from doorknobs at home.

God's Word
"For God so loved the world that he gave his one and only Son, that whoever believes in him shall not perish but have eternal life." John 3:16

For Younger Children:
"God so loved the world that he gave his one and only Son."

God's Word & Me
We can be a part of God's family because of God's love and forgiveness through Jesus.

Talk About

- Our Bible says, "God so loved the world that he gave his one and only Son." **What can we do to show we're glad God sent Jesus?** (Sing songs. Say, "Thank You" to God.)

- One reason to be thankful for Jesus is because He loves us. Alex, **who are some people Jesus loves?** You're right! Jesus loves you and your mom and your sister. Jesus loves us all.

- **Let's thank God together for Jesus.** Pray briefly, **Thank You, God, for Jesus. We love You! Amen.**

For Older Children

Print "God loves the world" on a length of butcher paper. Children draw pictures to illustrate the title. (Optional: Children make individual posters.)

© 2006 Gospel Light. Permission to photocopy granted. *Treasure Seekers*

 # Art Center

FOR OLDER CHILDREN
Selections from the Gospels

LESSON six

Collect

Bible, scissors, measuring stick, 20 or 24 gauge spool of copper wire (available at craft or hardware stores), small beads, chenille wires, short lengths of ribbon or string.

Prepare

For each student, cut a 30-inch (76-cm) length of wire and four to six short lengths of wire that vary from 2 to 6 inches (5 to 15 cm) long.

Do

1. Each child forms a cross shape from a 30-inch (76-cm) length of wire (see sketch a) to make a cross mobile.

2. Children string beads onto short wire pieces and/or shape wire in fun designs and twist ends around opposite sides of cross shape (see sketch b).

3. Distribute chenille wires to children. Children cut chenille wires in half and make small decorative shapes (hearts, stars, etc.). Children use the remaining lengths of wire to hang chenille-wire shapes to their cross mobiles (see sketch c).

4. Children tie ribbon or string loops at the top of the cross mobiles as hangers. Hang mobiles in classroom, or allow students to take them home.

God's Word

"For God so loved the world that he gave his one and only Son, that whoever believes in him shall not perish but have eternal life." John 3:16

For Younger Children:
"God so loved the world that he gave his one and only Son."

God's Word & Me

We can be a part of God's family because of God's love and forgiveness through Jesus.

a. b. c.

Talk About

- What are some of the things a cross reminds us of? (Jesus' death. God's love. Forgiveness for our sins.)

- Read John 3:16. **What can all people receive when they believe in Jesus' death on the cross and His resurrection from the dead?** (Live forever with Jesus. Become members of God's family.)

- **What might you say if someone asks you about the cross you made today?** (Tell the good news that Jesus is alive and gives us forgiveness.) Dear God, thank You for Your love and forgiveness for all people. In Jesus' name, amen.

 ## For Younger Children

Twist two lengths of chenille wire together to make a cross shape. Children string pony beads onto wires and bend and twist wire ends. Tie a yarn or ribbon loop at the top of the cross as a hanger.

© 2006 Gospel Light. Permission to photocopy granted. *Treasure Seekers*

Worship Center
Selections from the Gospels

LESSON six

Collect

Bibles, *Island Music* CD and player, song charts (pp. 250-251), marker, large sheet of butcher paper, wrapped candies, two beach chairs, colored strips of paper, pencils, tape.

Prepare

Draw a large cross shape on butcher paper.

Team Game

Divide class into two or more teams. Invite one child from each team to represent his or her team. Children choose "odd" or "even." Each child puts a hand behind his or her back and together they count "one-two-three." On "three," each student thrusts out a hand with one to five fingers showing. Player(s) who chose "odd" or "even" wins according to the total number of fingers that are showing. Winner wins candy prizes for his or her team.

God's Word
"For God so loved the world that he gave his one and only Son, that whoever believes in him shall not perish but have eternal life." John 3:16

For Younger Children:
"God so loved the world that he gave his one and only Son."

God's Word & Me
We can be a part of God's family because of God's love and forgiveness through Jesus.

Bible Verse Game

Place two beach chairs on one side of the play area. Six to eight volunteers from each team line up opposite chairs on other side of the play area. First child from each line runs to beach chair, sits in chair and says first word of John 3:16 then runs back to tag next player. Game continues until the entire verse is said.

Song

You, or another leader, lead children in singing "He's Alive Again!" adding motions and/or clapping if desired.

Prayer

When we think about what Jesus has done for us by dying on the cross, there are many ways we can respond. One way is to thank Him in prayer. Distribute paper strips and pencils to children. Children write thank-you prayers on strips and tape to cross shape drawn on butcher paper. (Optional: Younger children may write their names on paper strips and attach to cross to show thankfulness.) Close with the following prayer: **Thank You, Jesus, for Your great love and forgiveness. We love You! In Your name, amen.**

Song

Play "The Only One." Lead children in singing, adding motions and/or clapping if desired.

Lesson 6 ◆ Pattern Page

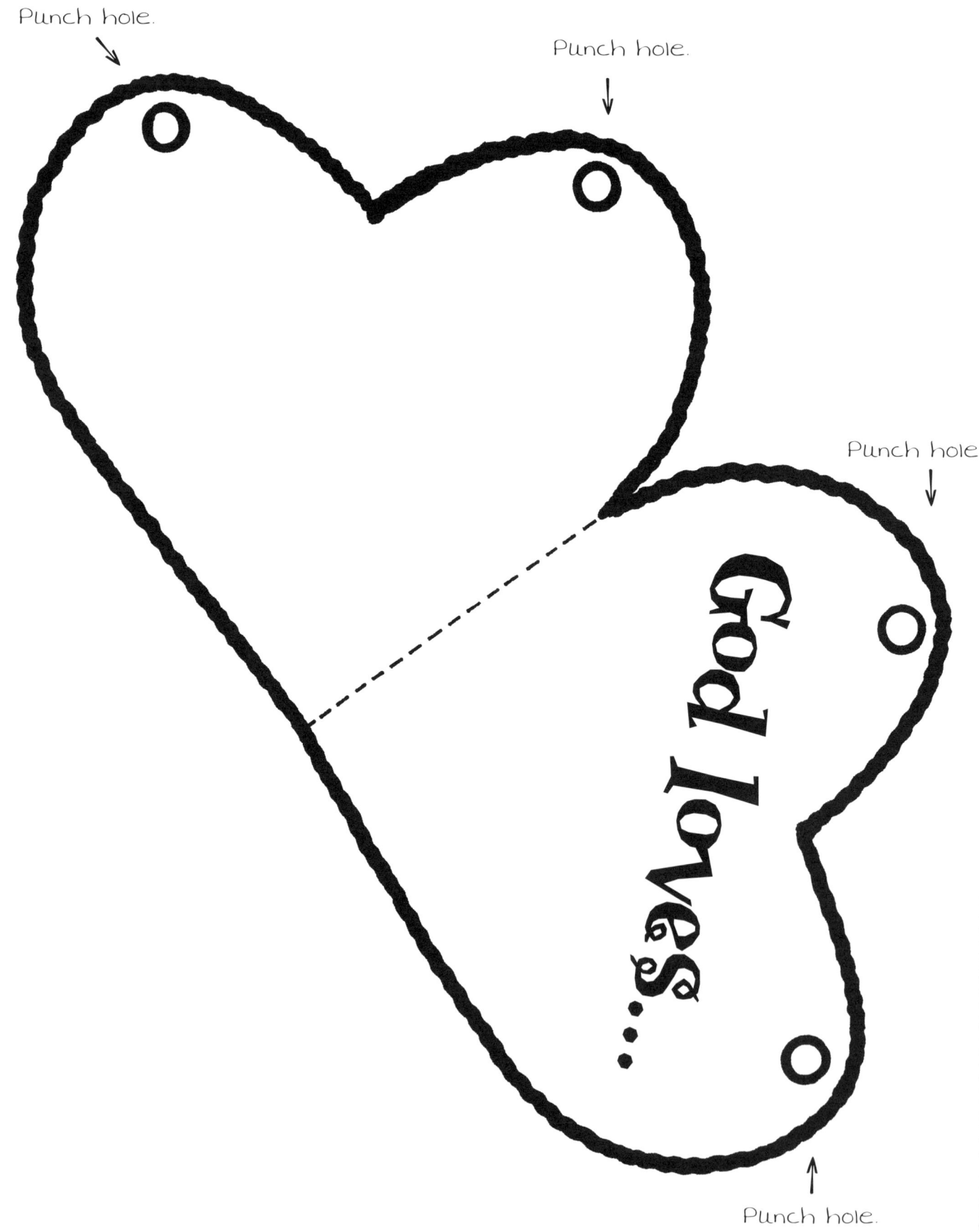

Heart Pocket Pattern

Lesson 6 ◆ Coloring/Puzzle Center
GOD'S LIFELINE!

Mark 16:1-8

 Unscramble the words in the rocks. Write the words in the rectangles according to their numbers. Find the message by reading the rectangles in numerical order.

Why was Jesus the only one who could die for our sins?

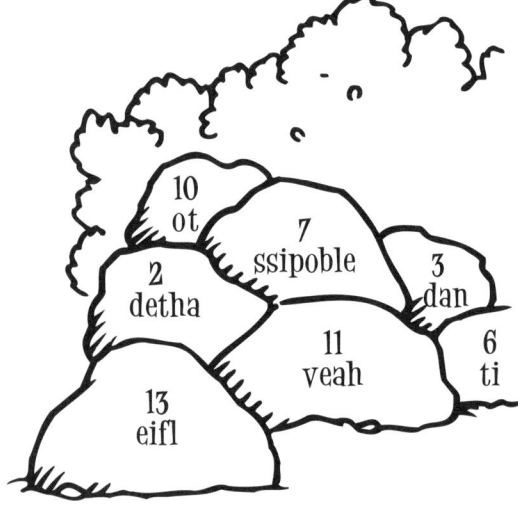
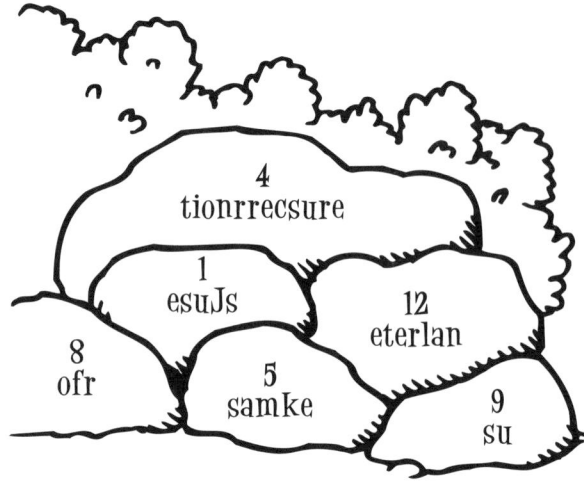

 What is the shape that is made when you connect the dots?

_____

BIBLE STORY ◆ 1 Kings 17:7-16

God Provides

LESSON seven

Teacher's Devotional

What comes to mind when you hear the word "abundance"? Throughout the Bible we see God's abundance in times of insufficiency and in circumstances of nothing and need. Even in the very first chapter of Genesis, God supplied the day and the night with a bounty of stars. With Abraham and Sarah, God abundantly provided by giving them Isaac and also by providing a sacrifice at Mt. Moriah in Isaac's stead. There, in that time of need, Abraham declared God's name as *Jehovah-Jireh*: "God will provide" (see Genesis 22:14). Time after time, God's people can testify to God's character and nature as the abundant provider!

God's Word
"My God will meet all your needs according to his glorious riches in Christ Jesus." Philippians 4:19

For Younger Children:
"My God will meet all your needs."

God's Word & Me
We can trust that God cares for us and will give us everything we need.

In 1 Kings 17, Elijah declared God's message of famine and drought in the land as the result of Israel's adulterous worship of idols. But now he found himself in the predicament of his prophecy's fulfillment. Hungry and thirsty, Elijah was promised food and sent by God to a Gentile widow in Sidon. Elijah found a woman collecting sticks, preparing to make her last meal and then to die. But from the little she had, God gave what was needed and supplied not only food for Elijah, but even more—an abounding source for the widow and her son.

Today, we can also testify to God working in the midst of insufficiency and circumstances of need, whether it be in our own daily lives and minute-to-minute personal needs or even in our children's ministry! What does the widow's last handful of flour and drop of oil represent in your life or ministry? In faith, are you able to surrender what little you may have at hand and take grasp of God's provisions available to you in Christ Jesus? Your students are very aware of their own insufficiencies and needs as well. From the youngest in your class to the oldest, a variety of needs will range from the physical and tangible to the spiritual and unseen. Before teaching today's lesson, ask God to give you insight into their needs. An abundance of hugs and smiles from you might be the way God chooses to reveal His providing character to your students today!

© 2006 Gospel Light. Permission to photocopy granted. *Treasure Seekers*

Planning Page

LESSON seven

Choose which centers you will provide and the order in which children will participate in them (see pp. 14-18 for schedule tips and pp. 24-25 for guidelines in combining older and younger children). Also plan who will lead each center (for staffing tips see pp. 19-21). Use the reproducible planning sheet (p. 238) to record your plans.

Bible Story Center

Bible Story
God Provides • 1 Kings 17:7-16

Younger Child Option
Use story objects to demonstrate story action

Older Child Option
Collect letters of a word that tells what God does to show His love and care

Art Center

Younger Child Option
Make play dough and name things God has given

Materials
Bible, measuring cup and spoons, large mixing bowl, flour, salt, cooking oil, warm water, large spoon, food coloring

Older Child Option
Create paintings using oil-like paints and discuss ways God cares

Materials
Bible, measuring spoons, liquid dishwashing detergent, water, powdered tempera in several colors, paper cups, paint brushes, large sheet of paper, markers, card stock or poster board

Game Center

Younger Child Option
Play a game like Cake Walk and tell good things God gives

Materials
Bible; *Island Music* CD and player; one paper plate for each child; red, orange, yellow and green markers

Older Child Option
Play a game like Fruit Basket Upset and tell why we can trust in God's care

Materials
Bible, Pattern Page (p. 140), scissors, lunch-sized paper bags

Coloring/Puzzle Center

Younger Child Option
Review the Bible story while completing coloring page

Materials
Lesson 7 Coloring Page (p. 141) for each student, crayons

Older Child Option
Review the Bible story while completing puzzle page

Materials
Lesson 7 Puzzle Page (p. 142) for each student, pencils

Worship Center

For the Younger and Older Child
Participate in large-group activities to review Bible verse and to worship God together

Materials
Bibles, *Island Music* CD and player, song charts (pp. 248, 251), markers, large sheets of butcher paper, construction paper, tape, two large containers filled with sand, 24 coins, two plastic shovels

© 2006 Gospel Light. Permission to photocopy granted. *Treasure Seekers*

Bonus Island Ideas

LESSON seven

Bonus Island Ideas can be used at any time during this session: as an additional activity center, to extend the session for a longer time, or for added island excitement.

Nutty for Coconuts

Before class, break open a real coconut. Place coconut halves on a paper plate. Use milk from the real coconut or purchase canned coconut milk and pour ¼ cup coconut milk into several small cups. Place coconut flakes and coconut snacks (chocolate-covered coconut candy bars, coconut cookies, etc.) in separate containers. Place markers and a blank sheet of paper by each coconut item. During class, distribute plastic spoons, small paper plates and napkins to each child. Children taste the various coconut items and then draw a happy face or sad face on the paper by each item to show if they liked or disliked the item. (Optional: Children place stickers on the papers by the items they liked.) **For older children:** Pour several kinds of fruit juice into separate paper cups and give each child a straw. Blindfold one child at a time and help him or her taste juices. Child tries to identify the flavors. Keep a running tally of children's guesses.

Post a note alerting parents to the use of food. Also, check registration forms for possible food allergies.

Island Snack

Before class, place pineapple chunks in several containers. In class, children peel and cut bananas into thick slices and add to containers. Children make kabobs with toothpicks or bamboo skewers, alternating the pineapple chunks and banana slices. **For younger children:** Children may string colorful circle-shaped cereal on a length of yarn or elastic cord and tie ends to wear as a bracelet or necklace—and eat!

Fruity Art Bulletin Board

On individual sheets of construction paper or on a large sheet of butcher paper, children use fruit-scented markers to draw things that God provides for them (water, food, the sun, rain, family, friends, etc.). Display in classroom. **For older children:** Print "God Provides" in large block letters across a length of butcher paper. Assign one or more letters to each child. Children decorate their letters. Display in classroom.

© 2006 Gospel Light. Permission to photocopy granted. *Treasure Seekers*

Bible Story Center

FOR YOUNGER CHILDREN
1 Kings 17:7-16

Collect

Bible.

Introduction

What foods do you like to eat? Volunteers answer. **Listen to find out about a time when someone did not have anything to eat.**

Treasure Chest Option

Place a bottle of cooking oil and a jar of flour in a treasure chest. At the appropriate times in the story, invite volunteers to remove objects from the treasure chest. Show objects to children and use them to demonstrate story action.

Tell the Story

God's helper Elijah had obeyed God. Elijah had told the king that there would be no rain for a long, LONG time, just as God had said. God told His helper just what to do: He told Elijah to stay by a little stream so Elijah would have water to drink every day. God made some big birds bring Elijah food every day! But soon there was not even one drop of water left in the stream. What would Elijah do now?

God told Elijah, "Go to a town. A woman there will give you food and water."

Step, step, step—Elijah walked to the town. When Elijah got to the town, he saw a woman picking up sticks to build a fire. Elijah asked the woman, "Would you please bring me some water?" Right away the woman went to get water for Elijah. As she left, Elijah called out, "And please bring me a piece of bread to eat."

The woman told him, "I have only enough flour and oil to make a little bread for my son and me. Then we won't have any food at all!" "Don't worry," Elijah said kindly. "God has promised that there will be enough food for all of us."

The woman used her little bit of flour and oil to bake the bread for Elijah. Then she looked in the jar where she kept her flour. There was still flour in the jar! She looked in her oil jar. The jar still had oil in it! There was enough flour and oil to make the bread she and her son needed for dinner.

Every day after that, there was enough flour and oil so that the woman could bake more bread. The jar of flour and the jar of oil NEVER became empty. God helped Elijah, the woman and her son to have food. How glad they were!

God's Word & Me

God showed that He cared for Elijah and the woman in today's Bible story. God gave them enough oil and flour to make bread every day! We can know for sure that God cares for all of us. Our Bible says, "My God will meet all your needs." God shows His care by helping us to have what we need every day. What can we say to God for caring for us? (Thank You.) Pray, **Thank You, God, for loving us and caring for all our needs! Amen.**

© 2006 Gospel Light. Permission to photocopy granted. *Treasure Seekers*

Bible Story Center

FOR OLDER CHILDREN
1 Kings 17:7-16

Collect

Bible.

Introduction

What would you want to eat or drink if you were REALLY hungry or thirsty? How would you get this food or drink? Today in our story we will hear about some people who almost had nothing to eat! As you tell the story, ask children on one side of the room to call out "ahhhh—refreshing!" when they hear the keyword **water** and children on the other side of the room to call out "mmm, mmm—good!" when they hear the keyword **food**. (Optional: Print phrases on separate poster board strips to use as cue cards. Invite two volunteers to hold up cue cards at the appropriate times during the story.)

Treasure Chest Option

Print each letter of the word "Provides" on a separate index card. Mix up cards and place cards in a treasure chest. At the end of the Bible story, invite eight volunteers to each take a letter card from the treasure chest. Volunteers stand in a line and hold up cards for other children to see. Children unscramble letters by helping volunteers stand in order to spell the word "Provides."

Tell the Story

God had asked His people in Israel to worship Him—the only true God. But now, in the time of King Ahab, the Israelites were worshiping false gods. They had forgotten all about following God's command and even had built altars to other gods! Because of their disobedience, God sent a message through Elijah that there would be no rain in Israel until He caused it to fall. That meant there would be no **water** to keep the rivers and lakes full. The ground would dry up and no **food** would grow.

During this time of no rain, God took care of Elijah. First God told Elijah to go to the Kerith Ravine, a place where he drank **water** from a brook and birds brought him **food**. Each day Elijah watched the brook get smaller and smaller and smaller—until finally one day there was NOTHING left but mud! Elijah couldn't even get one little drink! Elijah knew he couldn't live very long without **water**.

But God didn't forget Elijah. God knew just what Elijah needed and He had a plan to continue taking care of Elijah. God told Elijah to go and stay in a town named Zarephath in a region called Sidon. A widow there would give him some **food**. **What is a widow?** (A widow is a woman whose husband has died.)

Even though Elijah knew that most widows were very poor and would not have extra **food** to give to strangers, Elijah did what he always did when God spoke to him. When God said, "Go!" Elijah went where God told him to go!

When Elijah came to Zarephath, he saw a woman gathering sticks by the town gate. Elijah realized she was probably getting ready to build a cooking fire. *Could this woman be the widow God told me about?* Elijah wondered.

"Excuse me!" Elijah said. "Would you please bring me a drink of **water**?"

"Of course," the woman answered. "I'll be right back with some **water** for you!"

Surely, she MUST be the widow he was looking for! "Wait," he called. "Would you please bring me a piece of bread when you come back?" **What do you think most people would say if someone asked them for something to eat?**

© 2006 Gospel Light. Permission to photocopy granted. *Treasure Seekers*

The widow answered, "I don't have any bread—only a handful of flour in a jar and a little oil in a jug. I am gathering a few sticks to take home and make a meal for myself and my son, that we may eat it—and die." How could this poor woman help Elijah when she didn't even have enough for her and her son to eat?

But Elijah told her, "Don't be afraid. Go home and bake a small cake of bread for me first. Then bake bread for yourself and your son. God has promised that the jar of flour will not be used up and the jug of oil will not run dry until the day the Lord gives rain on the land." What astounding news—and hard to believe, too! **What do you think the woman did next? What would you have done?**

The woman went home and did as Elijah had told her. First she got out the flour and oil and baked one cake of bread. This bread was for Elijah. Then she probably stirred a little more flour and poured a little more oil to bake another cake of bread for her son. She was probably afraid to look in the flour jar for the third time! She was very hungry and would have to make her OWN cake of bread out of whatever was left! *What if there is no more flour?* she may have thought. The woman slowly looked in the flour jar. There WAS enough flour to make another cake of bread! And when she tipped the oil jar, there was just enough oil to mix the dough!

What was even more amazing was that EVERY DAY until God sent rain again, there was enough oil and flour to make bread for Elijah, the woman and her son! God showed His great power and love by supplying **food** for all three of them—even when there was no rain!

God's Word & Me

In today's Bible story, the widow and her son discovered what Elijah already knew. **What did God do to show Elijah that He was his provider—the one who would give what Elijah needed?** Read Philippians 4:19. **God is our provider, too. He loves us and cares for our EVERY need.**

- **What are some things that we need in order to live?** (Food and water. Air. Shelter. Love.)
- **Sometimes we might think that what we want is what we need. What are some things that we want?** (New video game. Cell phone. TV in bedroom.)
- **Why do you think God doesn't always give us everything we want?**
- **Why might God say no to our prayers?** (He knows what is best for us.) **We can ask for God's help to trust that He will give us what we REALLY need.** Pray with children, asking for God's help in trusting Him to provide for all their needs.

Game Center

FOR YOUNGER CHILDREN
1 Kings 17:7-16

LESSON seven

Collect

Bible; *Island Music* CD and player; one paper plate for each child; red, orange, yellow and green markers.

Prepare

Using the appropriate colored markers, print the words "red," "orange," "yellow" and "green" on separate paper plates, repeating colors as needed to prepare one plate for each child.

Do

1. Place paper plates facedown in a circle on the floor. (Note: If you have more than eight to ten children, you may wish to form additional game circles.) Children form a circle around paper plates.

2. Play "Treasure Forever." Children walk around paper plate circle as music plays. When music stops, children stop walking. Call out one of the colors on the paper plates. Each child turns over the nearest paper plate. Children who have turned over a paper plate with the named color tell a fruit or other food of that color. Repeat game as time allows.

God's Word

"My God will meet all your needs according to his glorious riches in Christ Jesus." Philippians 4:19

For Younger Children:
"My God will meet all your needs."

God's Word & Me

We can trust that God cares for us and will give us everything we need.

Talk About

- In today's Bible story, Elijah asked a woman to make bread for him. But the woman only had a little oil and flour to make bread with. God gave the woman enough oil and flour to make bread to share with Elijah and to eat every day!

- What is your favorite fruit? Favorite food? God has given us many different kinds of fruits and foods to enjoy! What are some other things that God gives to you? God also gives us our family and friends.

- Our Bible says, "My God will meet all your needs." He cares for us and gives us everything we need. Pray briefly, **Thank You, God, for giving us good things.**

For Older Children

Children play game as described above but with a Four Corners variation. Instead of calling out a color, call out four different items (e.g., pizza, fruit, salad, cheeseburger) from the same category (e.g., favorite foods) while pointing to each corner of the room. Each student tosses the nearest paper plate into a corner to indicate their favorite item. Children retrieve plates and play again with other categories (favorite ice cream, favorite animals, favorite cereal, etc.).

© 2006 Gospel Light. Permission to photocopy granted. *Treasure Seekers*

 # Game Center

FOR OLDER CHILDREN
1 Kings 17:7-16

LESSON seven

Collect
Bible, Pattern Page (p. 140), scissors, lunch-sized paper bags.

Prepare
Make a copy of the Pattern Page for each group of eight children. Cut cards from Pattern Page. Place cards in paper bag and shake bag to mix up cards.

Do
1. Children sit in a circle. One volunteer is selected to be the Caller and stands in the center of the circle. Each child takes a card from the paper bag.

2. Show Pattern Page to the Caller. Caller tells a way God provides for him or her. Caller then calls out a word that is listed on the page. Children with that word card jump up to trade places in the circle before the Caller can take one of the places. If the Caller calls out "God Provides!" all children must change places.

3. The child left without a place becomes the new Caller. Repeat play as described above. Game continues as time allows or until all children have had a chance to be the Caller.

God's Word
"My God will meet all your needs according to his glorious riches in Christ Jesus." Philippians 4:19

For Younger Children:
"My God will meet all your needs."

God's Word & Me
We can trust that God cares for us and will give us everything we need.

Talk About

- In today's Bible story, God helped a man named Elijah and a poor widow have enough bread to eat. The widow's flour and oil never ran out. **What words would Elijah and the widow have used to describe God after today's story? Why?**

- **What are some things that we need in order to live?** (Air. Food. Water.) **What are some other kinds of needs we have?** Sometimes we need God's care and help or an answer to a prayer. Share with students about a time God met a need you had.

- Read Philippians 4:19. **Why do we know that God will give us everything we need?** (Because God loves us and cares for us. God made everything. God promises to provide for all our needs.) Pray briefly, **Dear God, thank You for caring for all our needs. In Jesus' name, amen.**

 ## Younger Children
Number backs of cards. Group children in circles as described above. Caller calls out numbers instead of items. Children holding cards with the number called stand next to each other in the middle of the circle and complete the following sentence by naming people who care for them: **Thank You, God, for . . .** When the Caller calls out "God Provides!" all children find a new place to sit.

Art Center

FOR YOUNGER CHILDREN
1 Kings 17:7-16

LESSON seven

Collect

Bible, measuring cup and spoons, large mixing bowl, flour, salt, cooking oil, warm water, large spoon, food coloring.

Do

1. Pour 2 cups flour and 1 cup salt into large mixing bowl. (Note: Prepare one bowl of ingredients for each group of six children.) Pour 1 cup warm water and 2 tablespoons cooking oil into mixing bowl. Add a few drops of food coloring to create colored dough. Children take turns stirring mixture to make play dough. If dough is sticky, dust with additional flour. If dough is stiff, add a little water.

2. **The woman in today's Bible story made bread. Let's make bread together!** Demonstrate mixing, kneading and shaping dough into a bread loaf shape. Children use play dough to make bread shapes or other objects of their own choice.

God's Word

"My God will meet all your needs according to his glorious riches in Christ Jesus." Philippians 4:19

For Younger Children:
"My God will meet all your needs."

God's Word & Me

We can trust that God cares for us and will give us everything we need.

Talk About

- In today's Bible story, God gave a woman enough oil and flour to make bread to share with her son and a man named Elijah. God cared for them.

- God cares for you, too. One thing God helps us have are fingers and hands to play with the dough. And God gives us eyes to see the colors of the dough. What are some colors you can see in our room?

- Our Bible says, "My God will meet all your needs." **We can thank God for giving us so many good things.** Pray briefly, **Thank You, God, for giving us everything we need!**

 ## For Older Children

Children measure out the ingredients as well as mix the play dough. Children use play dough to make play dough people and Bible story objects to create Bible story displays.

© 2006 Gospel Light. Permission to photocopy granted. *Treasure Seekers*

 # Art Center

FOR OLDER CHILDREN
1 Kings 17:7-16

LESSON seven

Collect

Bible, measuring spoons, liquid dishwashing detergent, water, powdered tempera in several colors, paper cups, paint brushes, large sheet of paper, markers, card stock or poster board.

Prepare

Pour 2 tablespoons liquid dishwashing detergent and ½ teaspoon water in several paper cups. Add 2 tablespoons of powdered tempera to each cup, adding more for a thicker consistency as needed to make a paint that can be used like oil paints. Put a paint brush into each cup and mix well.

God's Word
"My God will meet all your needs according to his glorious riches in Christ Jesus." Philippians 4:19

For Younger Children:
"My God will meet all your needs."

God's Word & Me
We can trust that God cares for us and will give us everything we need.

Do

Brainstorm with children slogans that remind them that God provides for them ("God is good!" "I will survive because God will provide!" etc.). Print children's ideas on large sheet of paper. Each child chooses a slogan from the list and prints slogan on a sheet of card stock or poster board. Children use paints to decorate their sheets or create pictures of things God has provided. Encourage children to share paints with each other. Ask the questions below as children paint.

Talk About

- In today's Bible story, God provided for Elijah and a widow in need. God provided for their physical needs by giving the widow never-empty jars of oil and flour to make bread for them to eat.

- **What are some needs kids your age have?** (Need help in making friends. Need comfort when others make fun of me. Need strength to obey God.) **What is a way God might help a new kid in town have what he or she needs?** (Give him or her courage to make new friends.) **A kid who is sick in the hospital?**

- Read Philippians 4:19. **What has God done to show that we can trust Him to give us everything we need?** (Gave His one and only Son to die on the cross to take the punishment for our sins. Created the earth and everything in it for us to enjoy.) Pray briefly, **Dear God, thank You for providing for our every need! Help us to trust in Your love and care. In Jesus' name, amen.**

 ## For Younger Children

Photocopy Lesson 7 Coloring Page (p. 141) onto card stock for each child in the class. Children paint the Bible Story picture.

© 2006 Gospel Light. Permission to photocopy granted. *Treasure Seekers*

Worship Center
1 Kings 17:7-16

Collect

Bibles, *Island Music* CD and player, song charts (pp. 248, 251), markers, large sheets of butcher paper, construction paper, tape, two large containers filled with sand, 24 coins, two plastic shovels.

Prepare

Write the words of Philippians 4:19 in large letters on two separate butcher paper sheets. Tape construction paper sheets to butcher paper to cover words of the verse. Hide 12 coins in each container of sand. Place containers on one side of the classroom. (Note: Place large bed sheets under containers for easier cleanup.) Print letters of the alphabet down the side of another butcher paper sheet.

God's Word

"My God will meet all your needs according to his glorious riches in Christ Jesus." Philippians 4:19

For Younger Children:
"My God will meet all your needs."

God's Word & Me

We can trust that God cares for us and will give us everything we need.

Team Game

Divide group into two teams. Six to eight volunteers from each team line up and stand on one side of the room, opposite containers. At your signal, first child in each line runs to his or her team's container and uses shovel to dig for a hidden coin. When child retrieves a coin, he or she removes a sheet of construction paper from his or her team's butcher paper. Continue activity until a team uncovers all the words of the verse.

Bible Verse Game

Children remain in teams. Call out a phrase of Philippians 4:19 as you point to a team to echo the phrase. Team echoes the phrases as the team members stand up and then immediately sit down. Continue, saying one phrase of the verse at a time and pointing to teams. Repeat verse several times, increasing the speed of saying and echoing the verse in each round.

Song

Lead children in singing "You, O Lord," adding motions and/or clapping if desired.

Prayer

God has given us so many good things! Show alphabet paper you prepared. **Let's see if we can fill these letters with things that God provides for us.** Volunteers call out names of items God provides for them. Write items on paper next to the appropriate letters of the alphabet. (Enrichment Option: Assign points to each letter and teams compete to see who can obtain most points by filling in highest-scoring letters.) Invite children to complete the following prayer: **Thank You, God, for . . .**

Song

Play "He's Alive Again." Lead children in singing, adding motions and/or clapping if desired.

© 2006 Gospel Light. Permission to photocopy granted. *Treasure Seekers*

Lesson 7 ◇ Pattern Page

Family 	Water 
Friends 	Food 
Food 	Friends 
Water 	Family 

140

© 2006 Gospel Light. Permission to photocopy granted. *Treasure Seekers*

Lesson 7 ◆ Coloring/Puzzle Center

GOD FEEDS NEEDS!

Philippians 4:19

These papers have gotten all mixed up, but if you write the words from each paper in order on the numbered lines below, you will find the Bible verse. How would you say this verse in your own words? Tell someone your version.

1. My
2. God
3. will
4. meet
5. all
6. your
7. needs
8. according
9. to
10. his
11. glorious
12. riches
13. in
14. Christ
15. Jesus

BIBLE STORY ◆ Daniel 6:1-28

God Is with Me and Protects Me

LESSON eight

Teacher's Devotional

Big and small things can create fear and dismay within us: Whether enormous global disasters or unruly neighbors, there are plenty of sources of fear! What do we do when a fearful thought comes? Often, we mentally hold it tight like a quarterback with a football and run that thought to the end zone of its logical conclusion! Then we stand beneath the goal posts of dismay and doubt, thinking, *Things are hopeless! Is God really in control?* Because we are so used to the fear-based thinking of the world around us, this response almost seems normal. *Shouldn't we be concerned about (fill in the blank)?* The answer is always yes! But the difference between a person who trusts in God and a person who doesn't is what the person does with his or her concern. Rather than worrying, running our fearful thoughts into the end zone of dismay and doubt, we stop to hear God say, "Do not fear, I am with you; do not be dismayed" (Isaiah 41:10).

God's Word

"Do not fear, I am with you; do not be dismayed, for I am your God. I will strengthen you and help you." Isaiah 41:10

For Younger Children:
"I am with you; . . . I will . . . help you."

God's Word & Me

We can depend on God to protect us in times of worry or trouble.

Similar words were first spoken to Joshua as he stood at the edge of the flooding Jordan (see Joshua 1:9). The known risks of entering Canaan were tremendous. (Remember the giants from 40 years before? How many were there now?) Then there were the *unknown* risks, as well! With so much to inspire fear and dismay, there was only one solution: the presence and protection of God Himself!

God has not changed. When fears come, it's easy to forget (but powerful to remember) that God is not only with us in the sense of being present, but also He is *with us* in the sense of being on our side! Paul exults, "If God is for us, who can be against us?" (Romans 8:31). There is nothing He cannot do—and He is right here! Experience the power of His presence. Trust His powerful protection. Believe that He is completely able to do everything He says He can do; for God is just as able today as He was in Joshua's day. He has not changed!

© 2006 Gospel Light. Permission to photocopy granted. *Treasure Seekers*

Planning Page

Choose which centers you will provide and the order in which children will participate in them (see pp. 14-18 for schedule tips and pp. 24-25 for guidelines in combining older and younger children). Also plan who will lead each center (for staffing tips see pp. 19-21). Use the reproducible planning sheet (p. 238) to record your plans.

Bible Story Center

Bible Story
God Is with Me and Protects Me
• Daniel 6:1-28

Younger Child Option
Use an object to help tell the Bible story

Older Child Option
Unscramble letters taped on eight different items to spell out the word "protects"

Art Center

Younger Child Option
Create lion faces and thank God for people who help them every day

Materials
Bible, Pattern Page (p. 154), white paper, scissors, paper plates, crayons, glue, yellow decorating materials

Older Child Option
Make feet-shaped self-portraits to add to a mural as a reminder of God's help wherever they go

Materials
Bible, colored craft foam, pencils, scissors, decorating materials, butcher paper, tape, markers

Game Center

Younger Child Option
Tiptoe through pretend lions and name places where God is with us and helps us

Materials
Bible, tape, pictures of three different locations, three paper plates, a clean sock for each child, basket

Older Child Option
Play a game like Capture the Flag and tell times they need to depend on God's help and protection

Materials
Bible, masking tape, crepe paper streamers of two different colors, scissors

Coloring/Puzzle Center

Younger Child Option
Review the Bible story while completing coloring page

Materials
Lesson 8 Coloring Page (p. 155) for each student, crayons

Older Child Option
Review the Bible story while completing puzzle page

Materials
Lesson 8 Puzzle Page (p. 156) for each student, pencils

Worship Center

For the Younger and Older Child
Participate in large-group activities to review Bible verse and to worship God together

Materials
Bibles, *Island Music* CD and player, song charts (pp. 248-249), paper strips, markers, balloons, two large garbage bags, large sheet of butcher paper

Bonus Island Ideas

Bonus Island Ideas can be used at any time during this session: as an additional activity center, to extend the session for a longer time, or for added island excitement.

Island Animal Hunt

Write names of different island animals and birds (alligator, iguana, anteater, parrot, flamingo, cuckoo, etc.) on separate index cards. (Optional: You may also write one fact about each animal on the cards, collecting information from an encyclopedia or the Internet.) Cut each card into two puzzle pieces and hide pieces around the room. Children find and match pieces to discover names of the different island animals. **For Younger Children:** Find and cut out pictures of island animals from travel or nature magazines and cut into puzzle shapes for children to find.

Post a note alerting parents to the use of food. Also, check registration forms for possible food allergies.

Starfish Snacks

Children use star-shaped cookie cutters to cut star shapes from bread. Children pinch and shape points of shapes to look like starfish. Children spread whipped butter on starfish and sprinkle cinnamon and sugar on top. Provide sprinkles or raisins for children to add to starfish. Eat and enjoy! (Optional: Children create an edible beach scene on paper plates using bread to create starfish, crushed vanilla wafers for sand, blue colored Cool Whip for water, etc.)

Jungle Obstacle Course

Set up stations for an island jungle obstacle course using the following items: kid's pool filled ankle deep with water, sand box, green streamers placed in lines with a few feet between each, and jump rope. Create a challenge or task to do at each station (wade through the pool, search for hidden coins in the sand box, hurdle over green streamers, walk the jump rope.) Children take turns going through obstacle course.

© 2006 Gospel Light. Permission to photocopy granted. *Treasure Seekers*

Bible Story Center

FOR YOUNGER CHILDREN
Daniel 6:1-28

Collect
Bible.

Introduction
What do lions sound like? Lead children in roaring quietly and then loudly several times. **Listen to hear what happened when a man named Daniel was put into a cave with some lions.**

Treasure Chest Option
Place a stuffed toy lion or a picture of a lion in a treasure chest. Invite a volunteer to remove picture or toy from the treasure chest and show to others before you begin telling the Bible story.

Tell the Story

Daniel loved God. One way Daniel showed his love was by praying to God. Daniel prayed to God one, two, three times every day.

Daniel was an important helper to the king. The king liked Daniel very much. But there were some men who did not like Daniel. They were angry that the king liked Daniel better than the king liked them. These angry men thought of a plan to get Daniel in trouble with the king. They went to the king and said, "King, we think you should make a rule that everyone must pray only to YOU. If people pray to anyone else but you, they will be thrown into a cave filled with lions!"

The king thought this rule was a good idea. The king sent helpers to tell all the people they must pray only to him.

The next day Daniel opened his window, just like he always did. Daniel prayed to God, just like he always did. He did not pray to the king. The mean men watched as Daniel prayed to God. Then they ran to tell the king what they saw.

The king was sad. The king did not want Daniel to be hurt, but the king had to obey the rule, too. Daniel was put into a big cave where lions lived. All night long the king worried that the lions would hurt Daniel!

The next morning, the king ran to the lions' cave. He called, "Daniel! DANIEL!" He waited. He listened. Then he heard Daniel's voice!

"King, I am safe! God protected me and shut the lions' mouth!" said Daniel. The king was so glad that Daniel was not hurt!

Daniel came out of the cave. The king knew that God had helped Daniel. God had kept him safe from the lions. The king sent a message to all his people that they should pray to God as Daniel did.

God's Word & Me

In today's Bible story, Daniel needed God's help. And God helped Daniel by keeping him safe when he was put in a cave of lions! Our Bible says, "I am with you; . . . I will . . . help you." Every day, we need God's help, too. We can know that God loves us and will always help us.

© 2006 Gospel Light. Permission to photocopy granted. *Treasure Seekers*

Bible Story Center

FOR OLDER CHILDREN
Daniel 6:1-28

Collect

Bible.

Introduction

Who are some brave or courageous people you know? What did they do to be brave or show courage? **In today's Bible story, we will find out how someone showed true courage.** Divide class into three groups. Assign each group a character from the story: Daniel, officers and lions. Groups sit together, choosing a motion and/or sound to represent the character(s) they were assigned. ("Officers" may stand with their arms crossed and tap their feet. "Daniel" may kneel down and fold hands as in prayer. "Lions" may crawl around and roar.) Each time the characters are mentioned in the Bible story, signal groups to do their motions.

Treasure Chest Option

Tape each letter of the word "protects" to eight different kinds of protective items: umbrella, sunscreen, mouth guard, bike helmet, sunglasses, goggles, shoe and thimble. Place items in a treasure chest. At the end of the story, invite volunteers to remove objects, identify their purpose and then unscramble letters on objects to spell the word "protects."

Tell the Story

Daniel was a prophet of God. He was living in Babylon, where Darius was the king. Darius chose 120 men as governors and satraps (SAY-traps), or leaders over his kingdom. One man he chose was Daniel. Daniel was over 80 years old at that time.

Daniel was wise. He was experienced. He was a favorite of the king. Because the king liked Daniel so much, the king planned to make Daniel the leader of the whole kingdom. Well, that made some of the other leaders VERY jealous of Daniel! They tried hard to find something Daniel might have done wrong, so they could point it out to King Darius. But it was no use! Daniel had a reputation for never doing anything wrong or dishonest.

The leaders wanted to stop Daniel. They planned to get him in trouble for following God! Some of the officers went to see King Darius. "Your Majesty," they smiled, "ALL the governors and leaders of your kingdom have agreed that you should make a law. Give orders that for 30 days, no one can pray to any god or man except you. And whoever disobeys your law will be thrown into a den of hungry lions!"

Since the officers had said that ALL the leaders liked this law, Darius may have figured Daniel had approved of it, too. And since this law seemed like a good way to honor himself, King Darius wrote it and signed it, just as the leaders suggested he should do. As the leaders walked away, they must have thought, *Now we've got Daniel right where we want him!*

Daniel soon heard about the new law. Of course he would not obey it. *I will continue to pray to God just as I always have,* Daniel decided.

Daniel knew that disobeying the law meant he would be thrown into the lions' den. But he opened the window of his room and got down on his knees. He prayed, giving thanks to God—just as he had always done. Lions or no lions, Daniel knew what he had to do to obey God.

Daniel's enemies were ready and waiting outside Daniel's house. Would he open his shutters and pray, as he always did? Yes! There he was—kneeling down! They ran just as fast as they could—straight to King Darius.

"Oh, King Darius," they said, "Daniel does not respect you. He knows you made the law that no one could pray to anyone but you for 30 days. But still, Daniel prays to his God three times a day! We saw him!"

King Darius realized he had been tricked. He realized that the leaders had urged him to make this law so that Daniel would be KILLED! King Darius worked all day to find a way to change the law and rescue his friend Daniel, but it could not be done. So the king had to obey his own law. With a heavy heart, he gave the order. He watched as Daniel was thrown into the den full of lions. The king said to Daniel, "May the God you faithfully serve rescue you!" Then a large stone was rolled over the opening to the pit so that Daniel could not escape.

That night the king couldn't eat or sleep because he was thinking about Daniel. When the king got to the lions' den the next morning, he listened anxiously for any sound. Then he called out, "Daniel, servant of the living God! Was the God you serve able to save you from the lions?"

"Yes, your Majesty!" Daniel answered. "God sent His angel to shut the mouths of the lions, so they could not hurt me. He did this because He knew I did nothing against you!" The king was so happy to hear Daniel's voice! He gave orders to lift Daniel out of the den.

Then the king remembered the leaders who had tricked him into writing the law. The king yelled, "Arrest those men who tricked me. Throw THEM into the lions' den!" And the lions did not keep their mouths shut this time!

Right away King Darius wrote a special decree to all the people. The message told everyone to respect and worship the God of Daniel. Daniel continued as leader over all of Babylon. He also continued to pray to God three times a day—no matter what!

God's Word & Me

Daniel depended on God through the difficult circumstances and troubles he faced. He trusted in God's help and protection. In our lives, there are sure to be troubles we will face that might cause us to worry or feel afraid. But no problem or worry is too big for God to handle! We can trust and depend on God's help and protection as Daniel did.

- **When might Daniel have felt afraid or worried?** (When the king made a new law not allowing anyone to pray to any god or person other than the king. When Daniel was thrown into a den of lions.)

- **What do you think Daniel knew about God that helped him depend on God and have courage in the difficult circumstances he faced?** (God loved him. God would always be with him and help him.)

- **What kind of situations might someone face today that would require the kind of courage and trust that Daniel had?** Read Isaiah 41:10. **How can this verse help someone in these situations?** Pray with children, asking for God's help and protection in the situations mentioned.

Game Center

FOR YOUNGER CHILDREN
Daniel 6:1-28

Collect

Bible, tape, pictures of three different locations (house, park, beach, etc.), three paper plates, a clean sock for each child, basket.

Prepare

Tape each picture to a separate paper plate. Place socks in basket.

Do

1. Pass the basket of socks around and invite children to each take a sock and throw sock on the floor. Place prepared paper plates facedown in the middle of the socks. **Let's pretend that these socks are sleeping lions. Be careful not to wake up the lions on your way to the paper plates!**

2. Children line up and take turns tiptoeing around socks to reach paper plates. Other children roar like lions while waiting for their turn. When child reaches the paper plates, invite child to turn over one of the plates and name the place that is shown in the picture. Say, **God is with you when you are at (home).**

3. Continue until each child has had a turn tiptoeing through the socks, using a different plate after every few rounds.

God's Word

"Do not fear, I am with you; do not be dismayed, for I am your God. I will strengthen you and help you." Isaiah 41:10

For Younger Children:
"I am with you; . . . I will . . . help you."

God's Word & Me

We can depend on God to protect us in times of worry or trouble.

Talk About

- In today's Bible story, God kept Daniel safe when he was put in a cave of lions. Daniel knew that God was always with him and would help him.

- Kelly, where is some place you like to go? God helps you by giving you people to care for you at the park. Who takes you to the park and takes care of you there?

- Our Bible says, "I am with you; . . . I will . . . help you." God promises to always be with us wherever we go. Pray briefly, **Thank You, God, for Your promise to be with us and to help us wherever we go. In Jesus' name, amen.**

For Older Children

Brainstorm with children names of people, places and things. Write children's responses on separate index cards. Place each category of cards in a separate paper bag. Children throw socks on floor, making a sock maze. Place bags in the middle of the sock maze. Children form teams of five or six. Teams form lines, with team members placing hands on shoulders of the child in front of him or her. Teams take turns walking through sock maze to reach bags. Then one team member chooses one card from each bag and uses items on cards to describe a situation in which the promise in Isaiah 41:10 needs to be remembered.

© 2006 Gospel Light. Permission to photocopy granted. *Treasure Seekers*

Game Center

FOR OLDER CHILDREN
Daniel 6:1-28

Collect
Bible, masking tape, crepe paper streamers of two different colors, scissors.

Prepare
Use masking tape to make two goal lines 30 to 40 feet (9 to 12 m) apart on opposite sides of play area. Cut streamers into 12-inch (30.5-cm) lengths.

Do
1. Divide class into two teams. Assign teams a streamer color. Each player on team tapes one end of streamer to his or her back as a flag.

2. Teams line up facing each other on opposite sides of play area. At your signal, teams run toward the goal line facing them on the other side of the play area. (Optional: In smaller play area, children hop or jump towards goal line.) As teams are trying to get to their goal lines, players try to grab other team's flags while protecting their own. When a player's flag is captured, he or she becomes a part of the opposing team and aids that team in capturing flags. Game ends when one team captures all or most flags of the opposite team.

God's Word
"Do not fear, I am with you; do not be dismayed, for I am your God. I will strengthen you and help you." Isaiah 41:10

For Younger Children:
"I am with you; . . . I will . . . help you."

God's Word & Me
We can depend on God to protect us in times of worry or trouble.

Talk About

- What did you need to do in order to play this game? (Protect your flag.) **In today's Bible story, a man named Daniel depended on God to protect him from a den of lions.**

- **When are some times someone might need to depend on God's help and protection?** (When they are in danger. When they are uncertain about the future. When others might tease them for doing something they believe in.)

- Read Isaiah 41:10. **What are the reasons this verse gives for depending on God in times of worry or trouble?** (God promises to always be with us. God promises to strengthen us and help us.) Isaiah 41:10 is a good verse to remember in times of worry or trouble. Pray briefly, **Dear God, thank You for Your promise to always be with us, to strengthen us and help us. Amen.**

 ## For Younger Children

Children run around the room as leader tries to tag children's flags. Children keep streamers on throughout the game. After a few rounds, have children try to tag the leader.

© 2006 Gospel Light. Permission to photocopy granted. *Treasure Seekers*

Art Center

FOR YOUNGER CHILDREN
Daniel 6:1-28

Collect

Bible, Pattern Page (p. 154), white paper, scissors, paper plates, crayons, glue, yellow decorating materials (crepe paper streamers, yarn, tissue paper, etc.).

Prepare

Make copies of the Pattern Page, one for each child. Cut out lion faces from copies.

Do

Distribute lion faces and paper plates to children. Children color faces and glue faces onto paper plates. Children choose and glue yellow decorating materials around face.

God's Word

"Do not fear, I am with you; do not be dismayed, for I am your God. I will strengthen you and help you." Isaiah 41:10

For Younger Children:
"I am with you; . . . I will . . . help you."

God's Word & Me

We can depend on God to protect us in times of worry or trouble.

Talk About

- In today's Bible story, a man named Daniel was put into a cave of hungry lions. God helped Daniel by keeping him safe in the cave of lions.

- God helps us by giving people to care for us. Natalie, who is someone that takes care of you when you are at home? What does your (mom) help you do every day? Jason, who helps you when you are at the park? What does your (grandpa) help you do when you are at the park?

- Our Bible says, "I am with you; . . . I will . . . help you." We can thank God for giving us people who love us and help us! Rebecca, who do you want to thank God for? Lead each child in completing the following prayer by naming someone to thank God for: **Dear God, thank You for (Grandma). Amen.**

 ## For Older Children

Children glue lion faces onto paper plates. To decorate faces, provide different shades of yellow tissue paper or yellow paper. Children make tissue-paper collages around faces or cut yellow paper into ¼x6-inch (0.6x15-cm) strips, wrapping strips tightly around pencils to make curled paper quills to glue around faces.

© 2006 Gospel Light. Permission to photocopy granted. *Treasure Seekers*

Art Center

FOR OLDER CHILDREN
Daniel 6:1-28

LESSON
eight

Collect

Bible, colored craft foam, pencils, scissors, decorating materials (yarn, glitter glue, chenille wire, etc.), butcher paper, tape, markers.

Do

1. Give each child a sheet of craft foam. Each child removes shoe and sock from one foot and uses pencil to trace around his or her foot on craft foam sheet. Child cuts out foot outline. Child then uses decorating materials to create a self-portrait on the foot outline (see sketch).

2. When portraits are complete, invite children to tape feet onto prepared butcher paper, creating a path. Children use colored markers to write phrases of Isaiah 41:10 on the paper. Display paper in classroom or in a well traveled hallway in the church.

God's Word

"Do not fear, I am with you; do not be dismayed, for I am your God. I will strengthen you and help you." Isaiah 41:10

For Younger Children:
"I am with you; . . . I will . . . help you."

God's Word & Me

We can depend on God to protect us in times of worry or trouble.

Talk About

- **What are some things kids your age worry about?** (Getting a good grade on a math exam. Making the team at soccer tryouts.) **What kind of troubles might kids your age face? When we face situations that might cause us to worry or feel afraid, we can depend on God's promises in His Word, the Bible.**

- Read Isaiah 41:10. **What promise does Isaiah 41:10 give to us?** (God is with us. God will help us and strengthen us.) **What names could we use to describe God according to this verse?** (Helper. Protector. Shield.)

- **What are some things we can do when we are worried or afraid?** (Remember God's promise in Isaiah 41:10. Pray to God. Depend on God's help. Tell a parent, friend or Sunday School teacher about your situation and ask them to pray for you.) Pray, **Dear God, You are our protector, helper and shield! Thank You for Your promise to be with us and help us. Wherever we are and in whatever circumstance we may face, help us to depend on You. Amen.**

For Younger Children

Before class, cut out pictures of different places from magazines. In class, assist children in tracing around feet and cutting feet shapes from craft foam sheets. Invite children to identify the different places shown in the pictures as they glue pictures and feet shapes to butcher paper.

© 2006 Gospel Light. Permission to photocopy granted. *Treasure Seekers*

Worship Center
Daniel 6:1-28

LESSON eight

Collect

Bibles, *Island Music* CD and player, song charts (pp. 248-249), paper strips, markers, balloons, two large garbage bags, large sheet of butcher paper.

Prepare

Write phrases of Isaiah 41:10 on separate strips of paper and insert into balloons. Inflate and tie balloons closed. Make another set of verse strips and insert into balloons and tie balloons closed, making sure there are an equal number of balloons in each set. Place each set of balloons in separate garbage bags. Write Isaiah 41:10 in large letters across butcher paper.

God's Word
"Do not fear, I am with you; do not be dismayed, for I am your God. I will strengthen you and help you." Isaiah 41:10
For Younger Children:
"I am with you; . . . I will . . . help you."

God's Word & Me
We can depend on God to protect us in times of worry or trouble.

Team Game

Divide group into four teams. Each team stands in a different corner of the room. You, or another leader, stand in the middle of the play area and randomly point to different teams, signaling teams when to roar like lions. Choose another leader to judge which team roars the loudest.

Bible Verse Game

Place bags filled with prepared balloons on one side of the play area. Divide group into two teams. Several volunteers from each team line up opposite bags on the other side of the play area. At your signal, first child in each line runs to team's bag, removes a balloon and pops the balloon by sitting on it. Child picks up paper strip from balloon and places it on the floor next to bag. Next child in each line repeats action. Game continues until all balloons are popped and paper strips are arranged in correct verse order.

Song

Lead children in singing "You, O Lord," adding motions and/or clapping if desired.

Prayer

Read Isaiah 41:10 from the prepared butcher paper sheet. **When are some times we might need to remember this verse? Let's write our names around the verse to show that we know that God is with us and helps us in times of worry or trouble.** Several children at a time take turns writing their names around the verse on the paper. If time permits, lead children in saying Isaiah 41:10 as a prayer all together, inviting children to say their names in place of the words "you" and "your" in the verse.

Song

Play "Promises." Lead children in singing, adding motions and/or clapping if desired.

© 2006 Gospel Light. Permission to photocopy granted. *Treasure Seekers* 153

Lesson 8 ◇ Pattern Page

Lesson 8 ◇ **Coloring/Puzzle Center**

God protects Daniel in a den of lions.
Daniel 6:1-28

God helped Daniel by protecting him in a cave of lions.
Who does God give to help you?

© 2006 Gospel Light. Permission to photocopy granted. *Treasure Seekers*

Lesson 8 ◇ Coloring/Puzzle Center

SHAPE YOUR FAITH!
Daniel 6

Find the letter in each shape to discover something all God's children should do.

Why was Daniel able to do this with courage in today's Bible story? Look up Isaiah 41:10 to help find the answer.

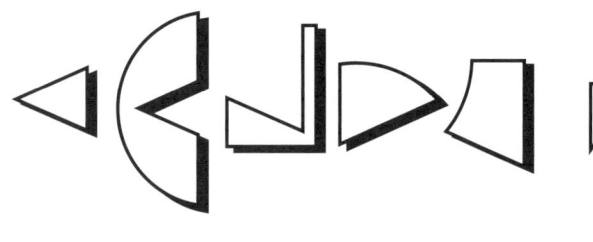

___ ___ ___ ___ ___ ___ ___   ___ ___ ___

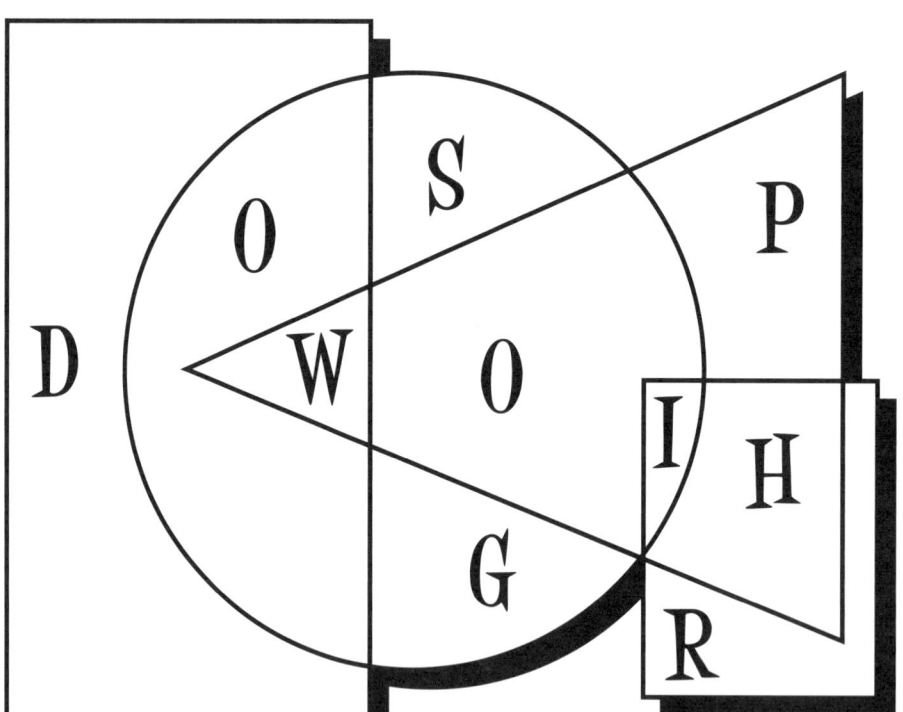

1. Which letter is in the rectangle, circle and triangle? _____
2. Which letter is in the rectangle and circle? _____
3. Which letter is in the small rectangle only? _____
4. Which letter is in the rectangle only? _____
5. Which letter is at the top of the circle? _____

Write your answers in order to find one way to worship God: With your _____ of praise!

156

© 2006 Gospel Light. Permission to photocopy granted. *Treasure Seekers*

Bible Story ◆ Acts 12:1-19

God Answers Prayer

LESSON nine

Teacher's Devotional

Have you ever noticed how we tend to emphasize some Scriptures over others? We're big on the Ten Commandments, and rightly so. We're unlikely to steal our neighbor's car or tell a lie in court. But there's one verse in Scripture we often forget or deemphasize when we are in the middle of a worrisome or difficult time: "Do not be anxious about anything, but in everything, by prayer and petition, with thanksgiving, present your requests to God" (Philippians 4:6).

God's Word tells us not to worry! And for a child of God, worry is not an option—but prayer is! We are to pray not only about our worries, needs and requests, but also to thank God as part of that process. We can rage, cry, whine and complain in prayer as King David did! David confidently says, "Listen to my cry for mercy. In the day of my trouble I will call to you, for you will answer me" (Psalm 86:6-7). Then, also like David, we must move on to praise the God who is big enough to not only listen to us rage, cry, whine and complain but also to completely change the situation we describe to Him! David didn't try to "nice up" his prayers for God but was sure that his loving Father heard.

Honesty, confidence and thanks may not always be features of our prayers. But God encourages us not only to be honest with Him, but also to thank Him in faith that He will *do something* about what we've asked! After all, God invites us to call upon Him and pray to Him (see Jeremiah 29:12). And He promises to listen and answer. We may not get the answer we expect, but that is because He loves us more than we love ourselves and is wiser than we ever can be. So certainly, He will do something that will result in our good and His glory—and surprise us every time! Anticipate that He will hear you when you call and will answer!

God's Word

"Call upon me and come and pray to me, and I will listen to you." Jeremiah 29:12

For Younger Children:
"Call upon me . . . and I will listen to you."

God's Word & Me

We can pray to God because He promises to hear and answer our prayers.

© 2006 Gospel Light. Permission to photocopy granted. *Treasure Seekers*

Planning Page

Choose which centers you will provide and the order in which children will participate in them (see pp. 14-18 for schedule tips and pp. 24-25 for guidelines in combining older and younger children). Also plan who will lead each center (for staffing tips see pp. 19-21). Use the reproducible planning sheet (p. 238) to record your plans.

Bible Story Center

Bible Story
God Answers Prayer • Acts 12:1-19

Younger Child Option
Use a lock and key to help tell the story

Older Child Option
Solve a telephone number code that tells what God does when He hears our prayers

Art Center

Younger Child Option
Make place mat collages and tell times to pray throughout the day

Materials
Bible, magazines, store ads, scissors, construction paper, Con-Tact paper, glue sticks, snack

Older Child Option
Create prayer journals and discuss ways God answers prayer

Materials
Bible, Pattern Page (p. 168), colored card stock, large sea shells, colored-ink stamp pads, hole punch, yarn or ribbon

Game Center

Younger Child Option
Play a knocking game and name things and people to thank God for

Materials
Bible, large sheet of butcher paper or bed sheet

Older Child Option
Play a game similar to golf and tell prayer requests

Materials
Bible, three long cardboard tubes, three golf or tennis balls, large index cards, marker, three containers

Coloring/Puzzle Center

Younger Child Option
Review the Bible story while completing coloring page

Materials
Lesson 9 Coloring Page (p. 169) for each student, crayons

Older Child Option
Review the Bible story while completing puzzle page

Materials
Lesson 9 Puzzle Page (p. 170) for each student, pencils

Worship Center

For the Younger and Older Child
Participate in large-group activities to review Bible verse and to worship God together

Materials
Bibles, *Island Music* CD and player, song charts (pp. 249, 252), large beach towel, Post-it Notes, marker

© 2006 Gospel Light. Permission to photocopy granted. *Treasure Seekers*

Bonus Island Ideas

LESSON nine

Bonus Island Ideas can be used at any time during this session: as an additional activity center, to extend the session for a longer time, or for added island excitement.

Pin the Treasure in the Chest

Draw an open treasure chest (see p. 234) on a large sheet of paper. Attach paper to wall. Lead children to play a game like Pin the Tail on the Donkey. Children take turns being blindfolded and turned around a few times before trying to place a sticker on the treasure chest. **For Older Children:** On the open treasure chest, draw stars or coin shapes and print numbers (10, 20, 50, 100, etc.) on the shapes. Divide class into two teams. Blindfolded children try to place stickers on these numbered shapes to collect points for their teams. The team that collects the most points receives a small prize (chocolate coins or other wrapped candies)!

Post a note alerting parents to the use of food. Also, check registration forms for possible food allergies.

Rolly Relay

Bring to class inflated swim rings (available at toy stores). Children form teams and play a relay game, rolling the rings as they run from one end of the play area to the other. **For Older Children:** Set up cones in a line from one end of the play area to the other. Children take turns rolling rings through cones, weaving in and out.

Lizard Snacks

Children create edible lizards using square crackers for heads, celery sticks filled with green cream cheese (add green food coloring to cream cheese) for bodies, four stick pretzels (each broken in half) or licorice sticks for legs, and raisins or jelly beans for spots on the bodies.

© 2006 Gospel Light. Permission to photocopy granted. *Treasure Seekers*

Bible Story Center

FOR YOUNGER CHILDREN
Acts 12:1-19

Collect

Bible.

Introduction

Knock on a door or wall. **When a friend comes to your house and knocks on your door, what do you usually do?** Volunteers answer. **Listen to hear what happened when a man knocked on the door of his friend's house.**

Treasure Chest Option

Place a lock and its key (or use a combination lock) in a treasure chest. Volunteer removes object(s). In the Bible story when you tell that the gates of the jail were opened, undo the lock.

Tell the Story

Every day more and more people believed that Jesus is God's Son. But some people wanted to stop Jesus' friends from telling others about Jesus. They even put some of Jesus' friends in jail, even though Jesus' friends had not done anything wrong.

One day Jesus' friend Peter was put in jail for teaching that Jesus is God's Son. Peter's friends began to pray to God for help. Peter had chains locked around him. But that couldn't stop God! One night God sent an angel to Peter.

"Quick—get up!" the angel said. Peter looked down. The chains around him fell off his arms! Peter got dressed and followed the angel. The guards were all asleep. The gates to the jail opened. Peter and the angel walked outside into the street. Then the angel was gone!

Peter knew that God had rescued him from the jail! Peter walked right to the house where he knew his friends were praying for God's help. Peter couldn't wait to tell them what God had done!

Peter knocked at the door. A girl named Rhoda came to answer the knock. Before she answered the door, she asked, "Who is it?"

"It's me!" said Peter.

Rhoda knew that voice! She was so excited, she forgot to open the door! She ran back to tell the people who were praying. "PETER is at the door!" she shouted.

Everyone looked up at her in surprise. "Peter? You're wrong," some of them said.

"No!" she said. "It's really Peter!" All this time Peter was still knocking at the door! Finally his friends opened the door. Peter's friends were amazed to see that God had heard and answered their prayers!

God's Word & Me

God heard the prayers of Peter's friends and answered their prayers by rescuing Peter from the jail. God loves to hear and answer our prayers! We can pray to God at anytime. He will always be listening! Our Bible says, "Call upon me . . . and I will listen to you." Pray, **Dear God, thank You for promising to listen and answer when we pray. Amen.**

Bible Story Center

FOR OLDER CHILDREN
Acts 12:1-19

LESSON nine

Collect

Bible.

Introduction

Tell children a Knock, Knock joke or invite a few children to tell any Knock, Knock jokes they know. **Listen to hear why someone was so surprised when she found out who was really knocking on her door.** As you tell the story, lead children in using their feet to create sound effects at different parts of the story (use both feet to make loud marching steps when it is mentioned that the soldiers were sent to arrest Peter; make two heavy stomps when it is mentioned that Peter's chains fell off; tap one foot quickly on floor to make knocking noises; quickly stamp both feet to make the sound of Rhoda running).

Treasure Chest Option

Draw a large copy of a phone's keypad onto a sheet of paper. Write the following numbers on the paper: 267-9377 and 772-9377. Place paper in a treasure chest. At the end of the story, volunteer removes paper and displays for others to see. Children work together to figure out the coded message: "answers prayers."

Tell the Story

It was time for the Passover, usually a joyful time to worship God in Jerusalem. But for God's growing family, it was a SCARY time. You see, Herod, the Roman ruler, had sent soldiers to arrest and KILL James, one of Jesus' followers! Everyone in God's family was very sad. And they were wondering what that cruel ruler Herod would do next!

It wasn't long before Herod did something else to make them afraid. He sent soldiers to arrest Peter, another one of Jesus' friends. Herod had Peter put in prison. Herod was planning to keep Peter in prison until the Passover holiday was over. Then Herod planned to accuse Peter of doing something wrong and put him on trial, so Herod could kill him, too.

Peter's friends knew that Peter might be killed. So guess what they did. They prayed! They met at the house of a woman named Mary and prayed and prayed with all their might, asking God to protect Peter and to help them.

The night before Herod was going to have Peter killed, God sent an angel to Peter's prison cell. The angel said, "Quick, get up!" And the chains around Peter's arms just fell off! Then Peter and the angel walked right past the guards—they were sound asleep and didn't wake up!

When Peter and the angel got to the huge iron gate leading to the city, the gate opened as if an invisible hand was pushing it! Peter followed the angel to the end of the street. Then the angel simply DISAPPEARED!

Peter hurried to the house where his friends were praying. He knocked on the door. A servant girl named Rhoda called out, "Who's there?"

"Peter!" he answered. Rhoda was so overjoyed that she ran to the room full of praying people without even opening the door!

"Peter's at the door! Peter's at the door!" she cried.

"WHAT?" they asked. "You must be crazy! Peter's in prison. He CAN'T be at the door."

But Peter kept knocking on the door! When Rhoda finally opened it, Peter's friends were amazed—and happy to see him!

© 2006 Gospel Light. Permission to photocopy granted. *Treasure Seekers*

Lesson nine

"God heard your prayers for me," Peter said. "God rescued me! God sent an angel in answer to your prayers!"

Everyone was VERY glad that Peter was safe. They knew then that God had heard and answered their prayers! And so they prayed again—to THANK God for sending Peter safely back to them!

God's Word & Me

Sometimes when we pray, we may think that God doesn't hear us because He doesn't answer us when we expect He will or in the way we expect He will. But God really DOES hear—and He DOES answer our prayers. Sometimes He answers our prayers in good ways that we don't expect! He loves us and He loves to surprise us!

- **What did Peter expect would happen? What did his friends do?**

- **How did God surprise Peter?** (Sent an angel to his prison cell.) **When were Peter's friends surprised?** (When Peter came to their house.)

- **What are some reasons we pray to God?** (To show our love for Him. To praise and thank Him. To ask Him for an answer or for understanding.)

- **What are some things kids your age might ask God to do?** (Help in getting along with others. Help when afraid of something at school.) **Thank God for?**

- **What might be a reason God doesn't answer every prayer with a "yes"?** (God knows what is best for us. Some things we ask for might not be good for us. God may have a better plan for us.)

- Read Jeremiah 29:12 aloud. **What does this verse say that God wants us to do? When we pray, we can pray knowing and trusting that God will hear and answer our prayers.** Pray, **Dear God, thank You for hearing and answering our prayers. Amen.**

© 2006 Gospel Light. Permission to photocopy granted. *Treasure Seekers*

Game Center

FOR YOUNGER CHILDREN
Acts 12:1-19

LESSON nine

Collect
Bible, large sheet of butcher paper or bed sheet.

Do

1. Invite another leader to help you hold up the butcher paper or bed sheet. Divide the class into two groups. Invite one group to sit on one side of the sheet and the other group to sit on the other side.

2. Secretly choose a child from one side of the sheet to say "knock, knock" as he or she taps the sheet. Children gathered on the other side call out, "Who is it?" Child answers by saying, "It's me!" Children try to identify the child by his or her voice. After a few guesses, remove or drop the sheet to reveal who was speaking. Ask the child one of the questions about prayer below. Continue, choosing a new child from alternating sides to answer each time.

God's Word

"Call upon me and come and pray to me, and I will listen to you." Jeremiah 29:12

For Younger Children:
"Call upon me . . . and I will listen to you."

God's Word & Me

We can pray to God because He promises to hear and answer our prayers.

Talk About

- In today's Bible story, Peter knocked on his friend's door just like we did! A girl named Rhoda answered the door. Rhoda was so surprised to see Peter because she and her friends had just been praying for Peter and—there he was!

- Jeremy, what is something you want to thank God for? Jessica, who is someone in your family that you want to pray for? Bennie, what is your friend's name? We can pray for our friends, too.

- Our Bible says, "Call upon me . . . and I will listen to you." God promises to listen to our prayers. And we can trust that God will answer our prayers, too! Pray, *Dear God, thank You for listening to and answering our prayers. In Jesus' name, amen.*

 ## For Older Children

Children play the game as described above with children on each side of the sheet asking and answering questions about prayer or the Bible story while disguising their voices.

© 2006 Gospel Light. Permission to photocopy granted. *Treasure Seekers*

 # Game Center

FOR OLDER CHILDREN
Acts 12:1-19

LESSON nine

Collect

Bible, three long cardboard tubes, three golf or tennis balls, large index cards, marker, three containers (shoe box, large cups, etc.).

Prepare

Place each tube and ball set on floor on one side of the play area. On separate index cards write the following phrases: "I'm thankful for . . ." "Prayer Request for Me" and "Prayer Request for Others." Place containers on their sides at various distances from the tube and ball sets and place each card next to a container.

God's Word

"Call upon me and come and pray to me, and I will listen to you." Jeremiah 29:12

For Younger Children:
"Call upon me . . . and I will listen to you."

God's Word & Me

We can pray to God because He promises to hear and answer our prayers.

Do

1. Invite children to stand in three lines behind tube and ball sets. First child in each line takes a turn using tube to lightly hit the ball towards any of the containers. From the place where the ball stops, next child takes his or her turn. When a ball is hit into a container, child gives a response to the prayer category indicated on the index card placed near the container.

2. Continue playing rounds of the game as time permits.

Talk About

- When's a time God answered a prayer of yours or someone you know? What is a prayer request that you are still waiting for God to answer?

- What are some ways God answers prayer? (Answering in a way different from what we expected.) **Why does God sometimes answer our prayers with a "no"?** (God knows what's best for us.)

- Read Jeremiah 29:12 aloud. **What does God invite us to do?** God wants us to call upon Him and pray to Him! **Why do you think God wants us to call upon Him and pray?** (To show love and trust in Him.) Sometimes, God may answer in ways we don't expect. But we can keep on praying, at all times and with all kinds of prayers! God will hear us and answer. Pray with children, mentioning children's prayer requests from the game and the discussion.

 ## For Younger Children

Children line up and take turns rolling ball into containers, switching containers after every few rounds. When ball lands in the container, child tells something for which he or she wants to thank God.

164

© 2006 Gospel Light. Permission to photocopy granted. *Treasure Seekers*

Art Center

FOR YOUNGER CHILDREN
Acts 12:1-19

LESSON nine

Collect

Bible, magazines, store ads, scissors, construction paper, Con-Tact paper, glue sticks, snack.

Prepare

From magazines and ads, cut out pictures of things for which children might be thankful (foods, toys, things in nature, animals, etc.). Cut construction paper into a variety of geometric shapes, making several 4- to 5-inch (10- to 12.5-cm) shapes for each child. Cut Con-Tact paper into 12x18-inch (30.5x45.5-cm) rectangles, making two for each child.

God's Word

"Call upon me and come and pray to me, and I will listen to you." Jeremiah 29:12

For Younger Children:
"Call upon me . . . and I will listen to you."

God's Word & Me

We can pray to God because He promises to hear and answer our prayers.

Do

1. Invite children to choose pictures of items for which they are thankful to God. **Today we're going to make "Thank You, God!" place mats.**

2. Each child glues pictures onto construction paper shapes. When children are finished, children place shapes onto one sheet of Con-Tact paper. Place second sheet of paper on top. Then distribute snacks, placing snack on child's place mat.

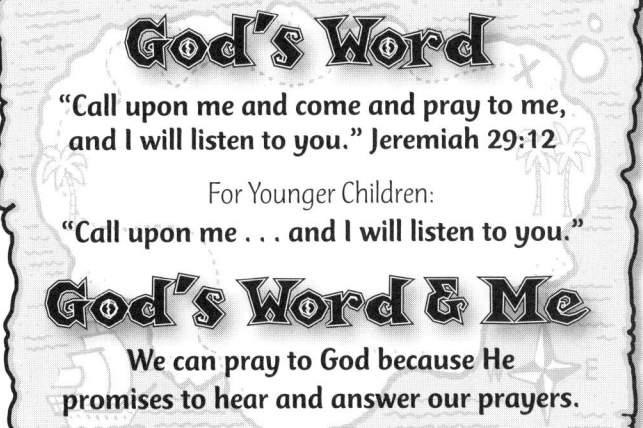

Talk About

- Tanya, which picture shows something that you thank God for? We can thank God for giving us yummy fruit like apples to eat!

- How many times do we eat each day? What can we say to God before we eat a meal? We can use the place mats to help us remember the things we want to say thank You to God for.

- Our Bible says, "Call upon me . . . and I will listen to you." God wants us to talk to Him. He promises to hear and answer our prayers! Pray, Thank You, God, for giving us this snack to eat. Amen.

 For Older Children

Children make woven place mats using two different colored sheets of construction paper. Child folds one sheet in half lengthwise, and then draws five to six wavy lines from the fold towards the paper's edge, stopping each line about 1 inch (2.5 cm) from the edge. Child cuts along the lines, keeping paper folded. Child then draws and cuts several wavy strips across the length of the second paper. Child weaves wavy strips under and over cut lines on other sheet, alternating pattern for each row. Cover with Con-Tact paper.

© 2006 Gospel Light. Permission to photocopy granted. *Treasure Seekers*

# Art Center

FOR OLDER CHILDREN
Acts 12:1-19

LESSON nine

Collect

Bible, Pattern Page (p. 168), colored card stock, large sea shells, colored-ink stamp pads, hole punch, yarn or ribbon.

Prepare

Make seven copies of the Pattern Page for each child, one copy for each day of the week.

Do

1. Distribute a sheet of blank card stock to each child. Children press the outside of shells onto ink stamp pads and then roll and press onto card stock to make a design. (Optional: If stamp pads are unavailable, children may color outside of shells with water-based colored markers with wide tips.) Children may need to press one side of the shell at a time, rolling left, then right to make one continuous print.

2. Distribute seven copies of the Pattern Page to each child. Children align cover and copies and punch three or four holes along the left edge of papers.

3. Children weave yarn or ribbon through holes to bind journal pages together. Children take home journals for families to use.

God's Word

"Call upon me and come and pray to me, and I will listen to you." Jeremiah 29:12

For Younger Children:
"Call upon me . . . and I will listen to you."

God's Word & Me

We can pray to God because He promises to hear and answer our prayers.

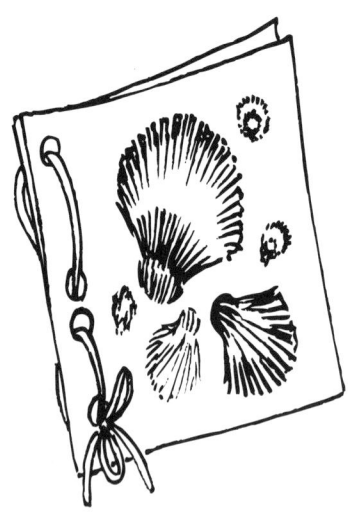

Talk About

- What are some things kids your age often talk to God about? (When help is needed to do something. To thank Him for having something good happen.)

- Why might God answer a prayer by saying "no" or "later"? (God knows what's best for us.)

- In what way has God answered a prayer for you or someone you know?

- Read Jeremiah 29:12. **What is something you want to talk to God about?** Invite children to complete one prayer journal page. Close with the following prayer: **Dear God, we trust that You hear our prayers and will answer us. Amen.**

For Younger Children

Provide stamps and stickers for children to use to decorate their journal covers. Provide blank paper for journal pages. Children may draw or glue pictures (cut from magazines) of things they thank God for.

© 2006 Gospel Light. Permission to photocopy granted. *Treasure Seekers*

Worship Center

Acts 12:1-19

LESSON nine

Collect

Bibles, *Island Music* CD and player, song charts (pp. 249, 252), large beach towel, Post-it Notes, marker.

Team Game

Lay out beach towel on the floor. Divide group into four to six teams. Invite a volunteer from each team to play. All players stand on towel. Then, players step off towel. Fold towel in half. Players gather to stand on towel again. Continue process so that the space for players to stand on gets smaller and smaller. Last player who is able to stand or stay on towel the longest is the winner! Repeat as time permits.

God's Word

"Call upon me and come and pray to me, and I will listen to you." Jeremiah 29:12

For Younger Children:
"Call upon me . . . and I will listen to you."

God's Word & Me

We can pray to God because He promises to hear and answer our prayers.

Bible Verse Game

Read Jeremiah 29:12 aloud. **This verse talks about God listening to our prayers. Let's play a game to see how good we are at listening.** Secretly choose two other leaders before the game and instruct leaders how to play the game. Create a rhythmic pattern by clapping hands, stomping feet or snapping fingers for children to follow. One of the leaders secretly changes the rhythmic pattern. Children follow the new leader's pattern. Later, the remaining leader starts another rhythmic pattern for children to copy. End the game. Ask children to identify who changed the rhythmic pattern during the game.

Song

You, or another leader, lead children in singing "Call Upon Me," adding motions and/or clapping if desired.

Prayer

Number Post-it Notes and distribute one to each child, inviting child to stick note to the front of his or her shirt. Call out pairs of numbers until each number written on a note has been paired. Children walk around room to find their partners. Partners exchange prayer requests or tell each other things for which they thank God. (For a large group: Children count off in fours. Children gather in their appropriate numbered groups and share prayer requests or praises.)

Song

Play "Promises." Lead children in singing, adding motions and/or clapping if desired. Close with the following prayer: **Thank You, God, for hearing and answering our prayers. Amen.**

© 2006 Gospel Light. Permission to photocopy granted. *Treasure Seekers*

Lesson 9 ◆ Pattern Page

My Daily Prayer Log

Today's Date: _____

Today I am feeling...

happy ☐ sad ☐ bored ☐ other ☐

Write or draw your prayer.
Dear God, Today I need...

Check the box to show how God answered:
☐ Yes ☐ No ☐ Wait

I'm sorry I...

Please help me...

I'm Thankful for...

168

© 2006 Gospel Light. Permission to photocopy granted. *Treasure Seekers*

An angel frees Peter.
Acts 12:1-19

Lesson 9 ◆ Coloring/Puzzle Center

Peter thanked God for answering his friends' prayers and rescuing him from the jail. What is something you want to thank God for? God answers our prayers.

Lesson 9 ◇ Coloring/Puzzle Center

FOLLOW THE CLUES!

1. It is not in any of the books which are laying flat.
2. It is to the left of Romans.
3. It is not a book which has the same name as another book.
4. It has more than four letters in its name.
5. It has the same name as something in an address.

One of the books below has a story about a talking animal. Find where the story is by reading the clues below.

Read _____ 22:21-34 for the story about what happened!
(book you discovered)

In one of the books below you can read about two miraculous escapes from prison.

1. It is not any of the books which are stacked in a pile.
2. It is to the right of Exodus.
3. It is not a book with a person's name.
4. It is not an Old Testament book.

Read _____ 12:5-11 and 16:16-40 to find out who prayed in these stories. What
(book you discovered) can you ask God for or praise Him for?

© 2006 Gospel Light. Permission to photocopy granted. *Treasure Seekers*

BIBLE STORY ◆ Matthew 8:23-27; Mark 4:35-41; Luke 8:22-25

God Is Powerful

LESSON ten

Teacher's Devotional

We are a culture fascinated with power: We buy power tools, take power-dressing seminars, eat power bars and schedule power lunches. We take power walks or do power lifting; we seek political power or the power of fame. Our culture constantly repeats, "Power is everything. You must gain power to be great."

What a contrast to Jesus Christ! Jesus showed His power in three ways: First, since He made this world by the word of His power, all power in heaven and Earth is His. Then while He lived on Earth, He exhibited power over every other power by stopping storms, feeding the hungry, healing the hopelessly sick and raising the dead. He left no doubt in any mind that His power was supreme: He even declared that no one could take His life; He would lay it down of His own accord (see John 10:18).

Jesus' exhibits of creative, absolute power prove He is God. But He taught us a third kind of power that turns our ideas about power upside down! He taught us by His humility—choosing to lay aside His rights to live in complete obedience to His Father right to death. In place of a sword, He carried the towel of a servant. In John 13:3, Jesus "knew that the Father had put all things under his power" so He wrapped a towel around His waist and began to wash His disciples' feet. He commands us to do the same—and told His disciples that the greatest one among them would be the servant of all!

Jesus so confidently walked in God's power that He did not need any of the window dressing of worldly power. When we serve and obey God not out of duty but out of dignity and delight, true power becomes ours. Jesus is ready to keep on turning the world's power structure upside down—through us! All power is His; we can trust His power in any situation to help us act as His servants.

God's Word

"No one is like you, O LORD; you are great, and your name is mighty in power."
Jeremiah 10:6

For Younger Children:
"LORD, you are great."

God's Word & Me

We can praise God for His help, because of His great power.

© 2006 Gospel Light. Permission to photocopy granted. *Treasure Seekers*

Planning Page

LESSON ten

Choose which centers you will provide and the order in which children will participate in them (see pp. 14-18 for schedule tips and pp. 24-25 for guidelines in combining older and younger children). Also plan who will lead each center (for staffing tips see pp. 19-21). Use the reproducible planning sheet (p. 238) to record your plans.

Bible Story Center

Bible Story
God Is Powerful • Matthew 8:23-27; Mark 4:35-41; Luke 8:22-25

Younger Child Option
Get sprayed by water to feel what it would be like to be in a storm

Older Child Option
Play Tic-Tac-Toe to collect letters of the word "powerful"

Art Center

Younger Child Option
Make windsocks as reminders of God's power and help

Materials
Bible, Pattern Page (p. 182), card stock, scissors, crepe paper streamers or thick ribbon in shades of blue, ruler, markers, yarn or thin ribbon, stapler or tape

Older Child Option
Create a wind-blown-painting mural and praise God for His greatness and power

Materials
Bible, newspaper, large sheet of butcher paper, extension cords, several blow-dryers, tempera paint in various colors, paper cups, markers

Game Center

Younger Child Option
Play a musical boat game and praise God for His greatness

Materials
Bible, *Island Music* CD and player, three or four hula hoops

Older Child Option
Play a wind blowing relay and identify ways God shows His power and help

Materials
Bible, pen, small waxed paper cups, string, scissors

Coloring/Puzzle Center

Younger Child Option
Review the Bible story while completing coloring page

Materials
Lesson 10 Coloring Page (p. 183) for each student, crayons

Older Child Option
Review the Bible story while completing puzzle page

Materials
Lesson 10 Puzzle Page (p. 184) for each student, pencils

Worship Center

For the Younger and Older Child
Participate in large-group activities to review Bible verse and to worship God together

Materials
Bibles, *Island Music* CD and player, song charts (pp. 250, 254), butcher paper, marker, two hula hoops

© 2006 Gospel Light. Permission to photocopy granted. *Treasure Seekers*

Bonus Island Ideas

LESSON ten

Bonus Island Ideas can be used at any time during this session: as an additional activity center, to extend the session for a longer time, or for added island excitement.

Melon Boats

Slice melon into wedges for each child. Place melon wedges on paper plates and distribute to children. Children use stick pretzels to make boat "masts," sticking one end of the pretzel in the middle of the melon wedge, and "sails" of precut cheese slices, securing with toothpicks (see sketch). Older children may cut their own sails. Children make "sailors" by sliding fruit (blueberries, strawberries or grapes) onto toothpicks and sticking toothpicks into melon.

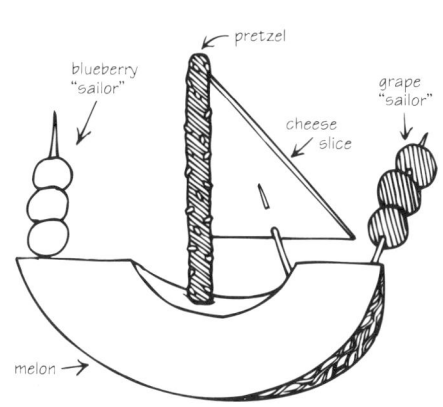

Post a note alerting parents to the use of food. Also, check registration forms for possible food allergies.

Staying Afloat

Fill a large dishpan with water. Provide various floating and nonfloating objects (small paper plate, sponge, thin paper, napkin, plastic yogurt covers, paper, aluminum foil) for children to experiment with to see how well objects float. Provide marbles or small stones for children to weight objects with. **For Older Children:** Children may design boats from straws, aluminum foil and tape. Children race their boats by blowing boats from one end of the dishpan to the other.

Children sit in a circle. Set a dishpan half-filled with water in the middle of the circle. Play music while children pass an ice cube around the circle as in the game Hot Potato. When the music stops, child holding the ice cube remains seated and tosses the ice cube towards the dishpan in the middle. If child misses, game quickly continues using the same ice cube. Play until ice cube melts or is successfully tossed in the dishpan. Repeat as time permits.

Cool Potato

© 2006 Gospel Light. Permission to photocopy granted. *Treasure Seekers*

Bible Story Center

FOR YOUNGER CHILDREN

Matthew 8:23-27; Mark 4:35-41; Luke 8:22-25

LESSON ten

Collect
Bible.

Introduction
What are some things you might hear if you were on a boat? (Waves splashing. Boat horn. Seagulls.) Listen to hear what happened to Jesus and His friends when they were on a boat and there were some BIG waves.

Treasure Chest Option

Place a spray water bottle in a treasure chest. Invite a volunteer to remove the water bottle. Mist children as you tell about the storm in the Bible story.

Tell the Story

Jesus spent all day teaching people about God. Now He was tired! Jesus and His friends were sailing across the lake in their boat. Jesus lay down in the back of the boat. Soon He was asleep. Splish, splish, splish.

Suddenly, the wind began to blow. Oooooo! Oooooo! The wind blew harder and harder. The little waves got bigger and bigger. Splish, splash! Splish, splash! The big waves hit hard against the little boat. Water splashed into the boat. The boat was filling with water.

"I'm afraid!" one of Jesus' friends might have shouted.

"Jesus! Help us!" shouted another friend. "Don't you care that our boat is sinking?"

Jesus woke up. He felt the strong winds blowing. He saw the big waves splashing. Jesus stood up and said, "Quiet! Be still!" And just like that, the wind stopped blowing. The big waves stopped splashing. Splish, splish. The little waves rocked the boat gently again.

"Why were you so afraid?" Jesus asked His friends. "Don't you know that you can trust Me to help you?"

Jesus' friends were surprised. Even the winds and the waves had obeyed Jesus! The friends were so glad Jesus had helped them in the big storm! Jesus had shown His love and power in a special way.

God's Word & Me

In today's Bible story, Jesus' friends learned about Jesus' great love and power. Our Bible says, "The Lord is great." "Lord" is another name for God. When we say God is "great," we mean that God is so strong and powerful, He can do anything! Jesus is strong. He is powerful and He can help us every day. Pray, **Dear God, thank You for Jesus' great power and for His help.**

© 2006 Gospel Light. Permission to photocopy granted. *Treasure Seekers*

Bible Story Center

FOR OLDER CHILDREN
Matthew 8:23-27; Mark 4:35-41; Luke 8:22-25

Collect

Bible.

Introduction

What are some of Superman's powers? Spiderman's? What are the powers of some other superhero comic characters you know? Volunteers respond. **Today we are going to hear a story about a real hero whose power is greater than any superhero.** Dress up in a Bible times costume and tell the story as one of Jesus' disciples caught in the storm. (Optional: Videotape someone ahead of time telling this story as Peter. Play video during class.)

Treasure Chest Option

Draw a large Tic-Tac-Toe board on butcher paper. Write in random order each letter of the word "Powerful" in a separate box on the Tic-Tac-Toe board. Write "Free" in the remaining box. Draw five Xs and five Os on separate Post-It notes. Place board and notes in a treasure chest. Invite two volunteers to remove items and use notes to play Tic-Tac-Toe. When a player gets three across, down or diagonal, he or she collects letters in that row. Write letters next to the board on the butcher paper, and cross out letters on board. Once all letters have been collected or when time is up, children work together to unscramble.

Tell the Story

Hi! My name is Peter. I'm one of Jesus' disciples. I'm sure you've heard of Jesus. He's the Son of God. I'll admit, I didn't always know that. But there was one time when I should have realized it. Let me tell you about it!

Jesus spent a lot of time teaching and healing people, mostly in the area near the Sea of Galilee. This particular day had been a VERY long one for all of us. People had come from all over to hear Jesus talk and to ask Him for healing. I could tell Jesus was exhausted, but the people just wouldn't go away. Along towards evening Jesus suggested that we take our fishing boat and go across the Sea of Galilee to the other side. That sure sounded like a good idea to me—that way maybe we all could get some rest before the crowd caught up with us! Once we all got on the boat, Jesus laid down on a bench in the stern and fell fast asleep.

Sailing at night was no big deal to me. We fishermen do most of our fishing at night—it's the best time to catch fish in the Sea of Galilee. While we sailed, we talked about Jesus.

"You think maybe He's the Messiah?" asked one of us. "Sure is hard to believe when you look at Him sleeping," said another. "He looks pretty ordinary."

"I've never seen an ordinary person who could perform miracles the way Jesus can," I said. "Remember that man who couldn't walk? Jesus just said, 'Get up and walk' and the man did!"

"Yeah," said another. "I couldn't believe the man's friends actually made a hole in the roof of the house so they could see Jesus!" We all laughed. Then I said, "Jesus sure is different from any ordinary person I know. I'm glad He picked me as His follower." **If you'd been with us in the boat that night, what would you have remembered about what Jesus said or did?**

Well, we kinda chatted on like that for a bit, when suddenly there was a great gust of wind. We knew we were in trouble! The Sea of Galilee is in a valley between some fairly steep mountains. When the wind comes blowing through, we get some really fierce waves.

© 2006 Gospel Light. Permission to photocopy granted. *Treasure Seekers*

First the wind knocked the boat back and forth. Then the waves came whooshing up, slapping the boat sideways. It was awful! The boat began to fill with water! **What do you think we did to try and save ourselves?** Those of us who weren't fighting to keep the boat steady were bailing out buckets of water as fast as our arms would go! But we weren't fast enough or strong enough. The boat was going down!

And guess who was sleeping through all of this? Jesus! You would have thought with all the noise the wind and the waves were making, He'd wake up. But He just kept on sleeping!

Finally we yelled for Him, "Teacher, don't You care if we drown?" We couldn't believe that Jesus hadn't heard what was happening! If He woke up, He could help us keep the boat from sinking!

What do you think Jesus did? Jesus got up and said to the waves, "Quiet! Be still!" The wind immediately died down. It was completely CALM. We were shocked! We sat there just staring at Jesus with our mouths open. I mean, He stopped the wind and everything!

"After listening to all I've said and seeing all I've done, you still don't have much faith!" Jesus said. "Don't you know you can trust Me to take care of you?"

Well, if you thought we were wondering about just who Jesus was before, you can imagine what went through our minds NOW! We asked one another, "Who IS this? Even the wind and the waves obey Him!" I know now how silly our thinking was, but you see, we didn't really know ALL about Jesus then. As far as we knew, only God could control the wind and the sea. We didn't really understand yet that Jesus IS God's Son!

God's Word & Me

In today's story, the disciples learned about God's amazing power. God shows His power to us in many ways. One way God has shown us His great power was in Jesus' death and resurrection. In forgiving all people's sins and conquering death, Jesus showed that God's power is greater than anything. Learning more about God and His amazing power helps us want to praise and thank Him!

- **What did Jesus do to show His power in today's story? How did Jesus' disciples respond when they saw Jesus' power?** (They were amazed. They wanted to learn more about Him.)

- **What are some other ways Jesus showed power in His life?** (Making sick people well. Forgiving sins.) **What are some ways Jesus shows His power in our lives today?** (Helping us choose to be honest. Giving us patience when someone wants to fight.)

- Read Jeremiah 10:6. **This verse praises God and tells how great and mighty He is! What are some ways we can say this verse in our own words to praise God for His greatness and power?** Close with prayer, using children's suggestions to paraphrase Jeremiah 10:6.

Game Center

FOR YOUNGER CHILDREN
Matthew 8:23-27; Mark 4:35-41; Luke 8:22-25

Collect

Bible, *Island Music* CD and player, three or four hula hoops.

Prepare

Lay hula hoops on floor, leaving a few feet between each hoop.

Do

1. Play "God Is So Strong" as children walk around the room. When music stops, children quickly move to stand inside one of the hula hoops.

2. **Let's pretend these hula hoops are boats.** Give children different motions to do, according to children's initials or color of clothing children are wearing. **Everyone whose name begins with a C or a J pretend to paddle your boat. Everyone wearing (green), pretend to rock your boat. Everyone who has (brown) eyes, pretend to steer your boat.** Repeat activity as time and interest permit.

Talk About

- Our Bible story tells about a time Jesus helped His friends on a boat!

- If you were in a boat, Samantha, what things would you see? How might you feel if there was a big storm? Jesus' friends were glad He helped them in a big storm. We can ask God for help anytime!

- Our Bible says, "Lord; you are great." "Lord" is another name for God. God is great because He is so strong! No one is stronger than Him. He always loves us and helps us. **What are some other words we could use to praise God?** Lead children in saying and completing the following sentence: **God, You are . . .**

God's Word

"No one is like you, O LORD; you are great, and your name is mighty in power."
Jeremiah 10:6

For Younger Children:
"LORD; you are great."

God's Word & Me

We can praise God for His help, because of His great power.

For Older Children

Use masking tape to mark numbers in the center of hula hoops on the floor. While music plays, children walk around the room. When the music stops, call out a number indicating the number of children to gather in hula hoops. Children in each hula hoop recite words of Jeremiah 10:6 together. Increase the challenge by calling out the number of children to gather in each numbered hula hoop (e.g., "5 in hula hoop 1," "3 in hula hoop 2," "2 in hula hoop 1!").

© 2006 Gospel Light. Permission to photocopy granted. *Treasure Seekers*

 # Game Center

FOR OLDER CHILDREN
Matthew 8:23-27; Mark 4:35-41; Luke 8:22-25

Lesson ten

Collect
Bible, pen, small waxed paper cups, string, scissors. (Note: If available, use fishing line instead of string for easier movement of the cup.)

Prepare
Use a pen to punch hole in center bottom of each cup.

Do
1. Divide group into teams of four to six players. Each team stands side-by-side in a line. Give each team a paper cup and a length of string that reaches the length of the line.

2. First player threads the cup onto the string, making sure the bottom of the cup is facing the next player (see sketch). At your signal, with the string held taut, the first player begins blowing into cup to send it toward the next player.

3. Each player continues blowing to race the "boat" to the end of the line. The first team to blow its boat to the end of the line calls out the words of Jeremiah 10:6.

God's Word
"No one is like you, O LORD; you are great, and your name is mighty in power."
Jeremiah 10:6

For Younger Children:
"LORD; you are great."

God's Word & Me
We can praise God for His help, because of His great power.

Talk About
- In today's Bible story, Jesus showed His power by commanding the stormy wind and the waves to be calm.

- **How does God show His power and help us today?** (Keeps us safe. Forgives our sins. Answers our prayers. Helps us when we have to do something hard.) **When is a time God has shown His power to you?** Share with children about a time God showed His power in your own life.

- **Why can we depend on God's power and help?** (He loves us. His power is greater than anything.) **Let's say Jeremiah 10:6 together as a prayer, praising God for His great power.**

 For Younger Children
Instead of playing a relay as described above, set up a few stations by tying ends of shorter lengths of string to pairs of chairs placed as far apart as the length of the strings. Groups of two to four children line up by each station and take turns blowing cup along string. Lead children in repeating Jeremiah 10:6.

Art Center

FOR YOUNGER CHILDREN
Matthew 8:23-27; Mark 4:35-41; Luke 8:22-25

LESSON ten

Collect
Bible, Pattern Page (p. 182), card stock, scissors, crepe paper streamers or thick ribbon in shades of blue, ruler, markers, yarn or thin ribbon, stapler or tape.

Prepare
Photocopy the Pattern Page onto card stock, making one copy for each child. Cut crepe paper or thick ribbon into 12-inch (30.5-cm) lengths.

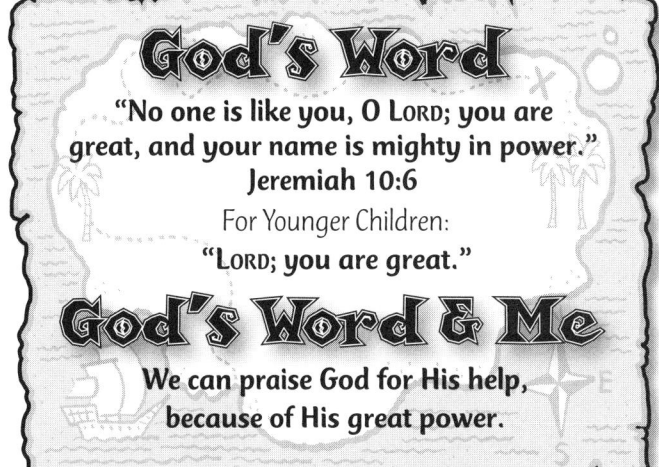

God's Word
"No one is like you, O LORD; you are great, and your name is mighty in power."
Jeremiah 10:6

For Younger Children:
"LORD; you are great."

God's Word & Me
We can praise God for His help, because of His great power.

Do
1. Distribute copies to children. Children color and decorate the pages.

2. Assist children in stapling or taping crepe paper streamers or thick-ribbon lengths to the bottom edge of the picture. Then help children roll the paper into a tube shape and staple or tape the side edges together. Staple or tape ends of a yarn or thin-ribbon length at the top for a hanger.

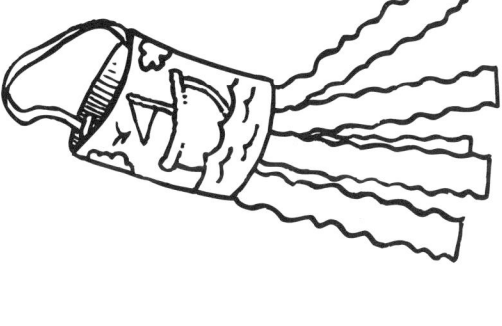

Talk About

- In today's Bible story, Jesus and His friends were in a boat. A strong wind began to blow. Jesus' friends were very afraid when the storm began. But they were glad when Jesus helped them!

- Caroline, when might you feel afraid? Jesus helps you when you are afraid.

- Jackson, where will you hang your windsock? When we see our windsocks moving in the breeze, we can remember today's story and Jesus' help.

- Our Bible says, "Lord; you are great." We can praise God for His help, because of His great power! *Pray briefly,* **Thank You, God, for Your great power. Thank You for helping us when we are afraid.**

For Older Children
Children decorate Pattern Page copies by gluing various shades of blue tissue paper squares to pages to make layers of ocean waves. After assembling windsocks, children decorate them with glitter glue.

 # Art Center

FOR OLDER CHILDREN
Matthew 8:23-27; Mark 4:35-41; Luke 8:22-25

LESSON ten

Collect

Bible, newspaper, large sheet of butcher paper, extension cords, several blow-dryers, tempera paint in various colors, paper cups, markers.

Prepare

Spread newspaper on the ground near electrical outlets in classroom. Lay butcher paper on top of newspaper. Use extension cords to connect blow-dryers to outlets and place blow-dryers around the paper. Preset blow-dryer controls to "Cool" and "High." Pour paint into several paper cups.

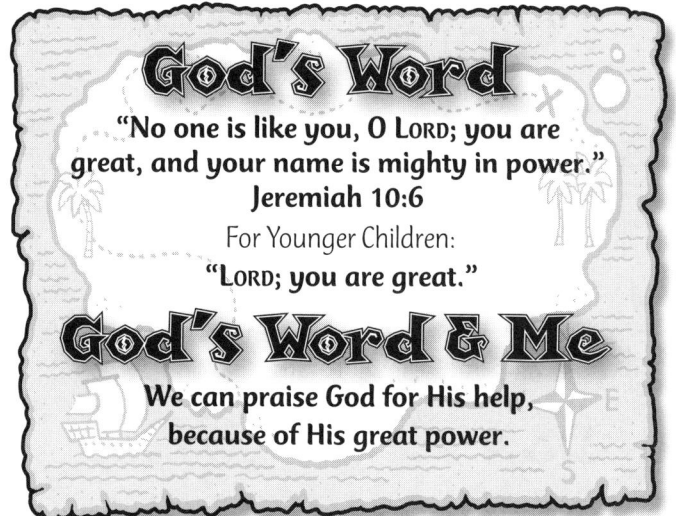

God's Word

"No one is like you, O LORD; you are great, and your name is mighty in power."
Jeremiah 10:6

For Younger Children:
"LORD; you are great."

God's Word & Me

We can praise God for His help, because of His great power.

Do

Children form lines behind blow-dryers to take turns pouring drops of paint onto the paper and then blowing paint across the paper to create interesting designs. (Optional: If blow-dryers are unavailable, children may use straws to blow paint.)

Talk About

- When mural is complete, ask, **What are some words that describe what you see? This mural can remind us of today's Bible story.**

- **What did Jesus do to show His power in the middle of the storm?** (He commanded the wind and waves to be quiet and still, and they obeyed.)

- **What are some words you would use to describe Jesus?** (Kind. Loving. Forgiving.) Read Jeremiah 10:6. **What words from Jeremiah 10:6 could we use to describe Jesus?** (Mighty. Great.) **What are some things we know from Jesus' life that show He is mighty and powerful?** (He gave sight to the blind. He healed the lame. He died and rose again.) Invite volunteers to complete the following sentence prayer by writing words on mural: **Dear Jesus, You are great and mighty because . . .**

 ## For Younger Children

Distribute a straw and sheet of paper to each child. Pour a few drops of colored paint onto sheets. Children use straws to blow paint across the paper to make designs

Worship Center

Matthew 8:23-27; Mark 4:35-41; Luke 8:22-25

Collect

Bibles, *Island Music* CD and player, song charts (pp. 250, 254), butcher paper, marker, two hula hoops.

Prepare

Write a large number 1 on the left side of the butcher paper sheet and write a large number 10 on the right side of the sheet. Create motions for words in Jeremiah 10:6. (Optional: Look up American Sign Language for the words in the verse.)

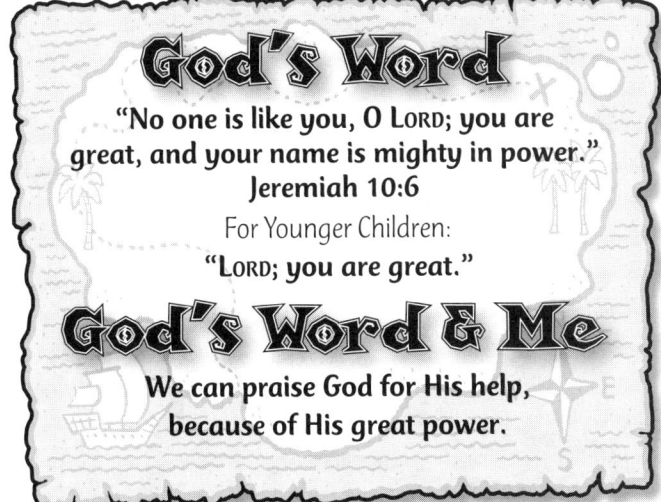

God's Word

"No one is like you, O Lord; you are great, and your name is mighty in power."
Jeremiah 10:6

For Younger Children:
"Lord; you are great."

God's Word & Me

We can praise God for His help, because of His great power.

Team Game

Invite six to eight children to form two teams of equal players to play a hula hoop passing relay. Players on each team join hands to form a circle, hanging a hula hoop from one person's arm in the circle. At your signal, the person holding hula hoop steps through hoop to try and pass hoop to the next player without letting go of teammate's hand on either side. Next player repeats action. Team that gets the hoop back to the starting player the fastest is the winner. Other children may cheer for either team.

Bible Verse Game

Demonstrate the motions and invite children to guess which words of Jeremiah 10:6 you are showing. Lead children in doing motions as you say words of the verse all together. Repeat motions and verse several times.

Song

You, or another leader, lead children in singing "God Is So Strong," adding motions and/or clapping if desired.

Prayer

Display prepared butcher paper sheet. **Let's name as many powerful items as we can think of and rate them from the least to the most powerful, 10 being the most powerful.** Children call out items. Write words between the numbers 1 and 10, writing items that are less powerful closer to the number 1 and writing items that are more powerful closer to the number 10. **God is even more powerful than all these things. Let's pray, praising God for His power that is greater than anything.** Invite children to complete the following sentence prayer: **Lord; You are . . .**

Song

Play "The Only One." Lead children in singing, adding motions and/or clapping if desired.

Lesson 10 ◊ Coloring/Puzzle Center

Jesus calms a storm.
Matthew 8:23-27; Mark 4:35-41; Luke 8:22-25

**What do you want to thank God for doing?
We can praise God for His great power and help.**

Lesson 10 ◇ Coloring/Puzzle Center

STORMY WEATHER!

The Challenge

Mark 4:35-41

Jesus is calming the storm. Can you break the code to tell the story?

CODE: B   M   X
REAL: A B C D E F G H I J K L M N O P Q R S T U V W X Y Z

Panel 1: QFBDF. CF TUJMM.

Panel 2: IF'T BTMFFQ. EPFT IF DBSF?

Panel 3: UIF TUPSN JT CBE. HP UFMM KFTVT.

Panel 4: IFMQ. XF'SF HPJOH UP EJF!

Panel 5: MFU'T HP BDSPTT UIF MBLF.

Panel 6: FWFO UIF TUPSN PCFZT IJN.

Now that you've broken the code, the story doesn't make sense. Put the story panels in the right order, so it does. Write the correct number of the panel in the bottom righthand corner.

 What is a way God shows that He is powerful in your life? Say a prayer, thanking God for showing His power.

184   © 2006 Gospel Light. Permission to photocopy granted. *Treasure Seekers*

BIBLE STORY ◆ Luke 15:11-32

God Is Merciful

LESSON eleven

Teacher's Devotional

Nearly every driver has had the experience: driving along, the reflection of justice appears in the rearview mirror—a police car! Lights flash, you check your speed, slow down and pull over, muttering that you weren't going that fast. Your mind scrambles with temptation to voice an excuse, to cry or to argue over what appears to be an inevitable speeding ticket! The officer begins by sternly announcing your error. He continues by listing the consequences that could result from such wrongdoing. But then, unexpectedly, the officer declares that no ticket will be given. You are free to go with a warning. You sink back in your seat as you drive slowly away. Your delight at receiving such mercy knows no bounds!

God's Word
"You are forgiving and good, O Lord, abounding in love to all who call to you."
Psalm 86:5

For Younger Children:
"You are forgiving and good, O Lord."

God's Word & Me
We can forgive others because God shows mercy and forgives us.

We love to receive mercy! But by its very definition, mercy is never deserved. And if we're honest, we know we deserve judgment (how many times have we been speeding and not been caught?). If we have joined God's family, God has shown us unfathomable mercy—He has forgiven our sin! However, even in our euphoria at being let off the hook, we don't always realize that because we have *received* mercy, we need to *give* it to those who might be equally euphoric to receive it from us!

Who have we chosen not to forgive? We have reasons, of course, good ones: We are trying to protect ourselves from further pain; we just can't seem to let go of our hurt feelings. But the character of God's family is to show His mercy to others. Our free and genuine forgiveness of others is one of the ways we acknowledge and express gratitude for God's mercy to us!

How has God forgiven you? Is there someone to whom you can show mercy today? For whom can you begin to pray, asking God to show you how to forgive? Expressing forgiveness can be a gut-wrenching process (much like being pulled over!). But the resulting joy from God's mercy flowing through you will be even greater than being let off the hook by the police officer!

© 2006 Gospel Light. Permission to photocopy granted. *Treasure Seekers*

Planning Page

eleven

Choose which centers you will provide and the order in which children will participate in them (see pp. 14-18 for schedule tips and pp. 24-25 for guidelines in combining older and younger children). Also plan who will lead each center (for staffing tips see pp. 19-21). Use the reproducible planning sheet (p. 238) to record your plans.

Bible Story Center

Bible Story
God Is Merciful • Luke 15:11-32

Younger Child Option
Use a toy ring to help tell the story

Older Child Option
Unscramble letters of a word that describes God and the father in today's story

Art Center

Younger Child Option
Make and move puppets as the Bible story is told

Materials
Bible, Pattern Page (p. 196), card stock, scissors, crayons, glue, large tongue depressors

Older Child Option
Create forgiveness logos and tell times kids their age can show mercy and forgiveness

Materials
Bible, large sheet of paper, marker, clear Con-Tact paper, scissors, variety of drawing utensils

Game Center

Younger Child Option
Play a game moving along a path in various ways and name family members to be kind and forgiving toward

Materials
Bible, masking tape

Older Child Option
Play a game trying to get team balloons "Home" and tell ways to show mercy and forgiveness to others

Materials
Bible, masking tape, inflated balloons in two different colors

Coloring/Puzzle Center

Younger Child Option
Review the Bible story while completing coloring page

Materials
Lesson 11 Coloring Page (p. 197) for each student, crayons

Older Child Option
Review the Bible story while completing puzzle page

Materials
Lesson 11 Puzzle Page (p. 198) for each student, pencils

Worship Center

For the Younger and Older Child
Participate in large-group activities to review Bible verse and to worship God together

Materials
Bibles, *Island Music* CD and player, song charts (pp. 247, 253), butcher paper, markers

Bonus Island Ideas

Bonus Island Ideas can be used at any time during this session: as an additional activity center, to extend the session for a longer time, or for added island excitement.

Treasure Hunt Family Fun Day

Send flyers home announcing a Treasure Hunt Family Fun Day (see p. 233 for sample flyers)! Get a copy of your church map or make one by drawing and marking buildings and obvious landmarks on the church grounds. Plan ahead of time where you will hide treasures (fun island-themed party favors) and mark Xs on the map to indicate general areas where treasures will be hidden. Make copies of the marked maps to distribute to families. Hide treasures and display signs nearby that reveal clues or that have riddles to be solved in order to find the exact location of the hidden treasure in that area. Have enough treasures hidden for each family that will be participating. (Note: Hide a special grand prize treasure ticket. For the family who found the ticket, give a prize that the whole family can enjoy together, such as a gift certificate to a favorite local family restaurant or amusement park.)

Post a note alerting parents to the use of food. Also, check registration forms for possible food allergies.

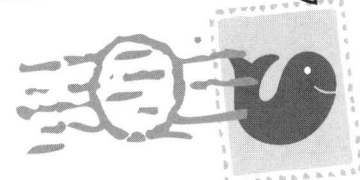

Ring Toss

Collect several inflated swim rings for children to use in playing a ring-toss game. Children form several lines and take turns tossing rings around cones set up several feet away. **For Younger Children:** Children may toss rings into wading pools placed a few feet away.

Banana Tacos

Make banana tacos kids will go loco for! Provide banana slices, vanilla pudding, taco shells, chocolate chips and sugar sprinkles. Children fill taco shells with vanilla pudding, then add banana slices and top off with chocolate chips and sugar sprinkles.

© 2006 Gospel Light. Permission to photocopy granted. *Treasure Seekers*

Bible Story Center

FOR YOUNGER CHILDREN
Luke 15:11-32

Collect

Bible.

Introduction

How many people are in your family? Volunteers answer. **Listen to hear a story Jesus told of a man who went far away from his home and family.**

Treasure Chest Option

Place a plastic toy ring in a treasure chest. (Optional: Provide a toy ring for every child in your class.) When it is mentioned in the story that the father gives the son a ring, invite a volunteer to open the treasure chest and remove ring(s) to wear.

Tell the Story

Once there was a father with two sons. They lived on a big farm. The father loved both of his sons. He took good care of them. One day the younger son said, "Father, you promised to give me money someday. I want it NOW!" So the father gave him the money.

The son wanted to live far away from his family. He packed his clothes. He walked away. The father felt sad. While the son was gone, the father waited and waited and WAITED for the son to come home.

When the son got to a new place, he spent his money until it was all gone. His nice clothes became dirty and torn. Soon he didn't have enough food to eat.

The son went to work caring for some pigs. As he worked, the son thought, *Even the men who work for my father have food to eat. The son decided, I'll go back home!*

So the son began walking home. He walked and walked and walked. Soon he saw his father's farm. When he was almost there, he saw someone running down the road toward him! It was his FATHER, running to meet him!

"Oh, Father," the son said, "I spent ALL the money you gave me. I did wrong things. I am very sorry."

The father loved his son and was glad he had come back home. The father gave him a ring, new clothes and had a party because he was so glad his son was home! How glad the son was that his father loved him and forgave him!

God's Word & Me

God is like the father in this story. God loves and forgives us, even when we do wrong. God wants us to be kind and forgive others, too. Our Bible says, "You are forgiving and good, O Lord." Pray, *Dear God, thank You for Your love and forgiveness. Help us to love and forgive others, too. Amen.*

© 2006 Gospel Light. Permission to photocopy granted. *Treasure Seekers*

Bible Story Center

FOR OLDER CHILDREN
Luke 15:11-32

LESSON eleven

Collect

Bible, bag with the following items placed inside: real or foil-wrapped chocolate coins, toy pig or garden pail, and toy ring.

Introduction

Where is the furthest place you have traveled from home? Volunteers respond. **Listen to hear about a son who left his home on a farm to go to a faraway city.** Invite children to sit in a circle as you tell the Bible story. Remove one item from the bag at a time to show children. Invite children to brainstorm and choose a sound to make for each keyword (e.g., "bling-bling" for the keyword **ring**, "cha-ching" for the keyword **money** and "oink-oink" for the keyword **pig** or **garden pail**). Return items to bag. During the story, each time you say one of the keywords, remove the appropriate item from the bag and hold up item for children to see. Children make the appropriate sound for that item.

Treasure Chest Option

Use permanent marker to write each letter of the word "Merciful" on separate foil-wrapped chocolate coins. Place coins in a lunch-sized bag and place in a treasure chest. At the end of the story, invite a volunteer to remove bag from treasure chest and unscramble lettered coins to spell a word that describes God and the father in today's Bible story.

Tell the Story

Once Jesus went to a dinner where there were many people who were proud of the way they obeyed God. Some of them said Jesus was wrong to care about people who didn't follow God's laws as well as they did. They thought God only loved people who obeyed God. So after dinner, Jesus told a story to teach what God's love is really like.

The story went something like this: A man had two sons and owned a big farm. He loved both his sons very much and planned to divide his **money** between them when they were older. But the younger son didn't want to WAIT for his share of the money. He wanted it NOW! He was eager to leave home and do what he wanted, even if it was wrong.

So the father gave the younger son his part of the **money**. The younger son said good-bye and headed to a faraway city. There, he started spending his money VERY foolishly—on wild parties and anything he thought would make him happy. He had lots of friends who enjoyed the parties he paid for!

But one day the younger son looked in his **money** bag. It was completely EMPTY! All of a sudden, people he thought were his friends didn't come to see him anymore. He was all alone. And he was in big TROUBLE. He had no money to buy food or to pay for a place to live. This was awful!

At last he found a job taking care of **pigs**! And he was so HUNGRY all of the time, he started thinking about eating the pigs' food!

One morning the younger son thought, *I am starving to death while the people who work for my father have plenty of food to eat!* The son decided to leave his job feeding **pigs** and return home. He was prepared to tell his father that he had done wrong and that he didn't deserve to be treated like his son anymore. He would then ask his father if he could be one of his father's servants.

© 2006 Gospel Light. Permission to photocopy granted. *Treasure Seekers*

Lesson eleven

Meanwhile, back on the farm, the father missed his younger son VERY much. Every day he looked down the road, just hoping his son might be coming home again. One day, he looked and someone was walking down the road! Could it be? YES! It was his son! The father was SO excited, he RAN to meet his son! He hugged him and kissed him. He couldn't hug him enough, even though his boy was smelly and dirty and ragged and didn't DESERVE to be kissed at all!

The father told his servants to bring his son new clothes and sandals and a **ring** of his own. Then the father threw a big party to celebrate! Even though the younger son had been foolish and selfish and wrong, his father still loved him and forgave him! But the older brother became angry and refused to go to the party. He didn't think the father should give his foolish brother a **ring** and a party. He didn't think his father should welcome his brother at all!

The people at the dinner who thought they were better than others were like that older brother. Jesus told this story because He wanted them to know that God is merciful and kind. God is so full of love for us, He wants to forgive us so we can be with Him always. When we do wrong, He will forgive us when we ask.

God's Word & Me

In today's Bible story, the father showed his son mercy and kindness. "Mercy" means showing more love or kindness to a person than he or she expects or deserves. God shows us His mercy and kindness, too. The greatest way God has shown His mercy is by sending His one and only Son, Jesus, to die on the cross to take the punishment for our sins. Because God has given us such mercy and kindness, He wants us to show mercy and forgive others.

- **What did the father do to show mercy and forgiveness?** (Welcomed his son when he came back home. Celebrated his son's return with a party. Forgave his son for the wrong things he had done.)

- **How do you think the son felt before he saw his father?** (Sorry for the wrong things he did. Worried that his father would not accept him.) **After he saw his father? When is a time you have felt like the son before he saw his father? What happened?**

- **What are some times kids your age can show mercy and forgive others? What are some of the different ways of showing mercy?**

- Read Psalm 86:5 aloud. **No matter what wrong things we do, God is merciful and forgiving. Since God is merciful and forgiving towards us, how can we treat others?** Pray, **Dear God, thank You for Your great mercy! Help us to show mercy and forgiveness to others. In Jesus' name, amen.**

Game Center

FOR YOUNGER CHILDREN
Luke 15:11-32

LESSON eleven

Collect
Bible, masking tape.

Prepare
Place a strip of masking tape (about 6 feet [1.8 m] long) on the floor in the middle of the playing area.

Do
1. Children gather at one end of the masking-tape strip. Invite children to take turns standing at the other end of masking-tape strip and moving along the path in various ways. Call out a different manner of moving along the path each time (tiptoeing, running, skipping, hopping, walking sideways or backward, etc.). (Optional: Challenge children to move along the line while balancing a paper cup or plate on their heads.)

2. When child reaches the end of the line, everybody cheers and says, "Welcome back!"

God's Word
"You are forgiving and good, O Lord, abounding in love to all who call to you." Psalm 86:5

For Younger Children:
"You are forgiving and good, O Lord."

God's Word & Me
We can forgive others because God shows mercy and forgives us.

Talk About
- Today's Bible story is about a father who was glad his son came home. The father forgave his son for all the wrong things he had done. The father was so happy, he ran down the road to welcome his son!

- Our Bible says, "You are forgiving and good, O Lord." "Lord" is another name for God. Sometimes we do wrong things, but God always forgives us when we ask Him. When God forgives us, it means that He forgets all about the wrong things we do.

- Sometimes people do wrong things to us. We can be kind and forgive others, even when they do wrong things. Stacy, who is in your family? You can be kind and forgive your little brother when he takes your toy. Elissa, who in your family can you be kind to? Lead children in completing the following sentence prayer by naming people in their families to whom they can be kind and forgiving: **Dear God, help me be kind to . . .**

For Older Children
Use masking tape to make a hopscotch grid of 8 to 12 squares on the floor. Print phrases of the verse on separate index cards and place cards faceup in each box on hopscotch grid. Children take turns tossing a stone or coin towards grid, turning over card in box the coin or stone lands on or near, and then saying words of verse while hopping through grid. Cards that have been turned over remain facedown throughout the game so that children are saying the entire verse from memory by the end of the game.

© 2006 Gospel Light. Permission to photocopy granted. *Treasure Seekers*

Game Center

FOR OLDER CHILDREN
Luke 15:11-32

LESSON eleven

Collect
Bible, masking tape, inflated balloons in two different colors.

Prepare
Use masking tape to make a 4- to 5-foot (1.2- to 1.5-m) circle on floor. Use tape to make block letters of the word "Home" in the middle of the circle.

Do
1. Divide class into two teams. Assign teams a balloon color. Teams sit on the floor. Toss balloons around the room.

2. At your signal, children crab walk around the room and try to get their team's balloons back "Home" by carrying balloons between their knees. After 10 to 20 seconds, call out "Stop!" Count balloons in the circle. Team with the most of their balloons in the circle wins that round. Ask a volunteer on the winning team to answer one of the questions below. Repeat game as time permits, varying the amount of time allowed for each round.

God's Word
"You are forgiving and good, O Lord, abounding in love to all who call to you."
Psalm 86:5

For Younger Children:
"You are forgiving and good, O Lord."

God's Word & Me
We can forgive others because God shows mercy and forgives us.

Talk About
- In today's Bible story, the father welcomed his younger son home with a big party, even when the son had been foolish and selfish in his actions. The father showed his son mercy and forgiveness.

- Showing mercy means showing more love or kindness to a person than he or she expects. What are some ways kids your age can show mercy and forgiveness to others? (Forgetting about the time when your brother or sister took your bike without asking. Accepting someone's apology.)

- Read Psalm 86:5. **How has God shown us His mercy and forgiveness? Who are people to whom you can show mercy and forgiveness?** Pray with children, asking God's help in showing mercy and forgiveness towards others.

For Younger Children
Children walk to balloons, pick up and carry balloons to the circle. Play music from the *Island Music* CD to cue children in starting and stopping.

© 2006 Gospel Light. Permission to photocopy granted. *Treasure Seekers*

Art Center

FOR YOUNGER CHILDREN
Luke 15:11-32

LESSON eleven

Collect

Bible, Pattern Page (p. 196), card stock, scissors, crayons, glue, large tongue depressors.

Prepare

Photocopy the Pattern Page onto card stock for each child. Make a sample set of puppets following the procedure below.

Do

1. Children cut out faces from Pattern Page, color faces and glue them onto tongue depressors. As children work, invite children to identify the different characters from the Bible story.

2. Lead children in moving the appropriate puppets as you retell the Bible story from Luke 15:11-24.

God's Word

"You are forgiving and good, O Lord, abounding in love to all who call to you."
Psalm 86:5

For Younger Children:
"You are forgiving and good, O Lord."

God's Word & Me

We can forgive others because God shows mercy and forgives us.

Talk About

- Today's Bible story tells about a kind father. The father was kind to his sons, even when one son had done something wrong. The father forgave the son.

- Our Bible says, "You are forgiving and good, O Lord." "Lord" is another name for God. God loves us and is kind to us. He wants us to show His love to others, too.

- We can be kind to people, even when they are not kind to us. When is a time someone in your family was kind by helping you? When might someone be unkind? When we forgive others, we can be kind and show God's love. We can ask for God's help to forgive others. Pray, **Dear God, help us to show Your love by being kind and forgiving others. Amen.**

For Older Children

Children lay paper bags horizontal and draw house scenes on one side of the bags and outdoor scenes of roads on the other side. Children open the bags and lay them on their sides. Children use the bags and puppets to act out the story.

© 2006 Gospel Light. Permission to photocopy granted. *Treasure Seekers*

 # Art Center

FOR OLDER CHILDREN
Luke 15:11-32

LESSON eleven

Collect

Bible, large sheet of paper, marker, clear Con-Tact paper, scissors, variety of drawing utensils (metallic or pastel paint pens, permanent markers in various colors, 3D paint, etc.).

Do

1. Brainstorm with children creative logos that might encourage people to show mercy and forgiveness to others ("Forgiving is forgetting." "Got mercy?" "4Give2Day!" etc.). Write children's ideas on paper. Children choose a logo and create a design for the logo. (Optional: Show children various sport [surf, skate or snowboard] magazines to give ideas of popular logo designs.)

2. Distribute sheets of Con-Tact paper to children. Children cut large or small shapes from Con-Tact paper and then write chosen logos and draw designs on shapes. Encourage children to give logo stickers to friends or to stick them onto objects they own to help remind them to show mercy and forgiveness.

God's Word

"You are forgiving and good, O Lord, abounding in love to all who call to you."
Psalm 86:5

For Younger Children:
"You are forgiving and good, O Lord."

God's Word & Me

We can forgive others because God shows mercy and forgives us.

Talk About

- In today's Bible story, the younger son didn't expect his father to welcome him home because of his foolish actions. But the father showed his son mercy and forgiveness by giving him new clothes, a ring and even a party to celebrate his return.

- When is a time someone has forgiven you? How did you feel? Why? When is a time you needed to forgive someone? Was it easy or difficult to forgive him or her? Why?

- Read Psalm 86:5. **Because God shows His mercy and forgiveness to us, we can show mercy and forgiveness to others. When are some times it might be difficult to show mercy and forgiveness? We can ask for God's help to be merciful and forgiving.** Invite volunteers to complete the following sentence prayer: **Dear God, help us to show mercy and forgiveness to others when . . . Amen.**

 ## For Younger Children

On 4-inch (10-cm) clear Con-Tact paper circles, children use markers to draw faces of people in their family to whom they can be kind and forgiving. Display faces by sticking onto windows in the classroom.

Worship Center
Luke 15:11-32

LESSON eleven

Collect
Bibles, *Island Music* CD and player, song charts (pp. 247, 253), butcher paper, markers.

Team Game
Invite four leaders to participate in a hog-snorting contest. Assign a number to each contestant. Contestants take turns giving their loudest, longest and best hog snorts! Children applaud and cheer for the best hog caller. (Optional: Award a blue ribbon to the best hog-calling contestant!)

God's Word
"You are forgiving and good, O Lord, abounding in love to all who call to you." Psalm 86:5

For Younger Children:
"You are forgiving and good, O Lord."

God's Word & Me
We can forgive others because God shows mercy and forgives us.

Bible Verse Game
Children stand in rows. First child in the row says the first word of Psalm 86:5 and then sits down. Next child in the row quickly says the second word of the verse and then sits down. Game continues with each child saying the next word of the verse and then sitting down. Continue until each child has had a turn. Repeat, giving new instructions each round (Say words of the verse in slow motion. Give a high-five as you say a word of the verse before sitting down. Call out words holding hands to mouth like a megaphone.). (Optional: Display words of the verse for children to refer to in the first few rounds of the game.)

Song
You, or another leader, lead children in singing "Love Like You," adding motions and/or clapping if desired.

Prayer
Write the word "Merciful" in large letters across a large sheet of butcher paper. Invite children to suggest names of people to whom they can show mercy. Using colored markers, write the names on the paper, adding them to the letters in the word "Merciful" and to the letters in the names added. Close in prayer, mentioning names of people to whom they can show mercy and forgiveness.

Song
Play "Before All Time." Lead children in singing, adding motions and/or clapping if desired. Close with the following prayer: **Thank You, God, for Your great mercy and forgiveness. We love You! Amen.**

Lesson 11 ◊ Pattern Page

Puppet Patterns

Lesson 11 ◊ Coloring/Puzzle Center

THE HAPPY WANDERER!
Luke 15:11-32

The Challenge → Find the message on the merchant's scroll. Take the first letter from each picture on the scroll and write it on the prodigal son's parchment. Draw lines to divide the letters into words.

On another sheet of paper, create your own picture code that spells out the name of someone who you might want to forgive. Pray for that person this week!

The Super Challenge → The prodigal son was a happy wanderer for a time. He spent his money foolishly. One day he spent exactly 205 shekels—no more, no less! The five things he bought were all different. Can you figure out what he got for his money?

_____ _____ _____ _____ _____

BIBLE STORY ◆ Acts 27:1-44

God Strengthens

LESSON twelve

Teacher's Devotional

In the parable of the sower (see Matthew 13), the seed (God's Word) flourished in three kinds of soil, yet in two of those, plants did not grow mature enough to bear fruit. Jesus pointed out that some people's hearts eagerly believe but then give up when times are hard. Others seek God's kingdom at first, but then growth is choked out by the daily distractions of life so that they don't mature to become fruitful. Jesus certainly knows us humans! In tough circumstances, it doesn't come naturally to us to keep on, to grow or to show the fruit of God's Spirit—those are *supernatural* responses!

God's Word

"The LORD is my strength and my shield; my heart trusts in him, and I am helped."
Psalm 28:7

For Younger Children:
"The LORD is my strength . . . and I am helped."

God's Word & Me

We can obey God and not give up, because He is our strength.

When Paul set sail for Rome, he probably didn't anticipate living through circumstances as overwhelming as weeks aboard a ship reeling out of control in a winter storm! Miserable and lost, the crew and the passengers had no reason to hope: They were dully waiting to drown. But Paul kept on trusting in this horrifying chaos. God then sent him a supernatural visitor as well as supernatural strength! Paul began handing out bread and cheerfully telling everyone that God had promised they all would survive! Relying on God's strength, Paul was free to focus on God, not the circumstances. Instead of letting fear choke him so that he was overwhelmed, he could bear the fruit of love, joy, peace and encouragement to everyone on board that ship.

Tough times come to all of us. No one is exempt! The question we need to ask before trouble comes is, *What will I choose to do in those times?* Choosing to rely on our own strength, our own solutions, we're *naturally* likely to give up or be overwhelmed. But choosing to look to God, we can ask Him for His strength and ability. Then we can let Him nourish our souls; we can take our direction from Him, and we can show the fruit of His Spirit in even the toughest circumstance!

© 2006 Gospel Light. Permission to photocopy granted. *Treasure Seekers*

Planning Page

Choose which centers you will provide and the order in which children will participate in them (see pp. 14-18 for schedule tips and pp. 24-25 for guidelines in combining older and younger children). Also plan who will lead each center (for staffing tips see pp. 19-21). Use the reproducible planning sheet (p. 238) to record your plans.

Bible Story Center

Bible Story
God Strengthens • Acts 27:1-44

Younger Child Option
Pretend to scoop out water from a boat as the story is being told

Older Child Option
Solve an object rebus to discover something God does when we obey Him

Art Center

Younger Child Option
Make a storm mural and name friends to help as a way to show love and obedience to God

Materials
Bible, large sheet of butcher paper, polyester batting or cotton balls, glue sticks, foil, thinned tempera paints in shallow containers, paintbrushes, paint smocks

Older Child Option
Make verse box reminders and ask God for His strength to obey

Materials
Bible, Pattern Page (p. 210), card stock, colored index cards, scissors, markers, decorating materials

Game Center

Younger Child Option
Play a game pretending to swim and ask for God's help to obey Him every day

Materials
Bible, *Island Music* CD and player

Older Child Option
Move through a fitness course and tell times they need God's strength to obey

Materials
Bible, four large sheets of paper, marker, tape, two jump ropes, four hula hoops, two dumbbells

Coloring/Puzzle Center

Younger Child Option
Review the Bible story while completing coloring page

Materials
Lesson 12 Coloring Page (p. 211) for each student, crayons

Older Child Option
Review the Bible story while completing puzzle page

Materials
Lesson 12 Puzzle Page (p. 212) for each student, pencils

Worship Center

For the Younger and Older Child
Participate in large-group activities to review Bible verse and to worship God together

Materials
Bibles, *Island Music* CD and player, song charts (pp. 253-254)

Bonus Island Ideas

LESSON twelve

Bonus Island Ideas can be used at any time during this session: as an additional activity center, to extend the session for a longer time, or for added island excitement.

Sandcastle

Provide one cupcake for each child in your class. Cut off tops of cupcakes and distribute bottoms to children. Children work together to build the castle base by placing cupcake bottoms in several rows of equal length, making a rectangular shape. Children may stack one additional layer of cupcakes on top of the cupcakes that make the base. Children cover top layer with vanilla frosting. For the sand castle walls, add graham crackers around the perimeter, using vanilla frosting to help graham crackers stand. Place a sugar cone at each corner of the castle. Fill cones with gumdrops or foil-wrapped chocolate kisses. After admiring their creation, children may dig in and eat!

Post a note alerting parents to the use of food. Also, check registration forms for possible food allergies.

Water Toss

Stay cool with this fun outdoor game! Fill resealable sandwich bags with water. Children form pairs and take turns tossing bag back and forth to one another. Each child takes one large step backward after each toss. Pairs may play until their bag bursts! **For Older Children:** Fill bags only ¾ full of water. Poke a small hole at the top of the bag using a push pin or needle. Distribute bags to pairs. Pairs play until the bag bursts or the water runs out!

Children gather in groups of six to eight. Groups stand in a circle. Each person reaches across the circle with his or her right hand and takes the right hand of the person standing across the circle and then takes the left hand of a different person. Without letting go of hands, groups try to untangle themselves. Invite several leaders to help groups untangle by directing children where to move.

Seaweed Tangle

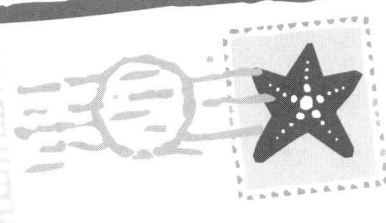

© 2006 Gospel Light. Permission to photocopy granted. *Treasure Seekers*

Bible Story Center

FOR YOUNGER CHILDREN
Acts 27:1-44

LESSON twelve

Collect

Bible.

Introduction

What do you think it would be like to be on a boat during a big storm? Volunteers tell ideas. **Listen to find out about Paul's trip on a boat.**

Tell the Story

Paul and many other people climbed into a big boat. They were going on a long trip across a big sea of water.

Treasure Chest Option

Before class, use masking tape to make a large boat outline on the floor. Place paper cups (one for each child) in a treasure chest. Invite a volunteer to remove cups from the treasure chest. Distribute cups and invite children to sit inside boat shape before you begin telling the story. Lead children in pretending to scoop out water from the "boat" as the story is being told.

While they were on the boat, the wind began to blow. It blew the boat out on the sea. The boat sailed with the wind for many days and nights.

Then the wind began to blow harder and harder. The waves splashed higher and higher. The waves rocked the boat up and down and from side to side. Splash! Splash! The waves splashed high in the air and into the boat. The waves almost knocked the boat over! Big dark clouds covered the sky. Rain came pouring down. It was very dark. No one could see the stars at night or the sun during the day. Everyone on the boat was afraid. They thought they were going to drown!

Paul cared for the people on the boat. He told them good news. "Don't be afraid," Paul said. "No one will be hurt." The people must have been amazed. Why would Paul say this?

"God sent an angel to talk to me. The angel said God will take care of all of us. He will keep us all alive. I know that God will do what He says He is going to do." Paul trusted God. He knew that God would take care of them.

Finally, one morning, the people saw land! They tried to sail the boat to shore. But the big strong waves pushed the boat into some sand just under the water. Crash! The boat began to break apart. All the people jumped into the water. Some people started swimming. Other people grabbed pieces of the broken boat to float on as they swam. They ALL found their way to the land. Every person was safe! No one had been hurt.

The people who had been on the boat must have been glad for what Paul had told them. And God had kept His promise! Everyone was thankful God had kept them safe.

God's Word & Me

During the big storm, Paul helped his friends on the boat. Helping others is one way to obey God. Our Bible says, "The Lord is my strength . . . and I am helped." God helps us to obey.

© 2006 Gospel Light. Permission to photocopy granted. *Treasure Seekers*

Bible Story Center

FOR OLDER CHILDREN
Acts 27:1-44

Collect

Bible.

Introduction

When is a time you have been caught in a big rain- or snowstorm? Volunteers answer. **Listen to hear what happened when a boat full of people got caught in a storm on the sea.** Divide the class into three or four groups and assign each group a sound effect to make (wind sounds, rain sounds, crashing wave sounds, etc.). As you tell the story, point to appropriate groups, cueing them to make sounds.

Place a piece of string, an envelope, a thermometer and a pen in a treasure chest. Invite a volunteer to remove objects from the treasure chest at the end of the story. Copy the parts of a rebus equation on separate index cards (see sketch). Children work together to assemble objects and cards to solve the rebus and discover the word "strengthen."

Treasure Chest Option

Tell the Story

Paul was on his way to Rome by ship. It wouldn't be a quick or easy trip, and as usual, Paul found himself in the middle of an adventure.

In Bible times, travel by ship was slow and unpredictable. One boat might only take people a part of the distance. The people who were traveling with Paul included a few of Paul's friends, some other prisoners, some soldiers and Julius, the Roman commander who was in charge of Paul.

At their second stop, in Myra, Paul and his traveling companions boarded a large Egyptian ship. It was sailing for Italy, across the great Mediterranean Sea. The ship's crew was busy loading many bags of grain, more cargo and all the passengers. All together there were 276 crew members and passengers on the large ship.

As soon as they left Myra, strong winds blew against the ship. After a difficult journey, the ship finally reached the harbor in Fair Havens. The sailors and passengers gratefully went ashore. But every day that they waited in Fair Havens, the risk of bad weather grew worse!

Paul knew that fierce storms came to the Mediterranean Sea at that time of year. He told Julius and the ship's captain that they should stay in Fair Havens. But the ship's captain disagreed. "Fair Havens is not a good place to stay!" he said. "We should go to a town called Phoenix and spend the winter there." Julius should have listened to Paul, but the captain seemed so sure. So they set off for Phoenix!

At first the calm sea made it seem as if the captain had been right. A gentle wind blew behind the ship and filled the sails. But then the gentle winds became great big GUSTS! The waves grew larger and tossed the ship from side to side. Then ENORMOUS waves began to crash against the wooden ship. The powerful winds caught the sails and blew the ship farther and farther off course.

Day after day angry waves pounded the ship. The sailors knew their ship would not hold together much longer, so they passed ropes under the ship to secure it and began to throw the cargo overboard. They hoped that

© 2006 Gospel Light. Permission to photocopy granted. *Treasure Seekers*

Lesson twelve

without the cargo, the boat wouldn't sink. But the ship was still blown wildly around. They had no idea where they were now! The terrible storm raged on as the passengers huddled together in terror.

"We're all going to die!" cried the sailors in despair. "Nothing can save us!"

In the middle of all this panic and hopelessness, Paul stood up. "Cheer up," Paul said. "I have good news!" Paul told everyone that an angel from God had promised that the ship would be destroyed but that everyone would live! *Amazing,* the sailors may have thought. *A promise from God that we won't die?!*

At midnight on the fourteenth day of the storm, the sailors discovered that they were sailing into shallow water. They were nearing land! The captain ordered his sailors to throw out the anchors. "That should slow us down," he said. "At daybreak we'll see what lies ahead!"

Paul brought bread to his shipmates and encouraged them to eat. They hadn't eaten during the last 14 days! Soon they were all eating and feeling hopeful. "Maybe we will make it after all!" they may have said to each other.

When it was fully light, the passengers and sailors on board the ship looked out across the sea toward the land up ahead. There was a sandy beach! They must have all cheered! The captain ordered the sailors to cut the anchors loose and head for shore. The sailors followed the captain's order, and it seemed as though the ship was going to land safely on the beach. But then the bow of the ship hit a sandbar and it stuck. As the huge waves crashed against it, the stranded ship began to break apart.

"We'd better kill all the prisoners," said the soldiers. "Otherwise they'll swim to shore and escape." But Julius wanted Paul to stay alive. He told the soldiers not to kill anyone and ordered those who could swim to jump overboard first to get to land.

One by one, the ship's passengers jumped into the cold, wild waves, floating on pieces of the ship or swimming toward the shore of the island of Malta. The ship was in pieces. The cargo had sunk. But not one person had been lost at sea, just as God had promised!

God's Word & Me

It would have been easy for Paul to be afraid and worried. But because Paul depended on God's strength, Paul was able to obey God by helping and encouraging his friends. Sometimes it might seem to us that obeying God and doing what's right is just too hard to do. But when we depend on God, He will give us the strength to do anything He asks us to do.

- **In today's Bible story, how did God strengthen Paul?** (God gave him a promise. He gave him hope and courage.)

- **Does God give kids your age strength to obey Him? Why or why not? When are some times kids your age need God's strength to obey? Why do you need strength to do that?**

- Read Psalm 28:7. **We can remember this verse when we need strength to obey.** Pray briefly, **Dear God, thank You for Your strength and help to do all that You ask us to do. In Jesus' name, amen.**

© 2006 Gospel Light. Permission to photocopy granted. *Treasure Seekers*

Game Center

FOR YOUNGER CHILDREN
Acts 27:1-44

LESSON twelve

Collect
Bible, *Island Music* CD and player.

Do
1. Invite children to stand along the wall at one end of the room. **We're going to pretend to go swimming today!**

2. **Let's swim to the other side of the room.** Play "God Is So Strong." Lead children in making swimming motions while walking across the room (back stroke, pretending to dive and jump like a dolphin, wiggling like a fish, etc.).

3. Continue, leading children in moving from one end of the room to the other doing various swim strokes or motions. Stop music as a cue to freeze before changing motions.

God's Word
"The LORD is my strength and my shield; my heart trusts in him, and I am helped."
Psalm 28:7

For Younger Children:
"The LORD is my strength . . . and I am helped."

God's Word & Me
We can obey God and not give up, because He is our strength.

Talk About

- In today's Bible story, God helped Paul and his friends swim to shore in a big storm. Paul knew that God would take care of him and his friends.

- Paul said kind words to his friends. Saying kind words is one way to obey God. Kaley, what are some kind words you could say to your family? (I'll help you. Thank you.) **God will help us obey Him.**

- Our Bible says, "The Lord is my strength . . . and I am helped." **Let's ask God for His help to obey Him every day.** Pray with children.

 For Older Children

Children participate in a "swim" relay. Divide class into four teams. Make swim lanes by placing long strips of masking tape on the floor that reach from one end of the room to the other. Teams line up by swim lanes. Place sets of swim equipment (goggles, swim fins, life jackets, etc.) near each team. Team members take turns putting on items, "swimming" to other end of lane and back, and then taking off items.

© 2006 Gospel Light. Permission to photocopy granted. *Treasure Seekers*

Game Center

FOR OLDER CHILDREN
Acts 27:1-44

LESSON twelve

Collect
Bible, four large sheets of paper, marker, tape, two jump ropes, four hula hoops, two dumbbells.

Prepare
On one sheet of paper, print "The Lord is my strength" and "Jump rope 5 times." On second sheet of paper, print "and my shield;" and "5 push-ups." On third sheet of paper, print "my heart trusts in him," and "Hop through hula hoops." On the fourth sheet of paper, print "and I am helped," and "5 arm curls." In each corner of the play area, display one of the four papers. Place sports equipment next to the appropriate papers.

God's Word
"The LORD is my strength and my shield; my heart trusts in him, and I am helped." Psalm 28:7

For Younger Children:
"The LORD is my strength . . . and I am helped."

God's Word & Me
We can obey God and not give up, because He is our strength.

Do
1. Divide class into pairs. Pairs line up along one wall of room. Demonstrate how to complete fitness course: Run to one station, do the exercise printed on the sign while saying verse phrase and then run to the next station. Continue to complete all exercises.

2. At your signal, first pair begins course. Once they move to next station the following pair may begin course. Ask the questions below when all pairs have completed the course.

Talk About
- What kind of strength did you need in order to do the fitness course? (Physical strength. Arm and leg strength.) **In today's Bible story, Paul needed a different kind of strength—God's strength. Paul's actions showed that he depended on God's strength, because he didn't give up and he trusted in God's promises.**

- When are some times we need God's strength to do what is right? (When we need to forgive someone. Obeying our parents when we want to do something our own way. Standing up for a friend.)

- Read Psalm 28:7. **When are some times we might need to remember this verse?** (When we face a task that is hard to do. When we can't do something on our own. When we face difficult times.) Pray briefly, **Dear God, please give us the strength to obey and follow You. We love You. Amen.**

For Younger Children
Give children simpler fitness tasks to do (jumping jacks instead of jumping rope, running in place instead of doing push-ups, etc.) and do each task with children while saying words of the verse.

Art Center

FOR YOUNGER CHILDREN
Acts 27:1-44

Collect

Bible, large sheet of butcher paper, polyester batting or cotton balls, glue sticks, foil, thinned tempera paints in shallow containers, paintbrushes, paint smocks.

Do

1. Children work together to create a storm mural. Help children create by asking, **What could we use to make clouds? Lightning?** Children may pull apart batting or cotton balls and glue them to the paper to make clouds. To make lightning, children may crumple pieces of foil into zig-zag shapes and glue them to paper. Children may paint raindrops on the paper.

2. Display completed mural on bulletin board or hallway wall. You may also use the mural as a backdrop when telling the Bible story for the Bible Story Center.

God's Word

"The LORD is my strength and my shield; my heart trusts in him, and I am helped." Psalm 28:7

For Younger Children:
"The LORD is my strength . . . and I am helped."

God's Word & Me

We can obey God and not give up, because He is our strength.

Talk About

- In today's Bible story, a strong wind blew Paul's boat out to sea. The boat was in danger of sinking. It then crashed into sand and broke apart. Paul helped his friends on the boat by saying kind words. He helped his friends to know that God would help them.

- Helping our friends is a way to show that we love and obey God. Kenneth, Sara needs to use the glue. How can you help her? Thank you for handing her the glue! Who are some other friends you can help?

- Our Bible says "The Lord is my strength . . . and I am helped." We can ask God to help us obey Him every day. Pray, **Dear God, we love You. Please help us to obey You. Amen.**

For Older Children

Invite children to choose parts of the mural to work on. Children use paint brushes or sponges to paint their hands and fingertips and make prints on paper for water and waves, clouds, raindrops, etc.

© 2006 Gospel Light. Permission to photocopy granted. *Treasure Seekers*

# Art Center

FOR OLDER CHILDREN
Acts 27:1-44

LESSON
twelve

Collect
Bible, Pattern Page (p. 210), card stock, colored index cards, scissors, markers, decorating materials (glitter glue, metallic pens, sequins, stamps, etc.).

Prepare
Copy Pattern Page onto card stock, making one copy for each child in your class. Cut index cards to fit center square on pattern.

Do
1. Distribute a copy of the Pattern Page to each child. Child cuts out shape, folds along indicated lines and hooks panels together in numerical order to assemble wave box.

2. Children then unfold and decorate the outside of the boxes with given materials. Children write phrases from today's verse and other verses from the Bible that tell about God's strength on index card pieces and place in boxes and close. (Lead children in reading the following verses in the Bible about God's strength: Psalm 46:1; 2 Corinthians 12:9; Ephesians 3:16; Philippians 4:13.) Encourage children to refer to verse cards when they need strength to obey.

God's Word
"The LORD is my strength and my shield; my heart trusts in him, and I am helped."
Psalm 28:7

For Younger Children:
"The LORD is my strength . . . and I am helped."

God's Word & Me
We can obey God and not give up, because He is our strength.

Talk About
- In today's Bible story, God strengthened Paul by giving him a promise. God's promise strengthened Paul by giving him hope and encouraging him to obey.

- When are some times we need God's strength to obey Him at home? At a friend's house? (When we need to be patient with a younger brother or sister. When we need to forgive someone. When we need to say no to something we know we shouldn't try or do.)

- Read Psalm 28:7. **We need God's strength to obey!** Invite volunteers to complete the following sentence prayer: **Dear God, I need Your strength when . . .**

 ## For Younger Children
Cut a box for each child in the class. Each child decorates his or her box. Child then draws a picture of him- or herself on a sheet of paper and folds picture to place in box. Talk with children about ways to obey God as children draw. Assist children in assembling boxes and folding pictures to place inside boxes.

© 2006 Gospel Light. Permission to photocopy granted. *Treasure Seekers*

Worship Center
Acts 27:1-44

LESSON twelve

Collect
Bibles, *Island Music* CD and player, song charts (pp. 253-254).

Team Game
Divide group into four or six teams. Teams choose a team leader to participate in the following game. Players compete in a balancing contest with increasing challenges after every round. Round 1: Players stand like flamingoes, balancing on one leg for as long as they can without falling over. Round 2: Players remain in the flamingo position and jump up and down on one leg. Round 3: Players hop on one foot to move from one end of the room and back. Children cheer for their team leaders.

God's Word
"The LORD is my strength and my shield; my heart trusts in him, and I am helped."
Psalm 28:7
For Younger Children:
"The LORD is my strength . . . and I am helped."

God's Word & Me
We can obey God and not give up, because He is our strength.

Bible Verse Game
Invite children to sit in a large circle. Designate a child to start a stadium "wave," standing and slowly raising arms above his or her head while everyone says the first word of Psalm 28:7. Child to his or her right continues the wave as the next word of the verse is said, and so on. The pace can be slow at first and then quicken after a few rounds. Occasionally call out "Shipwreck!" Children run to find a new place to sit in the circle and begin the verse again.

Song
You, or another leader, lead children in singing "God Is So Strong," adding motions and/or clapping if desired.

Prayer
We can ask for God's strength when we pray to Him. Invite children to tell prayer requests about times they need help to obey God. Pray, mentioning children's requests. (Optional: Divide class into groups of four to six children. Invite one leader to join each group. Each leader shares with his or her group a prayer request about needing God's strength. Leaders then invite volunteers from their group to share requests and then close in prayer.)

Song
Play "Love Like You." Lead children in singing, adding motions and/or clapping if desired. Close with the following prayer: **Thank You, God, for Your great strength. We love You! In Jesus' name, amen.**

Lesson 12 ⋄ Pattern Page

Paul's ship wrecks in a storm.
Acts 27:1-44

Lesson 12 ◆ Coloring/Puzzle Center

**Paul helped his friends on a boat during a big storm.
Who is a friend you can help?**

Paul's Letters

Lesson 12 ◆ Coloring/Puzzle Center

The apostle Paul wrote letters to Christians who lived in a variety of cities. Read each clue and then find the square on the map where the letter and number meet. Write the name of the city or region in that square. Draw a line from each city or region to the name of Paul's letter.

1. The region of Galatia (B9, B10).
2. The church in Rome (A1).
3. The Christians in Ephesus (C6).
4. The city of Philippi (B5).
5. Paul wrote two letters to the church in Thessalonica (B4).
6. Colossae is in D7.
7. The city of Corinth (C4).

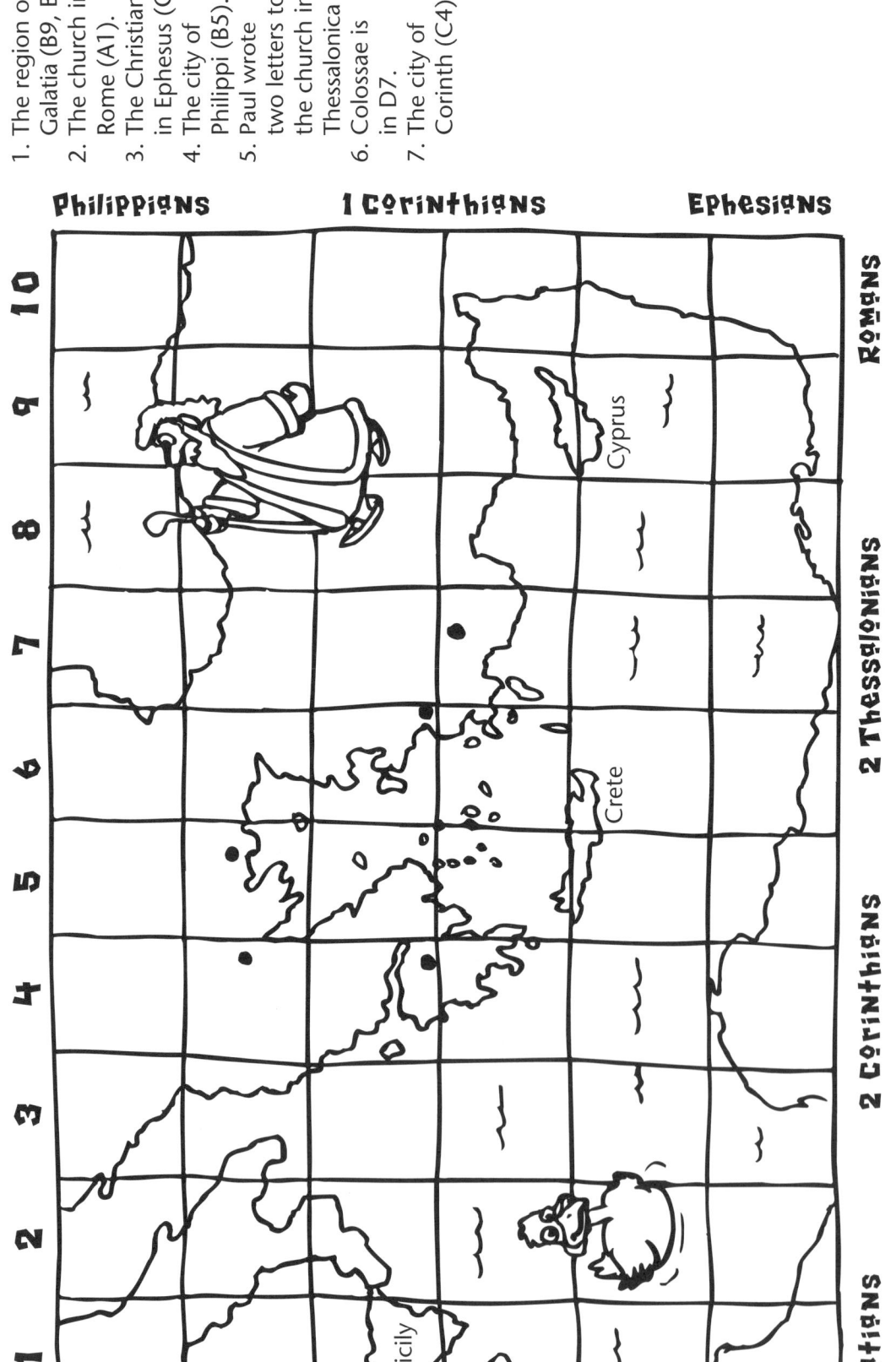

Paul depended on God's strength in his travels, even in a shipwreck on his way to Rome. When do you need God's strength?

BIBLE STORY ◆ 1 Kings 18:16-39

God Is the One True God

LESSON thirteen

Teacher's Devotional

In an outwardly polytheistic culture, life revolves around trying to please many gods. But when pleasing one god conflicts with pleasing another, which god should one try to please first? In our more subtly polytheistic culture, the gods might be named wealth, power, fame, and so on, but the effect is the same: In trying to please many little gods, we collapse into fear. There is simply no way to please everybody! Trying to please false gods creates only conflict and fear!

Scripture reveals only one true God, who not only made us but also declares that He is love. He even tells us He loves us so much that there is nothing we can do to make Him love us more. What a relief!

God's Word

"The LORD is the true God; he is the living God, the eternal King."
Jeremiah 10:10

For Younger Children:
"The LORD is the true God."

God's Word & Me

We can worship God because He is the one true God who loves us.

Elijah's organized contest had confident opponents: priests of Baal. They were sure they could convince Baal to prove he was the true god; after all, they knew all the prayers and rituals. They were even willing to cut themselves to please Baal! But their daylong prayer-and-wounding ritual ended without Baal's response. Then, in a "drum roll" moment, Elijah called everyone to watch as he repaired God's altar, dug a trench, poured gallons of water over the sacrifice and prayed, "O Lord, answer me so these people will know that you, O Lord, are God" (1 Kings 18:37). The fire that fell from God burned up the sacrifice—and everything around it! The people fell on their faces, shouting, "The Lord—he is God!" (v. 39).

So whatever little god we may be tempted to worship (however casual the worship may seem), remember that only the one true God loves us. Instead of bowing to little gods who will bring us to fear, run to the arms of the one true God, our loving Father. Rest there in the true love of the one true God!

Planning Page

LESSON thirteen

Choose which centers you will provide and the order in which children will participate in them (see pp. 14-18 for schedule tips and pp. 24-25 for guidelines in combining older and younger children). Also plan who will lead each center (for staffing tips see pp. 19-21). Use the reproducible planning sheet (p. 238) to record your plans.

Bible Story Center

Bible Story
God Is the One True God • 1 Kings 18:16-39

Younger Child Option
Show a picture of a mountain as the story is told

Older Child Option
Solve a math equation that has only ONE answer and discuss how God is the ONE true God

Art Center

Younger Child Option
Decorate minibooks and name people God loves

Materials
Bible, Pattern Page (p. 224), colored paper, scissors, crayons or markers

Older Child Option
Assemble and decorate unique picture frames and tell reasons to worship God

Materials
Bible, poster board, ruler, scissors, ribbon, stapler, glue, decorating materials

Game Center

Younger Child Option
Show various facial expressions and tell ways they can show they are glad the one true God loves them

Materials
Bible, two mirrors

Older Child Option
Play a game of Frisbee-baseball and tell ways God shows that He is the one true God

Materials
Bible, four pieces of cardboard or carpet, Frisbee or paper plate

Coloring/Puzzle Center

Younger Child Option
Review the Bible story while completing coloring page

Materials
Lesson 13 Coloring Page (p. 225) for each student, crayons

Older Child Option
Review the Bible story while completing puzzle page

Materials
Lesson 13 Puzzle Page (p. 226) for each student, pencils

Worship Center

For the Younger and Older Child
Participate in large-group activities to review Bible verse and to worship God together

Materials
Bibles, *Island Music* CD and player, song charts (pp. 250, 254), masking tape, jump rope, large sheet of paper, marker

Bonus Island Ideas

LESSON thirteen

Bonus Island Ideas can be used at any time during this session: as an additional activity center, to extend the session for a longer time, or for added island excitement.

Family Photo Day

Create lasting memories at Family Photo Day! Set a date and send flyers home ahead of time, inviting families to bring their cameras and smiles! Set up fun photo backdrops in several areas outdoors or in a large gathering area indoors. Use the following suggestions to create scenic backdrops: (1) Use a blue bedsheet for an underwater scene. Attach colorful paper fish and shells to sheet. Attach sheets of sand-colored paper at the bottom of the sheet to look like the ocean floor. Use glitter glue to make water bubbles. (2) Paint large surfing waves on butcher paper or a canvas painting tarp. Add fun summer props to each photo backdrop: treasure chest, surfboards, fishnets, snorkeling or scuba diving equipment, etc. For patterns and additional backdrop ideas, refer to the decorating ideas on pages 29-32, 234-237.

Post a note alerting parents to the use of food. Also, check registration forms for possible food allergies.

Wealth of Health

Before class, slice up various vegetables and fruits into small circular shapes to resemble coins (carrots, zucchini, cucumbers, bananas, etc.). Provide cheese and circle-shaped crackers. On a large platter, create a treasure chest using large rectangular matzo crackers. Use cream cheese to hold the sides and top of the treasure chest together. Fill the treasure chest with vegetable dip. Then arrange vegetable and fruit coins around the treasure chest, filling the platter. Kids will enjoy this snack (without even knowing how healthy it is)!

Sand Games

Plan a beach day! Play some fun games in the sand: (1) Play Tic-Tac-Toe. Children draw large Tic-Tac-Toe grids in sand and use pebbles and shells as game markers; (2) Have a sandcastle building contest; (3) Go on a nature hunt! Children gather in groups. Distribute one plastic jar to each group. Groups hunt for nature items (shells, rocks, pieces of driftwood, etc.) in and around the sand and place items in jars.

Bible Story Center

FOR YOUNGER CHILDREN
1 Kings 18:16-39

Collect

Bible.

Introduction

What do you think you would see if you were on the top of a mountain? Volunteers answer. **Listen to find out about what some people saw when they were on top of a mountain.**

> Place a picture of a mountain in a treasure chest. Invite a volunteer to show the picture at the beginning of the story. Show the picture when the mountain is mentioned in the Bible story.
>
> **Treasure Chest Option**

Tell the Story

A long time ago in Bible times, there was a king named Ahab who stopped worshiping the one true God. King Ahab and the Israelites began to love other things more than they loved the one true God. They worshiped a false god named Baal, who wasn't even real.

Because King Ahab and the Israelites prayed to this false god, there was no rain for a very long time. Because there was no rain, the people and animals were very hungry and thirsty.

One day, King Ahab went to look for some water and food for his animals. He met a man named Elijah who loved God very much.

Elijah wanted King Ahab and the people to see that God is the one true God. Elijah decided to have a contest at the top of a mountain. Everybody wanted to see the contest, so they walked up and up the mountain until they reached the top.

First, the people who loved Baal, the false god, prayed to Baal to send fire. But Baal was not the one true God. So nothing happened! There was no fire. Nothing! Baal couldn't answer their prayers. Baal couldn't do ANYTHING!

Then it was Elijah's turn. Elijah prayed to God, and God sent fire from heaven! Now the people knew who the real God is. The real God answers prayers! All the people worshiped God.

It finally began to rain! God sent the rain because the people once again worshiped the one true God.

God's Word & Me

Elijah loved God very much and wanted everyone to know and love the one true God, too. Our Bible says, "The Lord is the true God." One way we know that God is the one true God is by His love! God loves each one of us! I'm glad that the one true God loves us. Lead children in saying the following prayer: **Thank You, God, for loving me! Amen.**

© 2006 Gospel Light. Permission to photocopy granted. *Treasure Seekers*

Bible Story Center

FOR OLDER CHILDREN
1 Kings 18:16-39

Collect

Bible, giant foam finger used at sporting events.

Introduction

Show the giant foam finger. **Fans of some sports teams like to hold up these giant foam fingers to show that their team is number one. We're going to use it in our Bible story today to show that God is number one!** During the story, hold up the foam finger each time you say the keyphrase: **one true God**, cueing children to cheer, "God is the one true God!"

Treasure Chest Option

Write the following instructions on separate index cards and place cards in chest: "(1) Multiply the number of people in your family by 10"; "(2) Add the total number of shoes you own"; "(3) Subtract the the number of years you have been in school"; "(4) Divide the last number by itself." Place cards in a treasure chest. At the end of the story, volunteer removes cards from chest and reads each instruction. Write the equation on a large sheet of paper. Tell children that there is only ONE answer to the equation. Discuss how God is the ONE true God.

Tell the Story

God's people were in serious trouble! Because their king, King Ahab, had led them to worship false gods, called idols, there had been no rain for THREE years! The plants had died. The streams had dried up. Everything was DRY, just like God said it would be! King Ahab was DESPERATE to find some water! He called his servant Obadiah and instructed him to search the land in one direction for water as Ahab searched in another direction.

As Obadiah walked along, he saw Elijah, the prophet who had told King Ahab this would happen. Elijah told Obadiah to tell King Ahab that he wanted to see him.

Elijah had a message to give to Ahab from the living God: "We're going to have a contest. Gather all the prophets of Baal and meet me on Mount Carmel. This contest will prove who the **one true God** is!"

A large crowd gathered at Mount Carmel. Elijah, King Ahab, 450 prophets of Baal and many other people were there. Before starting the contest, Elijah said to the people, "How long will it take you to decide? If the Lord is God, follow him; but if Baal is God, follow him."

"Now," Elijah continued, "here are the rules of the contest. Give a young bull to the prophets of Baal and give a young bull to me. Each of us will prepare a sacrifice. But we won't burn the offering. You prophets of Baal can call on your god, and I will call on the living God. The god who answers prayers by sending fire to burn up the sacrifice is the **one true God**!"

"Great!" shouted the people. "Let's begin!"

The prophets of Baal went first. They got their sacrifice all ready and began to call to Baal. They waited and listened. But there was no answer.

They called again. Still no answer! They called louder and louder. They shouted and danced from morning until noon! Still NO voice and NO fire came from Baal.

© 2006 Gospel Light. Permission to photocopy granted. *Treasure Seekers*

Lesson thirteen

Elijah called to the prophets of Baal, "Maybe your god has gone to sleep and he has to be awakened. Or then again, maybe you aren't calling loud enough. Maybe he went for a walk and can't hear you!"

But the prophets of Baal kept right on shouting and dancing until late afternoon. Finally Elijah said, "You might as well give up. You've prayed all day without any answer. Now I will talk to the **one true God**."

Elijah got his sacrifice ready. He repaired the altar with 12 stones and dug a ditch around it. Then he had some men fill four large jars with water and pour it on the offering and on the wood. He told them to do it a second and then a third time.

Water was very valuable because it hadn't rained for THREE YEARS! But Elijah wanted the wood to be soaking wet. He wanted the people to know that only the **one true God** could start a fire on that wet wood!

Elijah confidently stepped forward and said a very simple prayer. "Oh Lord," he prayed, "let these people know that I am telling the truth and that You are God. Let them know that I have done all of these things at Your command. Please bring these people back to You."

Then the fire of the Lord came down and burned up everything on the altar, including all the water the men had poured on the altar. When the people saw what happened, they fell on their faces and worshiped the Lord. "The Lord—He is God!" they exclaimed. "The Lord—He is God!"

Elijah told King Ahab, "Go home now and get ready for rain! God will send it soon." Elijah prayed as he eagerly waited for God to do as He promised. Soon a tiny cloud got bigger and bigger until the whole sky was dark. Suddenly thunder boomed! The wind started to blow! Then the heavy rain came! The rain came because the people had finally acknowledged the **one true God**.

God's Word & Me

Elijah dared to challenge the prophets of Baal to a contest because he believed that God would show Himself as the one true God. Just like Elijah, our actions and attitudes show what we believe about God. When we obey God, we show that we believe that what God tells us to do is important. When we pray to God, we show that we believe that God answers prayer. When we worship God, we show that we believe that God does good things in our lives for which we want to thank and praise Him. Talk with interested students about showing their belief in God by becoming members of His family (see "Leading a Child to Christ" on p. 12).

- **In the story, how is God different from Baal?** (God has power and answers prayer. Baal does not. God is the one true God.)

- **How did Elijah show that he believed in the one true God?** (He worshiped God.)

- **What are some ways God shows He is the one true God in our lives?** (God sent His one and only Son to die on the cross to forgive our sins. God answers our prayers. We experience His love and help.)

- Read Jeremiah 10:10. **This verse tells us the reason we worship God. What are some other reasons we worship God?** Pray, **Dear God, we worship You because You are the one true God who loves us.**

© 2006 Gospel Light. Permission to photocopy granted. *Treasure Seekers*

Game Center

FOR YOUNGER CHILDREN
1 Kings 18:16-39

LESSON thirteen

Collect
Bible, two mirrors.

Prepare
Place mirrors at one end of the classroom.

Do
1. Divide class into two groups. Groups line up and stand opposite mirrors on the other side of the room. At your signal, first child in each line walks to the mirror. Ask, **How does your face look when you are glad?** Children show glad faces in the mirrors.

2. Continue with each child in line taking turns to walk to mirrors and make various facial expressions (sad faces, sleepy faces, surprised faces, etc.).

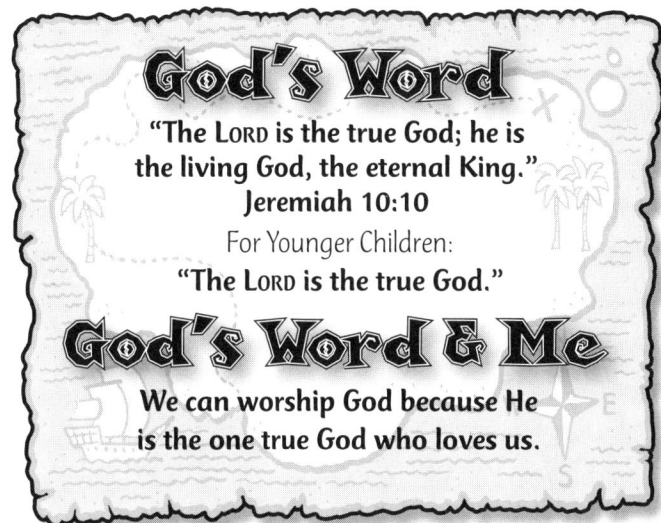

God's Word
"The LORD is the true God; he is the living God, the eternal King."
Jeremiah 10:10
For Younger Children:
"The LORD is the true God."

God's Word & Me
We can worship God because He is the one true God who loves us.

Talk About

- Steven, when did you feel glad today? Kara, when do you feel sad? God loves us when we're happy or sad. God always loves us!

- Our Bible tells us a reason to be glad. The Bible says, "The Lord is the true God." And the one true God loves each and every one of us! Jeremy, God loves you! Repeat, saying different children's names.

- What is a way we can show we are glad for God's love? We can show how glad we are that God loves us by thanking Him. Pray briefly, **Thank You, God, for Your love. Amen.**

For Older Children

Bring two instant or digital cameras to class. Invite two volunteers to be photographers. Photographers sit on chairs placed at one end of the room. Children play game as described above, taking turns walking to chairs and making various facial expressions that you name. Photographers take pictures of children making the various faces instead of children making faces in mirrors. Display pictures on a large sheet of butcher paper labeled "God loves me even when I'm . . ." Display paper in the classroom or church hallway.

© 2006 Gospel Light. Permission to photocopy granted. *Treasure Seekers*

Game Center

FOR OLDER CHILDREN
1 Kings 18:16-39

Collect

Bible, four pieces of cardboard or carpet, Frisbee or paper plate.

Prepare

Lay pieces of cardboard or carpet in a baseball-diamond shape on the ground in a large open area.

Do

1. Divide class into two teams. Children play Frisbee-baseball according to regular baseball rules. Children may only throw Frisbee or paper plate under one leg, whether at bat, playing the bases or in the outfield. If time is limited, give each team only three times "at bat" before switching sides.

2. When a team scores a run, volunteer from that team answers one of the questions below about worshiping the one true God.

Talk About

- In today's Bible story, God showed that He is the one true God by answering Elijah's prayer and showing His power by sending fire from heaven.

- What are some of the ways God shows He is the one true God? What are some ways we can show that we believe in the one true God? (Sing songs of praise to God. Pray to God. Thank God for all the good things He has done and continues to do for us. Obey Him.)

- Read Jeremiah 10:10. **What reasons does Jeremiah 10:10 give for worshiping God?** (God is the one true God. God is the living God.) **Let's worship God by thanking Him for who He is and for all the great things He has done and continues to do in our lives!** Invite volunteers to complete the following sentence: Thank You, God, for . . .

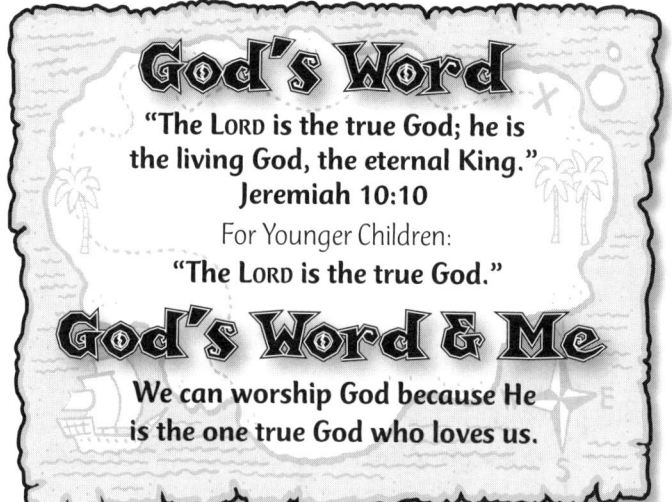

God's Word

"The LORD is the true God; he is the living God, the eternal King."
Jeremiah 10:10

For Younger Children:
"The LORD is the true God."

God's Word & Me

We can worship God because He is the one true God who loves us.

For Younger Children

Children take turns tossing Frisbee or paper plate towards numbered squares that are placed a few feet away. Depending on the numbered square the Frisbee or paper plate lands on or near, lead children in saying names of one, two or three children in the class whom God loves!

Art Center

FOR YOUNGER CHILDREN
1 Kings 18:16-39

Collect

Bible, Pattern Page (p. 224), crayons or markers.

Prepare

Photocopy the Pattern Page for each child in your class. Fold pages as indicated to make minibooks.

Do

Distribute prepared minibooks to children. Lead children in reading each page of the book. Children color and decorate minibooks.

God's Word

"The LORD is the true God; he is the living God, the eternal King."
Jeremiah 10:10

For Younger Children:
"The LORD is the true God."

God's Word & Me

We can worship God because He is the one true God who loves us.

Talk About

- In today's Bible story, a man named Elijah loved God very much! He wanted others to love God, too.

- Stacy, who is someone you love? God loves you and your (grandma), Stacy! Marcus, who in your family loves you? God loves you, too!

- The books that we made today say that God loves us even MORE than He loves the bananas in a banana tree! What else does God love us MORE than? (Note: Lead children in pointing out pictures shown in their minibooks.)

- Our Bible says, "The Lord is the true God." I'm glad that the one true God loves each one of us. Let's point to the people God loves. God loves (children point to a friend in the class). Repeat several times, encouraging children to point to a different friend each time. Then lead children in prayer, thanking God for His love.

 For Older Children

Children create their own minibooks about God's great love following the "More than . . ." rhyming pattern in the book. Give books to a younger class in the church along with uncolored copies of the minibook from the Pattern Page.

Art Center

FOR OLDER CHILDREN
1 Kings 18:16-39

Collect

Bible, poster board, ruler, scissors, ribbon, stapler, glue, decorating materials (wrapping paper, newspaper, magazine, markers, fabric scraps, colored yarn or string, rick-rack, sequins, feathers, straws, buttons, doilies, pom poms, glitter, etc.).

Prepare

Cut two 6-inch (15-cm) squares from poster board for each child. Cut a 3-inch (7.5-cm) square opening from the center of half the squares to make frames. Cut one 12-inch (30.5-cm) length of ribbon for each child.

Do

1. Give each child one cut and one uncut poster-board square. Children staple the ends of ribbons onto the corners of uncut poster-board pieces. Children spread glue along sides and bottom of frame pieces. With the staples and ribbon ends facing in, children place uncut poster-board piece on top of frame.

2. Using the given materials, children decorate frames. Invite children to insert a picture of themselves in the frame when they get home. (Optional: Use an instant camera to take a picture of each child.)

God's Word

"The LORD is the true God; he is the living God, the eternal King."
Jeremiah 10:10

For Younger Children:
"The LORD is the true God."

God's Word & Me

We can worship God because He is the one true God who loves us.

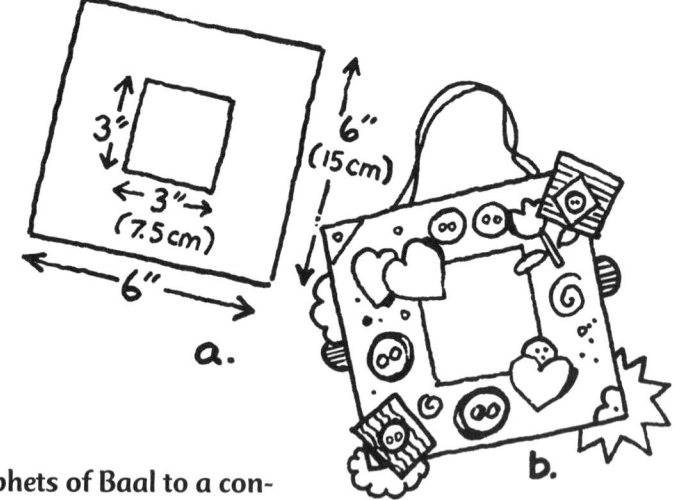

Talk About

- In today's Bible story, Elijah challenged the prophets of Baal to a contest to show that God is the one true God. Elijah did this because He believed that God is the one true God and wanted the people to worship God only.

- Read Jeremiah 10:10. **What are some ways we know that God is the one true God?** (We experience His love and forgiveness. He keeps His promises.) **Why does God want us to worship Him?** (He is the one true God. He loves us.)

- How does it feel to know that the one true God loves you? You may place your photo in the picture frame you made today to remind you that God loves you. Pray, Dear God, thank You for knowing and loving us. Help us to show our love for You as we come to know You more each day. Amen.

For Younger Children

Before class, assemble frames for each child in your class. During class, children decorate frames.

Worship Center

1 Kings 18:16-39

LESSON thirteen

Collect

Bibles, *Island Music* CD and player, song charts (pp. 250, 254), masking tape, jump rope, large sheet of paper, marker.

Prepare

Place a strip of masking tape on the floor.

Team Game

Divide group into two teams. Invite two volunteers from each team to participate in a Double Trouble Tug-of-War contest. Two volunteers stand and hold opposite ends of the jump rope. Player who pulls the opposing player over the masking-tape line wins the round. Players participate in several rounds of increasing challenge (Round 1: Stand backwards and pull the rope; Round 2: Hold rope with one hand; Round 3: Hold rope with one hand and stand on one foot; etc.). Use different volunteers for each round. Player who pulls the opposing player over the masking-tape line wins the round. Keep a tally of points. (Optional: For each round of increasing challenge, double the number of points you give to the winning player.)

God's Word

"The LORD is the true God; he is the living God, the eternal King."
Jeremiah 10:10

For Younger Children:
"The LORD is the true God."

God's Word & Me

We can worship God because He is the one true God who loves us.

Bible Verse Game

Divide class into four groups and number each group. Instruct Group 1 to say "The Lord is" when you hold up your right arm. Instruct Group 2 to say "the true God" when you hold up your left arm. Instruct Group 3 to say "he is the living God" when you hold up your right leg. Finally, instruct Group 4 to say "the eternal king" when you hold up your left leg. Each time you hold up an arm or leg, the appropriate group says their phrase of the verse. Practice several times so that each group remembers when it's their turn. Quicken the pace after several rounds.

Song

You, or another leader, lead children in singing "The Only One," adding motions and/or clapping if desired.

Prayer

One way we can worship God is by telling Him why we think He is great. What are some things God has done that we are thankful for? (Forgives our sins. Always loves us. Created the world. Sent Jesus to take the punishment for our sins.) List students' ideas on paper. Invite volunteers to complete the following sentence: **God, I worship You because You . . .** Children may refer to ideas listed on paper.

Song

Play "God Is So Strong." Lead children in singing, adding motions and/or clapping if desired.

© 2006 Gospel Light. Permission to photocopy granted. *Treasure Seekers*

Lesson 13 ◆ Pattern Page

More than
the fish in
the big
blue
sea...

(1)

I KNOW
GOD
LOVES
ME!

This book was colored by:
_____

(4)

Fold first.

Fold second.

More than finding a treasure chest's key...

(3)

More than bananas in a banana tree...

(2)

Lesson 13 ◆ Coloring/Puzzle Center

God is the one true God.
1 Kings 18:16-39

What can we do to show love for God?
We can worship the one true God who loves us.

© 2006 Gospel Light. Permission to photocopy granted. *Treasure Seekers*

Lesson 13 ◇ Coloring/Puzzle Center

TREASURE TROVE!

JEREMIAH 10:10

The Challenge

Ahoy there, mateys! Solve this puzzle and our pirate friend won't make you walk the plank. Use the letter and number under each line to find the coordinate on the map. When you've found each coordinate, unscramble the letters in the square to make a word. Do all 14!

Solve the puzzle and then draw a circle around one of the words that describes God's love. What are some other words or phrases that describe God's love?

Resources

Look in this section to find helpful resources that you can customize for use in your church. You will find theme-related art, decorating patterns, a lesson planning page, song charts, publicity flyers and more!

Certificates
Use these certificates to recognize and honor children, teachers and helpers.

Family Treasure Talk

Today's date _____

What we read _____
_____

One thing we already knew _____
_____

One thing we did not know _____
_____

One truth about God _____
_____

One way we can obey _____
_____

One thing to thank God for _____
_____

One thing to ask God for _____
_____

Parent Letters

Help parents become familiar with *Treasure Seekers* and encourage their child's attendance by sending a letter to each family several weeks before the program begins. Use this sample letter as inspiration to create your own letter. On page 233 you'll find two invitations you can modify to invite parents to join in on the fun at *Treasure Seekers*.

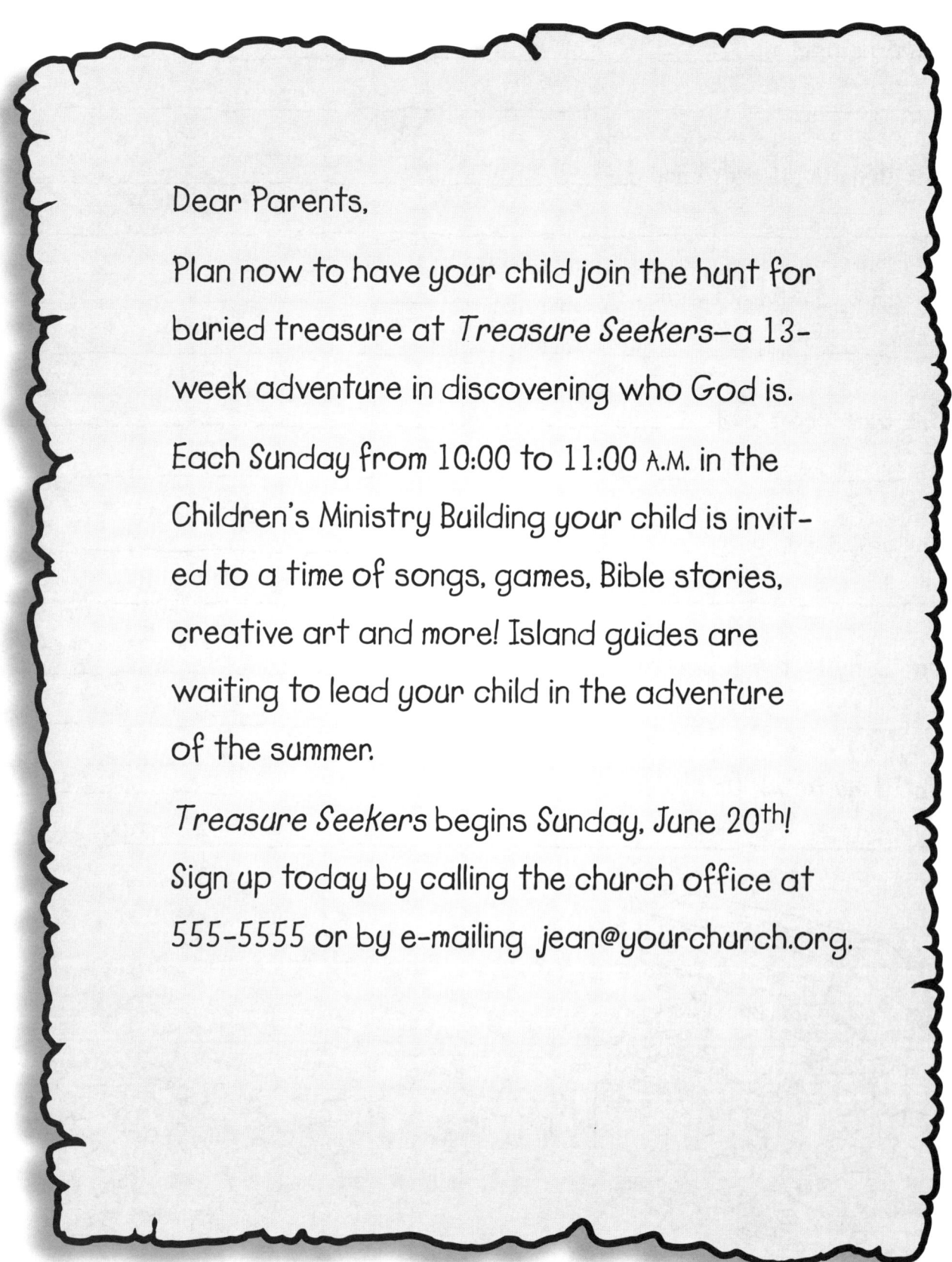

Dear Parents,

Plan now to have your child join the hunt for buried treasure at *Treasure Seekers*—a 13-week adventure in discovering who God is.

Each Sunday from 10:00 to 11:00 A.M. in the Children's Ministry Building your child is invited to a time of songs, games, Bible stories, creative art and more! Island guides are waiting to lead your child in the adventure of the summer.

Treasure Seekers begins Sunday, June 20th! Sign up today by calling the church office at 555-5555 or by e-mailing jean@yourchurch.org.

You're invited to Family Day at *Treasure Seekers!*

Date _____

Time _____

Place _____

Come join your kids for a treasure-chest full of fun!

Call Jean Brown at 555-5555 for more information.

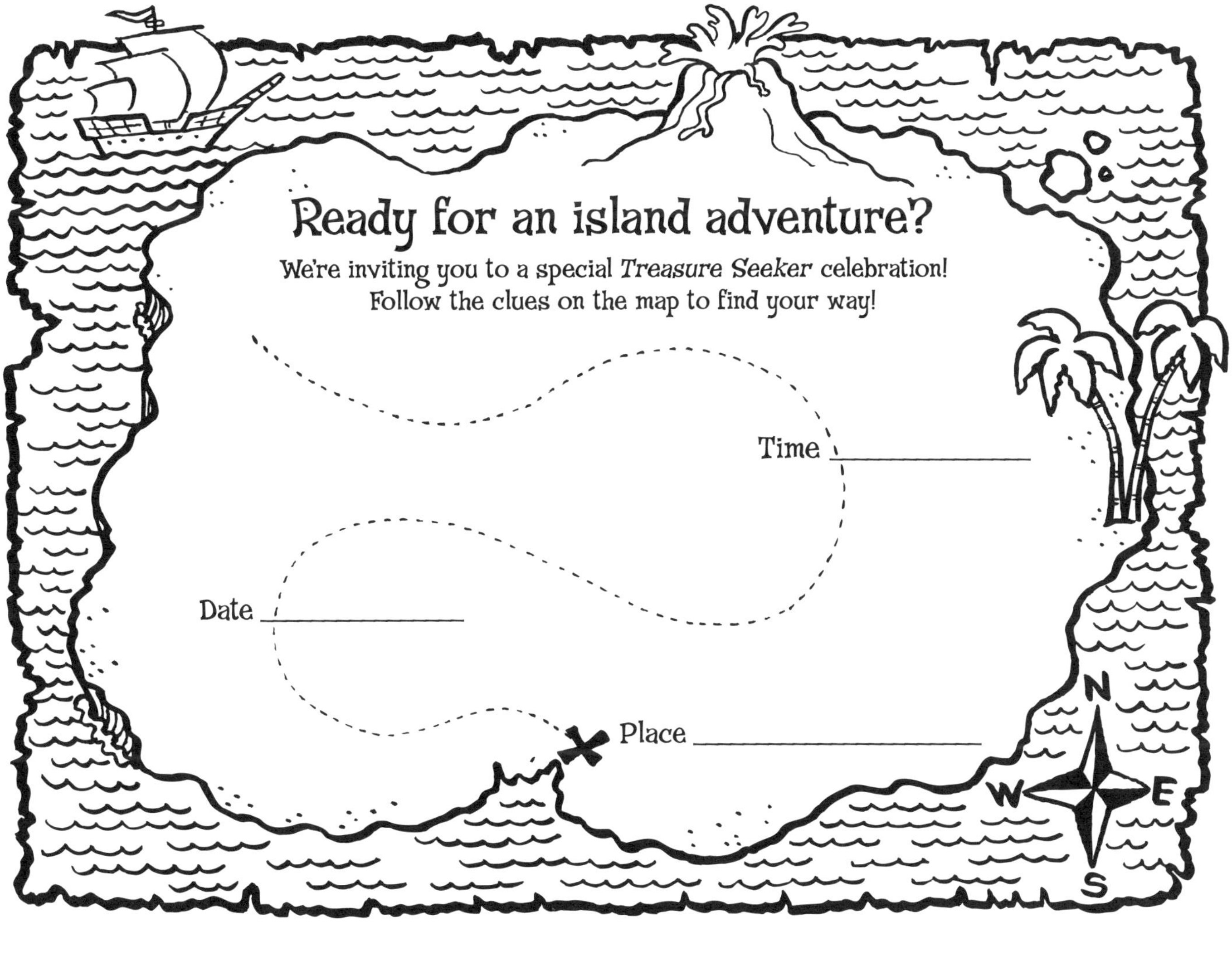

Ready for an island adventure?

We're inviting you to a special *Treasure Seeker* celebration!
Follow the clues on the map to find your way!

Time _____

Date _____

Place _____

Patterns

Use these patterns to enhance bulletin announcements, forms and flyers. Pattern can also be used to decorate bulletin boards, classrooms, hallways and church buildings. Follow these three easy steps to enlarge patterns:

1. Make overhead transparencies of the patterns using a photocopier, and project patterns onto butcher paper taped onto wall or onto portions of large appliance boxes.

2. Trace patterns with pencil.

3. Cut out patterns and then use markers or paint to color them. (Hint: To save time, you may also project patterns directly onto construction paper.)

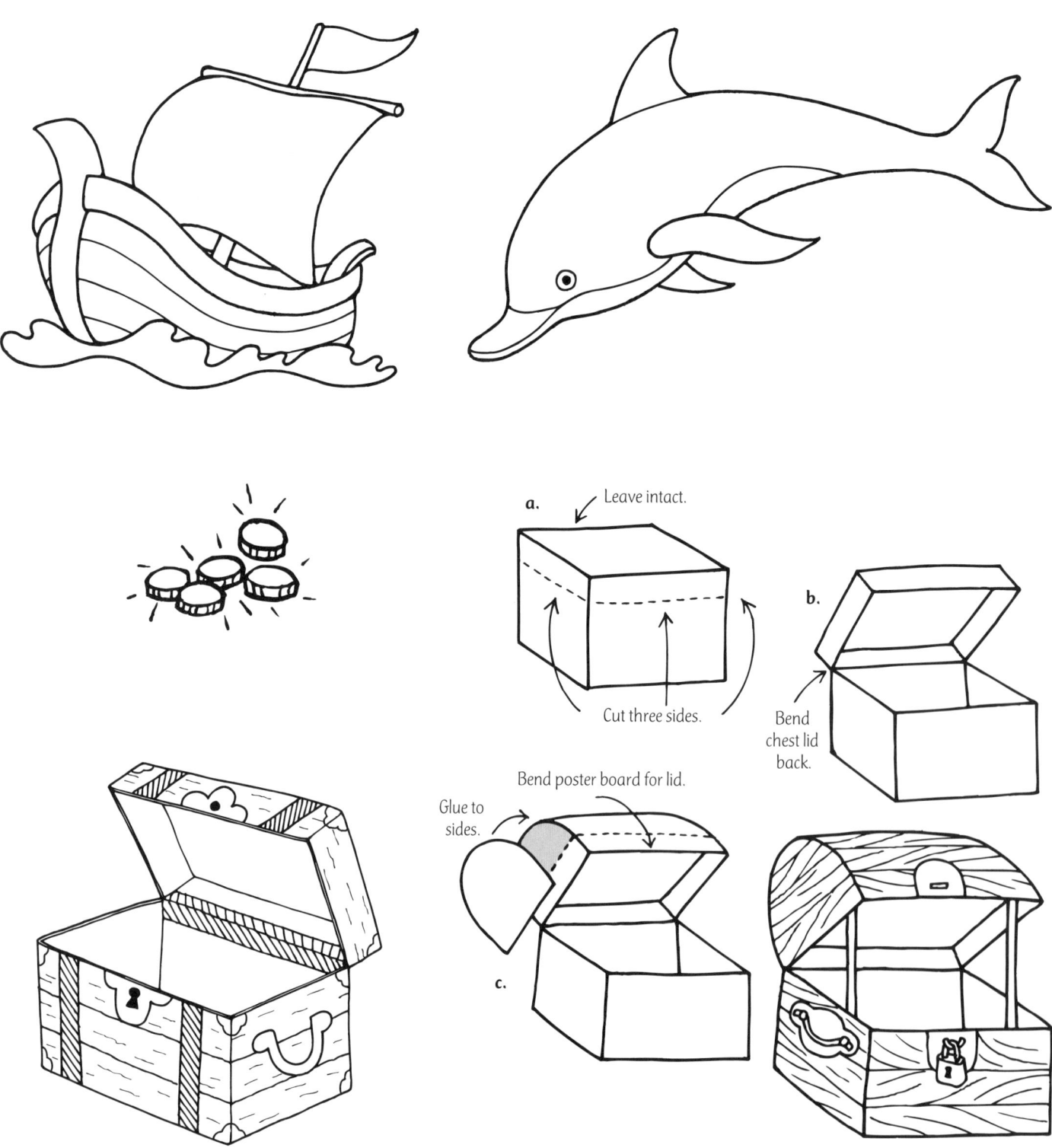

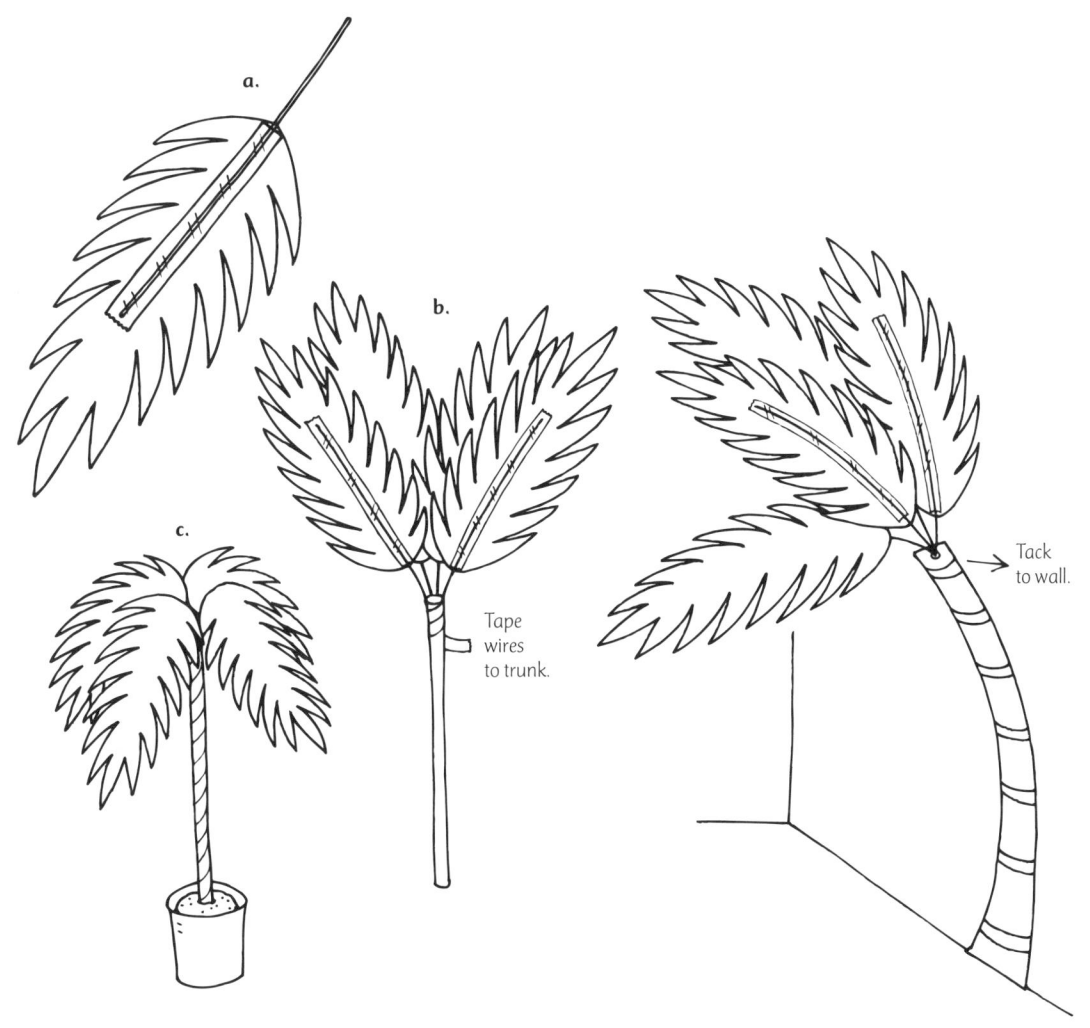

a.

b. Tape wires to trunk.

Tack to wall.

c.

© 2006 Gospel Light. Permission to photocopy granted. *Treasure Seekers*

Planning Page

Treasure Seekers

Date(s) _____

Lesson # and Title _____

Teaching Team _____

Time

Center

Materials

Teachers

Helpers

Publicity Flyers

Calling All *Treasure Seekers*

Discover a great treasure!

Date_____ Time_____

Place_____

Sign up now!

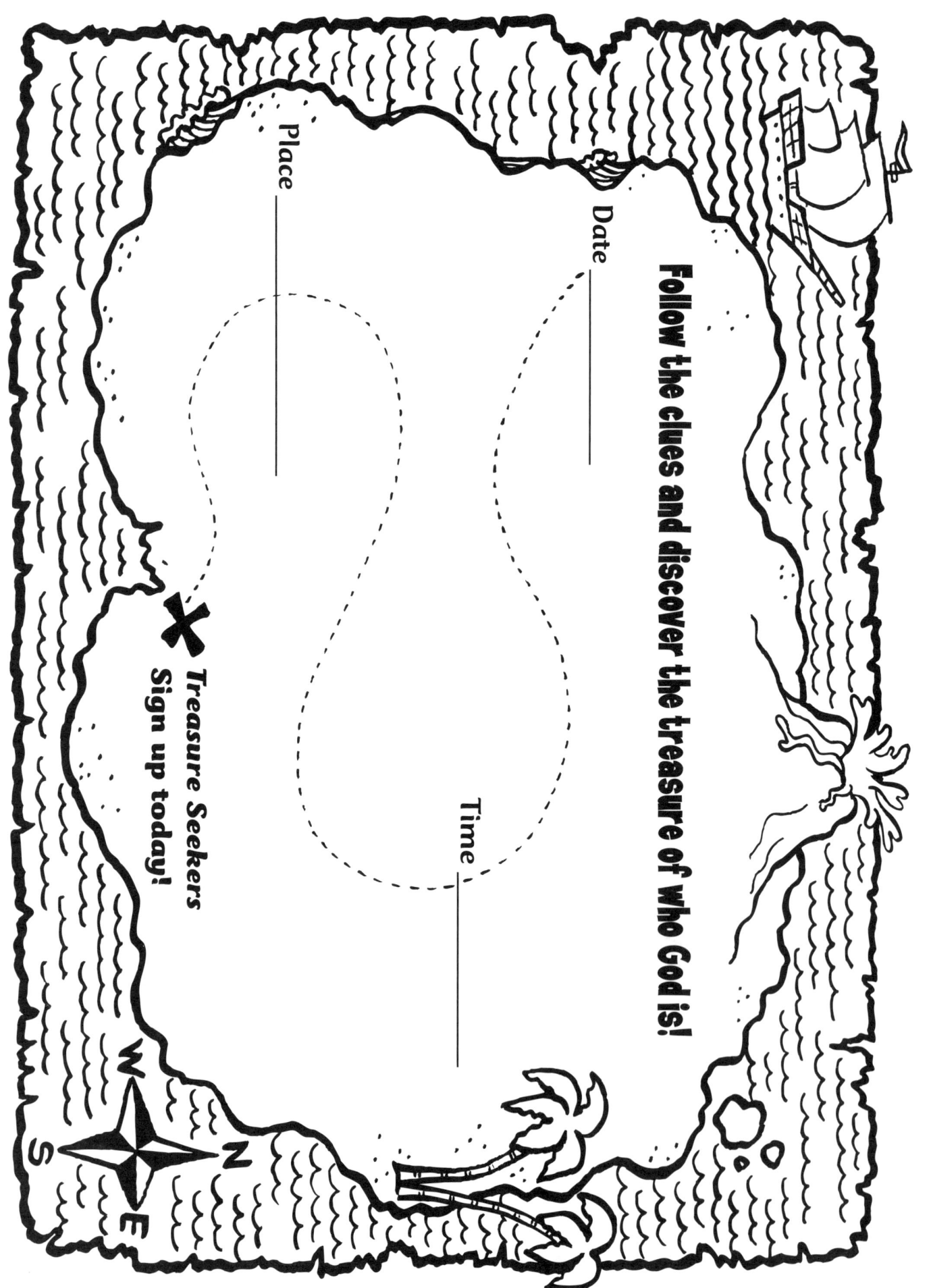

Listen up!

Join the adventure at *Treasure Seekers*.

Date_____

Time_____

Place_____

Sign up now!

Island Adventure

Board the ship, follow the clues and dig for treasure at *Treasure Seekers!*

Date_____

Time_____

Place_____

Sign up today!

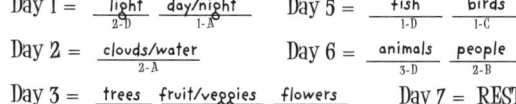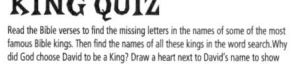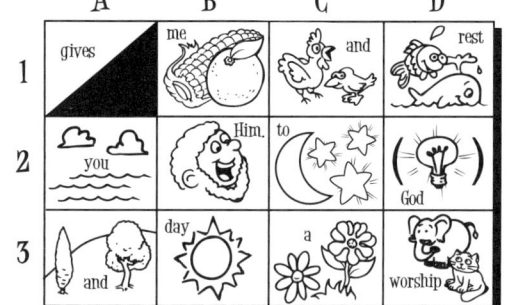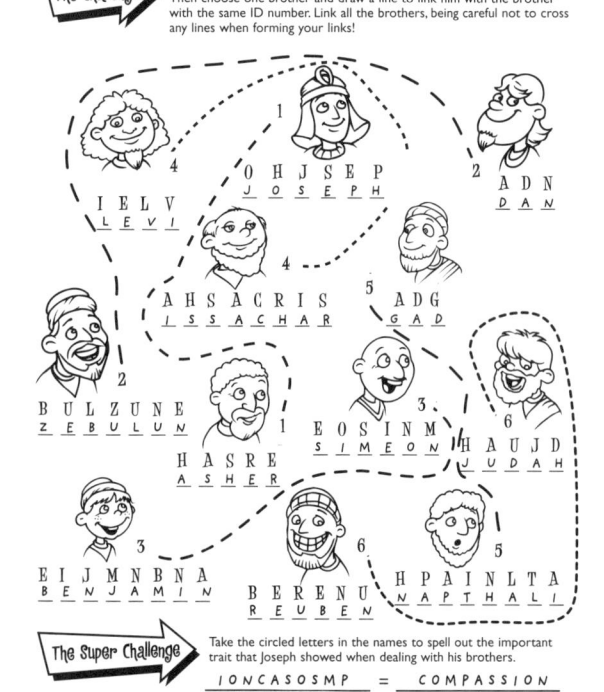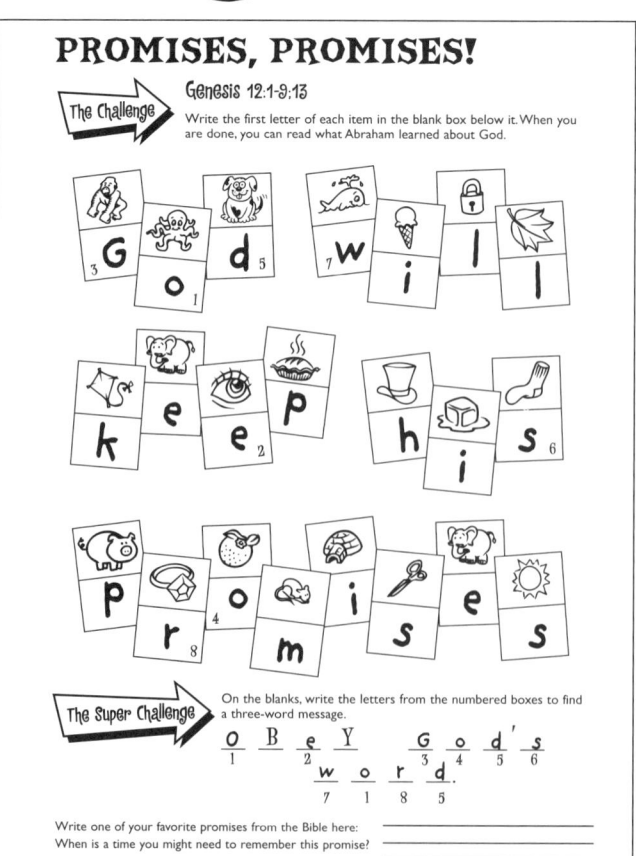

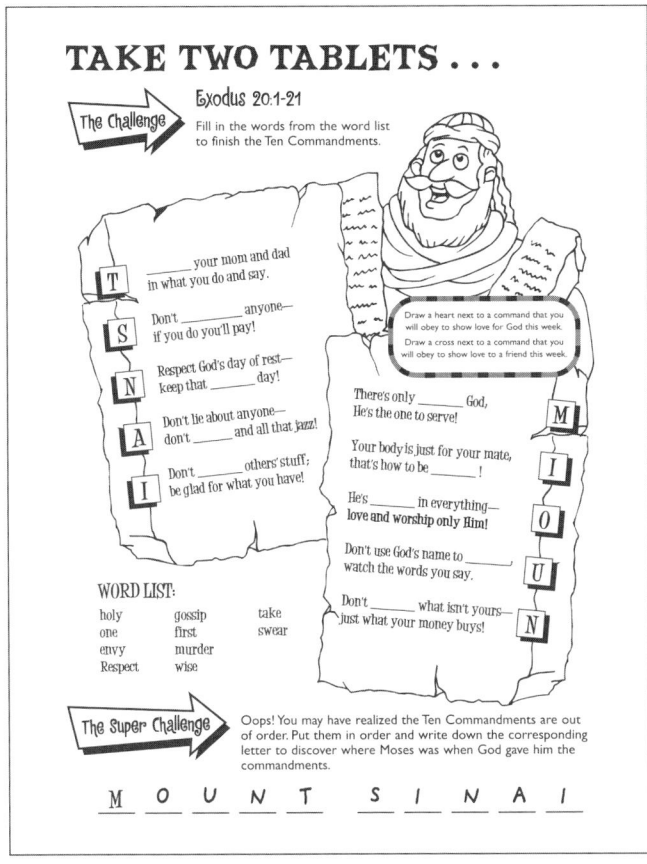
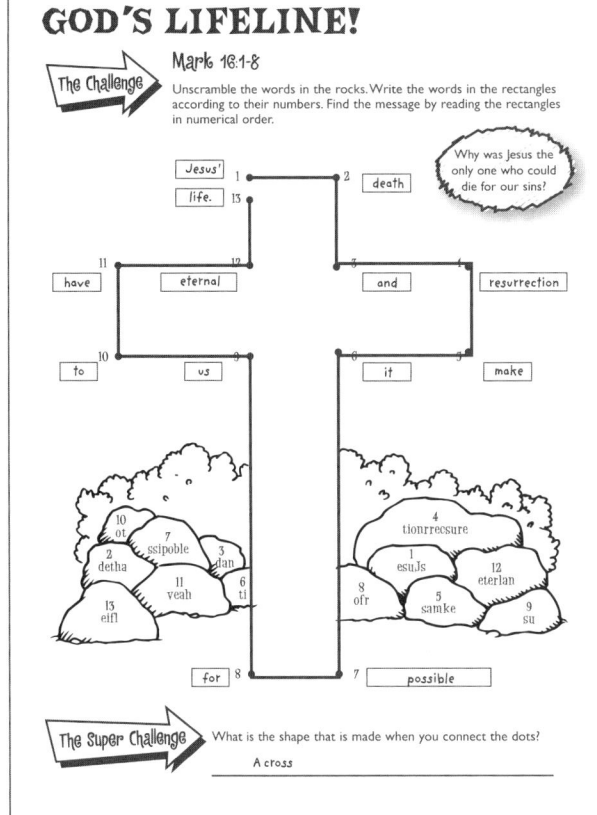
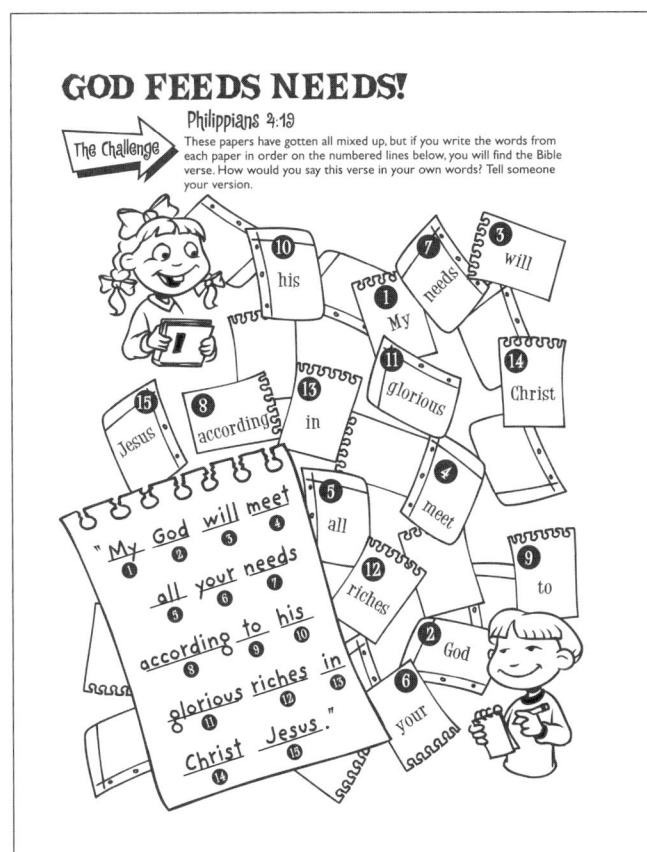

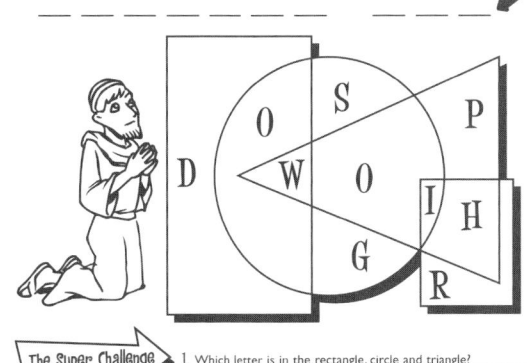

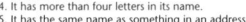

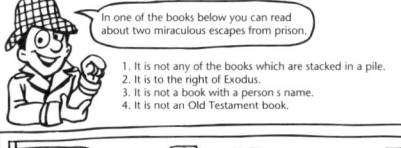

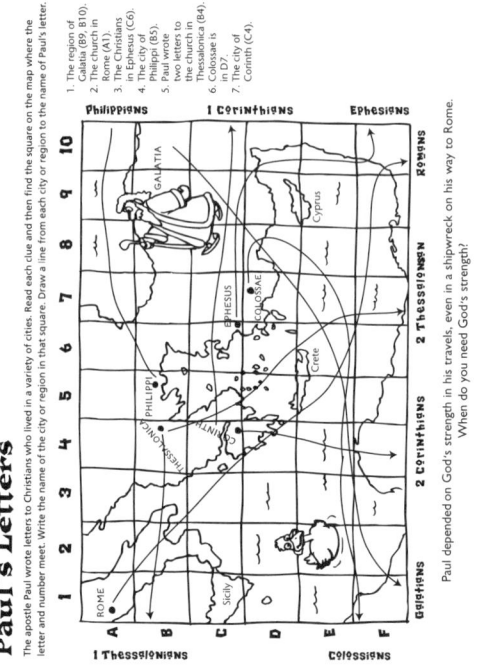

TREASURE TROVE

JEREMIAH 10:10

The Challenge: Ahoy there, mateys! Solve this puzzle and our pirate friend won't make you walk the plank. Use the letter and number under each line to find the coordinate on the map. When you've found each coordinate, unscramble the letters in the square to make a word. Do all 14!

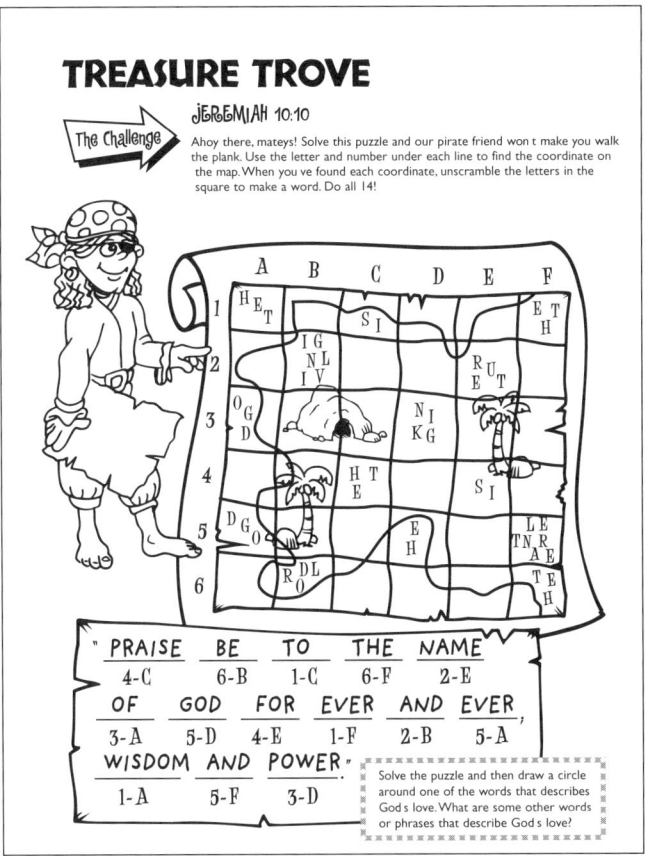

" PRAISE   BE   TO   THE   NAME
   4-C   6-B   1-C   6-F   2-E
  OF   GOD   FOR   EVER   AND   EVER,
  3-A   5-D   4-E   1-F   2-B   5-A
  WISDOM   AND   POWER."
   1-A   5-F   3-D

Solve the puzzle and then draw a circle around one of the words that describes God's love. What are some other words or phrases that describe God's love?

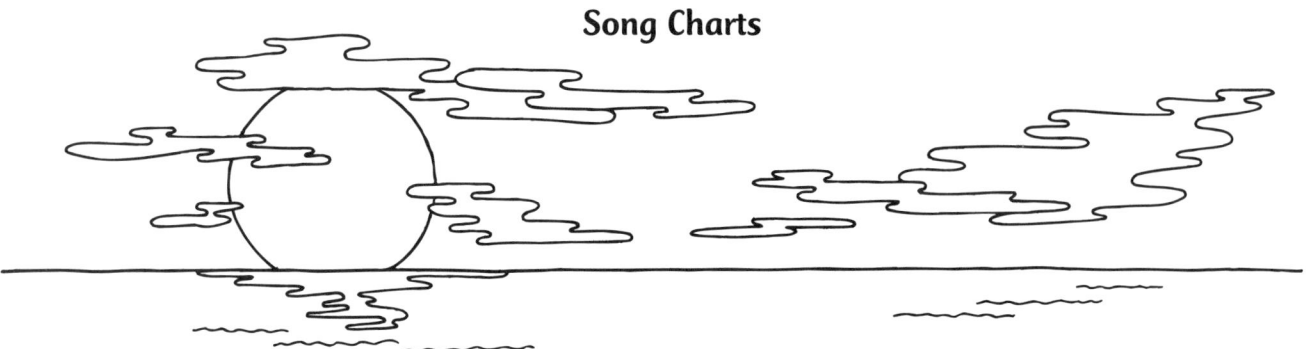

Treasure Forever

by Jamie Owens Collins

Welcome to our island home, just feel the ocean breeze.
We're so glad you've come to laugh and play-o, hey-o.
But there is more than meets the eye beneath the golden seas,
The love you will discover if you stay-o, hey-o.

Come on an island adventure.
We'll search for the world's greatest treasure.
It can't be bought or sold.
It's worth more than purest gold.
God's love is treasure forever, treasure forever.

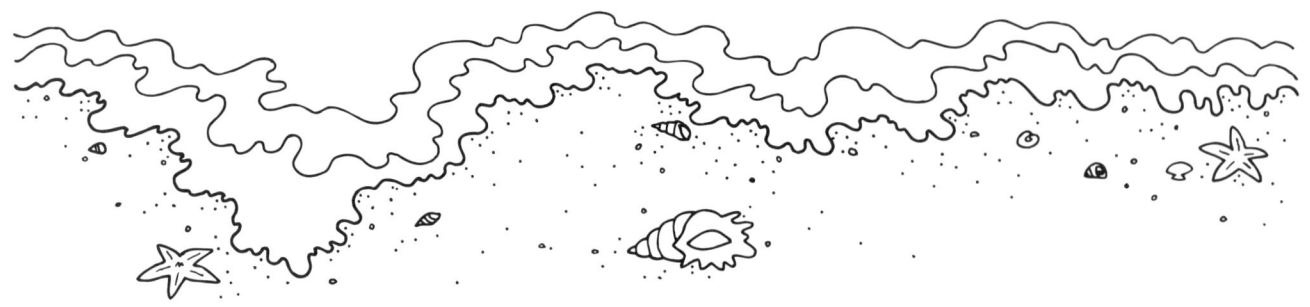

Before All Time

by Rob Evans, The Donut Man

1. Before the beginning,
Before there was time,
Before there was earth
And before there was sky,
Before He made the mountains,
Before He made the sea,
Oh, God loved you and me.

2. Before He made the sunshine,
Before He made the sand,
Before He made the waters,
Before He made dry land,
Before He made the islands
Or a coconut tree,
Oh, God loved you and me.

Chorus:
God's love, wider than the ocean,
God's love, higher than a mountain,
God's love, brighter than sunshine,
God's love, deeper than the sea,
God's love, stronger than the strongest man could ever be,
Oh, God loves you and me!
Repeat 1st Verse
Chorus

© 1998 Rob Evans, The Donut Man. Used by permission. Permission to photocopy granted. *Treasure Seekers*

You, O Lord

(Psalm 86:17)

by Gary Pailer

You, O Lord, You, O Lord,
You have helped me;
You have comforted me.
You, O Lord, have helped me and comforted me.

You're always there; You always care!

You, O Lord, You, O Lord,
You have helped me;
You have comforted me.
You, O Lord, have helped me and comforted me.
You, O Lord, have helped me and comforted me.

Promises

Words and Music by Judy and Marc Roth and Mary Gross Davis

Chorus

Promises, You keep Your promises;
Promises, O God, Your Word is like rock.
Promises, You keep Your promises;
Promises, O God, Your Word is like rock.

1. I know You love me; I know You listen;
   I know You hear me when I pray!
   You say You will forgive me and help me;
   You always do what You say!

Chorus

2. Sometimes I'm scared; sometimes I'm angry;
   Sometimes I feel all alone.
   But You have said You will be with me always;
   Your Word is stronger than stone!

Chorus

The Only One

by Gary Pailer

1. He's the only One
Who split the dark with light;
He's the only One
Who pushed up mountains with His might.
He's the only One
Who created you and me;
He is God Almighty!

2. He's the only One
Who commands the rain and wind;
He's the only One
With no beginning or end.
He's the only One
Who really knows me;
He is God Almighty!

3. Lord, You're the only One
And I worship You today;
You're the only One;
You hear me when I pray!
You're the only One;
You know what's best for me.
You are God Almighty

He's Alive Again!

by Dan McGowan

1. This is quite an amazing story.
We believe it because it's true!
Oh, what a victory!
For all the world to see!
Jesus died and rose to set us free!

2. Three days after they buried Jesus,
His friends came running to see the grave.
What a big surprise!
They couldn't believe their eyes.
The stone was rolled away, "He is alive!"

Chorus:
Jesus rose up from the dead,
He's alive again!
Jesus rose up from the dead,
He's alive again!
He's alive again!

3. Now He lives with the Lord in heaven,
Reigns forever, our loving King!
He died and rose again,
He took away our sin.
He lives eternally for you and me!
Chorus twice

Call Upon Me

(Jeremiah 29:12)

by Judy and Marc Roth

"Call upon me and come and pray to me,
And I will listen to you.
Call upon me and come and pray to me,
And I will listen to you."

God will hear and answer you.
He loves you; He will listen to you.
God will hear and answer you.
He loves you; He will listen to you.

And God says,
"Call upon me and come and pray to me,
And I will listen to you.
Call upon me and come and pray to me,
And I will listen to you."

Love Like You

by Jamie Owens Collins

Chorus:
Love like You,
I want to love like You
With patience and kindness,
Forgiveness, too.
Love like You,
I want to love like You.
O Lord, won't You help me to love like You.

When I'm feeling glad,
Help me to love like You.
When I'm feeling bad,
Help me to love like You.
When I don't get my way,
Help me to love like You.
At school or at play,
Help me to love like You.

Chorus

When mom needs some hugs,
Help me to love like You.
When my brother bugs,
Help me to love like You.
In all that I say,
Help me to love like You.
Every day,
Help me to love like You.

© 2005 Fairhill Music, Inc. Used by permission. Permission to photocopy granted. *Treasure Seekers*

God Is So Strong

by Judy and Marc Roth, Lynnette Pennings and Mary Gross Davis

1. Stronger than a redwood tree is my God.
   Stronger than Earth's gravity is my God.
   Stronger than a hurricane is my God.
   Stronger than a mountain range is my God.

Chorus:
He's stronger than you can imagine—
How can I describe?
God is so strong, He can make the dead alive!
He's stronger than you can imagine—
How can I describe?
God is so strong, He can make me new inside!

2. When I know I've won the race, He's my God.
   When I know I'm in last place, He's my God.
   When I know that I've done wrong, He's my God.
   When I know I can't be strong, He's my God.

Chorus

He's the place where I can hide,
'Cause His love's so big and wide.